ASIAN LOOT

Unearthing the Secrets of Marcos,
Yamashita and the Gold

Charles C. McDougald

San Francisco Publishers

FIRST EDITION

ISBN: 0-940777-08-8
LCCN: 92-83783

93 94 95 96 97 10 9 8 7 6 5 4 3 2 1

Library of Congress Cataloging-in-Publication Data

McDougald, Charles C., 1940-
    Asian Loot : Unearthing the Secrets of Marcos
Yamashita and the Gold.
    Bibliography : p.
    Includes Index.
    1. Philippine - History. 2. Marcos, Ferdinand E.(1917-1989).
3. Yamashita, Tomoyuki. 4. Treasure - trove - Asia.
I. Title.

DS686.5 1993 959.9046 P931000002
ISBN 0-940777-08-8

IN MEMORIAM

Raul Copino
Casiano B. "Sonny" Garcia
Mark Navales
Aurelio Sayson

Acknowledgments

I would like to thank the people that made this book possible. Congressman Boni Gillego started me in the right direction, Noel Soriano made me stay the course, and Mario Ongkiko kept my pursuits within the confines of Philippine law.

Gustavo "Tabo" Ingles, who survived imprisonment and torture at Fort Santiago, led me back through the chambers and cells of the old fort despite the painful memories it dredged up every time he went back.

Ophelia Soliven at the Central Bank patiently fielded all my critical questions about international reserves and the gold.

Caesar Parlade was my initial contact in the Presidential Commission on Good Government library. He allowed me access to their documents which helped in the initial stages of my research. David Castro later became head of the PCGG and continued to be available when I needed assistance.

Mike Salamon, an old friend and the head of Reuters News Agency in Tokyo at the time, let me use his resources when trying to track down information in Japan.

James Black shared his vast library and depth of knowledge about the island of Corregidor during World War II.

Aida Alejandrino provided me with her scrapbook of maps, engineering drawings, and other data on Fort Santiago.

Despite his busy schedule at the psychology department of Ateneo University, Jaime Bulatao always had time to regress an eye-witness or discuss the Japanese occupation.

Lewis Gleeck is the author of many excellent books about Americans in the Philippines. He is also the curator of the American Historical Collection library. He allowed me the use of the library and provided some invaluable background information on pre-war Manila.

Steve Psinakis, who had conducted his own intensive research and broke the story about the Leber Group treasure hunt in 1978, helped me with the background of Leber Group.

General John K. Singlaub kindly provided me with a lot of the background on the Nippon Star treasure hunting group.

Gabriel "Gabe" Casal, head of the National Museum, and Eustacio "Jun" Orobia, head of the Intramuros Administration at the time of the Fort Santiago excavation, helped with their recollections of the Fort Santiago excavation.

Felix Imperial, architect and Intramuros expert, introduced me to the Intramuros Archives and let me roam around at will.

Doctor Serafin Quiason, head of the National Historic Institute, provided invaluable information and documentation of Intramuros and Fort Santiago.

Joan Orendain took time away from her many duties as Enrique Zobel's public relations manager to provide all the documents I requested. She also introduced me to ginger tea which is a great fortifier during the rainy season.

Enrique Zobel, despite his life-threatening injury, graciously agreed to be interviewed and provided many insights into Marcos and the $35 billion in gold.

Gary Thompson and Arlene Friedman, two intrepid researchers, conducted their own investigation and travelled the world as a team. Arlene gathered information for her law firm, Magaña, Cathcart, and McCarthy, who is handling Roger Roxas' lawsuit, and Gary, the former managing editor of the *Las Vegas Sun*, gathered material for his newspaper article. Our common interest brought us together and we shared a lot of our research material.

The opinions expressed in this book are mine and should not be construed as those of any of the above-named individuals or of any agency of the Philippine government.

Contents

CHAPTER ONE

Fort Santiago

"**O**h God!" the colonel muttered, as the jeep pulled over. This meant he was in for special treatment. It was August 1943 and the place was Fort Santiago in the Philippines. The colonel was a Filipino guerrilla. The Japanese had arrested him two months earlier and turned him over to the *Kempei Tai*, the dreaded secret police. Since then he had been taken to several places of detention and questioned but apparently he didn't give the right answers. He didn't look so good as a result. Both eyes were black and blue; his nose was swollen; and his cheek was bloody from the beatings he had taken.

Two burley Japanese guards, one on each side, dragged him up the dozen stone steps of the Bastion de San Lorenzo. They stopped briefly at a wooden guardhouse while the two guards gave the prisoner's name. Then he was escorted across the roof, down the back stairs, and marched three hundred meters to the front of the fort.

"Maybe I'm going to New Bilibid. That would be nice," the colonel said to himself as they headed toward the entrance. Bilibid was the federal prison. Anything was nicer than this. People disappeared in here. Those that survived spoke of horrible torture and beatings.

They turned left and walked over to a barbed wire gate. A shout brought two sentries running. The prisoner was turned over to them. "March," one of the sentries yelled, as he was kicked and shoved forward. They led him to a long wooden building, past a dozen or so doors, and stopped at one. "No talking or sleeping in the daytime," he was told. One guard unlocked the door. The other shoved him inside, and the door was slammed shut.

Today Tabo Ingles is still slim and trim, with the ramrod posture of a colonel. He was twenty when they arrested him. Now he had returned to recall his imprisonment. These were not fond memories. His voice cracked occasionally, but he composed himself and continued.

"There was only one man in the cell when I arrived but soon it filled up to twelve. Only eight of us could lie down at one time, so we took turns sleeping. We had it pretty good. In some cells there were twenty. It was always hot, like an oven, and quiet except for the sound of the flies buzzing around, and those who had tuberculosis coughed constantly. The smell was terrible — unwashed bodies, sweat, urine, and feces.

"They brought me to the torture chamber the next day. I had been told what to expect and I hoped I wouldn't talk. But now I was here and it was terrible. The fear gnawed at my bowels and I couldn't control them. I saw the interrogator smile when he smelled the odor. I'm sure he thought, 'This one is going to be easy.' I wasn't."

For the next seven months they questioned him. All he would say is that he was a messenger and didn't know anything. So the torture began. First they tried *jiu jitsu*, throwing him around on the concrete floor. Then they beat him with wooden slats and burned him with cigarettes. Next came the splinters under the fingernails and the electrodes hooked to the testicles. Still he wouldn't talk. Finally they tried the water cure, the worst of all. Water was forced down his nose and mouth, giving the effect of drowning. When his belly was bloated they beat him, forcing the water out all orifices. The pain was excruciating. Then it would be repeated, again and again.

The colonel was in good company. Most of the famous names of the guerrilla movement had passed this way. He knew what had happened to them so he tried to prepare himself. He had heard about the execution chamber down the hall and the truck rides to the Chinese cemetery. The execution chamber was for summary executions. The truck rides were for those who, for some reason, needed to go through the semblance of a trial, be found guilty, and sentenced to death. Usually this treatment was reserved for soldiers. At the cemetery each prisoner was made to dig his own grave and then kneel down beside it to await his beheading.

"Many nights I lay awake wondering what it would be like," Tabo said. He never got to find out. In February 1944 he was tried and sentenced to thirteen years at hard labor. He took a truck ride to the main prison at New Bilibid but at least it didn't stop at the cemetery. He survived. But to this day he still has nightmares about the fort and the Chinese cemetery.

When the tour was over Tabo and I left the peaceful serenity of the fort, crossed the street, and went out into the hustle and bustle of the Manila traffic, back to the present. As we said goodbye I didn't realize this was the beginning of a journey for the truth about former President Ferdinand Marcos and his incredible wealth, and that the fort would play a key role.

Tuesday, 25 February 1986, was not a good day for President Marcos. After more than twenty years in power the Filipino people had turned against him. He had tried to fake the returns of a presidential election just once too often. Now he sat in his second-floor bedroom in Malacañan Palace listening to the unruly crowd outside the gates. Their shouting and screaming was occasionally punctuated by the crack of a rifle shot or the roar of a rocket exploding on the palace grounds. Inside there was pandemonium as the staff rushed around gathering possessions and packing boxes.

Down the hall, General Fabian Ver, armed forces Chief of Staff, was busy in Marcos' office directing soldiers in one last obscene parting gesture, directed at the people he wanted to hurt if he couldn't control. He had already shown his ugly side the day before when he pleaded with Marcos on national television to bomb and strafe the crowd on E. De Los Santos Boulevard in front of Camp Crame. Marcos had said no then, but now he was too busy and too sick to care what Ver and his soldiers were doing.

"Put the books back," Ver ordered, and the men gingerly replaced them on the shelves. Now the bombs could not be detected and everything looked normal. Carefully the soldiers ran the trip-wires across the doorway and finished their job. "Good. Now let them come," Ver said as he inspected his handiwork one last time, and walked out.

Later that evening the crowd outside at the gates heard the distinctive whump-whump-whump sound of helicopters landing and taking off a few hundred meters away directly across the Pasig River in Malacañan Park. The park was Marcos' private golf course and also the home of the Presidential Security Command, Marcos' personal bodyguard outfit commanded by Ver.

As those sounds died away the word spread that Marcos was gone. The crowd moved slowly, hesitantly at first, toward the gate. Not meeting any resistance, they surged forward, scaled the fence, and stormed the palace. Now they were an unruly mob. Their angry shouting reached a fever pitch, and drowned out the screams of the few unfortunate Marcos loyalists who stayed behind and had not yet scampered to safety. Some were beaten to death. Others were smart enough to hide and then melt into the crowd. It was get even time in old Manila as the poor exacted their own tribute from a tyrant who kept them downtrodden for so many years.

Anything that wasn't nailed down was fair game. Chairs, tables, curtains, rugs, ashtrays, even trash cans were taken away. Television camera crews recorded the event and relayed their footage back to the states in time for the six o'clock news. One scene showed a Filipino standing in a window on the second floor wrestling with a large picture of Marcos. He struggled for a moment, then raised it over his head and heaved it out the window. A roar went up from the crowd as it fell to the ground. A picture of Imelda sailed out moments later. The people below rushed to trample, spit on, and curse the pictures. As they took their revenge on two pieces of cardboard, U.S. helicopters sped the real things to Clark Air Base.

The pillaging went on for several hours, but no one tripped any wires or detonated any explosives. They were at the wrong building. The actual palace, where the first family lived and where Marcos had his office, was next door. The crowd had stormed Maharlika Hall, the executive building, a few meters away. It was more visible from the road and could easily be mistaken for the palace at night. It was a fortunate mistake. While the crowd celebrated soldiers loyal to President Aquino quietly moved in and secured the palace. They found the bombs in Marcos' office and defused them.

Order was restored the next day. Because of the booby-traps
that were found the palace was meticulously searched room by room.
Downstairs in the courtyard by the fountain another trip-wire was
discovered and the bomb defused. Finally the palace was declared
safe. Aquino said that she didn't want to live there, but, she
announced, everyone should come and see the intimate details of
the place Marcos called home for twenty years. Soon the world
would come to know the wretched excesses of a man consumed
by greed and his wife who tried to spend it all.

Marcos and Imelda had separate bedrooms similar in only two
details. Instead of walk-in closets both had walk-in vaults. And both
had large triangular-shapes on their wood floors. These shapes also
decorated Marcos' bedroom ceiling and Imelda's dressing room
ceiling. They believed, like the Egyptians of old, in the magical
properties of the pyramid. Marcos' bedroom exposed the lie that
he was a well man. There was a normal double bed, and beside
it was a hospital bed. Nearby were two dialysis machines for his
failing kidneys, a portable toilet, and stacks of diapers. There was
also a cabinet built into one wall, about three meters high and six
meters long, full of medicine.

Only a doorway separated Marcos' quarters from Imelda's. Her
bedroom was dimly lit and contained no reading lights. Her
oversized bed was actually two queen-size beds side by side with
a tulle canopy overhead. The headboard was elaborately carved.
The bed cover and pillow cases were made of expensive *piña* (a cloth
made from fibers of the pineapple plant). The entire affair was laid
out on a platform raised about twenty-five centimeters off the floor
and surrounded by a low balustrade. This was supposedly a copy
of the bed in which Marie Antoinette slept. Beside the bed was
a cylinder of oxygen. She thought an occasional whiff would make
her skin soft. The singer Michael Jackson had recommended it.
Doctors didn't agree but no one bothered to tell her.

Directly in front was her vault, which had contained some
of her favorite jewelry pieces and *objets d'art*. Imelda liked to take
the pieces out and play with them, especially late at night — she
suffered from insomnia — with her friends. She loved the *ooohs*
and *aaahs* of the admiring crowd as she tried on the rings, necklaces,
and earrings, and told them where this piece came from or how

much that piece cost. After she left a receipt from Bulgari's was found inside the vault for six pieces of jewelry worth $1,431,000. Unfortunately the jewelry was gone. The value of her total jewelry collection may never be known because it was stored in many different places. After the revolution twenty-two Louis Vuitton suitcases were found at a home in the exclusive suburb of Dasmariñas Village. The suitcases were secured with locks and tape and appeared ready to be shipped somewhere. An inventory placed their value at ₱236 million ($11.5 million). In addition, a Greek jeweler was stopped at the airport before he could leave with several suitcases of jewelry which he admitted belonged to Imelda. They were valued at ₱15 million ($732,000). More pieces were found stored in the vault at the Central Bank.

Off to the left was her bathroom. There were gold plated fixtures and a walk-in tub. Displayed on the shelves were gallon jars of the most expensive perfumes. To the left of this was the sitting room. The centerpiece was a large grand piano, especially tuned for her friend, Van Cliburn. He played here often after an evening's performance at the Cultural Center. Seven grand pianos were found in the palace.

To the right of the bedroom was her dressing room. On the shelves were more gallon jars of perfume. Behind was a large walk-in closet containing about 200 dresses and some shoes. But this was just one week's supply. Downstairs was a room about the size of a basketball court that resembled some smart house of fashion in New York. First there were the dozen odd racks of evening wear. Some had the distinct butterfly shoulders of the *terno*, the formal attire favored by the Filipina. Others had the mark of fine tailoring from Paris or Rome. There was exquisite hand-sewn beadwork, and gold and silver lamé. Then came the dozens of racks of day dresses of different colors and various styles. The numbers were overwhelming — 2,900 gowns and dresses were counted. Imelda could not have worn all these in two lifetimes. Fifty four sable and mink coats were also found in the cold storage lockers of several hotels. Marcos' clothes occupied a modest corner of the room. There were racks of pants and *barong tagalogs*, the formal Filipino attire, along with a dozen or so pairs of elevator shoes. He was a short man, 1.6 meters, and vain despite the immense power he wielded.

Of the 122 racks of clothes, sixty-seven were empty. That was all they had time to pack. All of Imelda's bullet-proof bras were still on their hangers. Nearby were her shoes. None were elevated. She was a tall woman, 1.7 meters, and beautiful in her youth. But now that youth was gone and what remained was a yearning, for shoes, size eight. Actually there were only 1,200 pair found in the palace. The other 2,800 pair were found in the forty guest houses which the Marcoses maintained all over the country.

Next to the wardrobe room was Marcos' private hospital. It contained two more dialysis machines and more medicines in the laboratory. Three trucks were needed to cart them away. Outside there was a bus equipped as well as some hospitals and containing another dialysis machine. It followed Marcos everywhere during his last run for the presidency. Now it sat unused, a reminder of a sick president and his last campaign. His staunchest enemies begrudgingly admitted he was the best since Manuel Quezon, president at the start of the second world war, when it came to politicking. There would be Marcos at some rally standing on the podium, bringing the crowd to a frenzy with one of his speeches. When it was over sometimes he would have to be carried off the podium to that hospital bus. That took incredible courage, yet he would never admit he was sick.

Between Marcos' booby-trapped office and the office of his private secretary was the secure communications room. It was from here that the telexes had been sent in 1983 to the foreign creditors, announcing that the Philippines could no longer meet its foreign obligations. That shook up a few big banks. It was the first inkling that something wasn't right, that dollars were becoming scarce, that somebody was pillaging the government institutions of U.S. greenbacks. Over in the corner were four shredding machines, their mechanisms burned out from overwork. Confetti was scattered on the floor, the remains of thousands of pages of documents that could have proved where a lot of the dollars went.

A few steps away was Marcos' private study, and then his bedroom. A wall panel hid the secret door to his walk-in vault. Inside were four filing cabinets containing documents, not about affairs of state, but about other matters such as Swiss bank accounts and real estate located all over the world. Up to now the estimates

of Marcos' wealth were just guesswork. The evidence gathered over
the years didn't come close to adding up to the five or ten billion
dollars that some said he was worth. But here in these filing cabinets
was proof of serious wealth, and that was just the start.

Across Manila civilian groups that had assisted Aquino in her
presidential bid now took on a new role. During the campaign they
had armed themselves with hand-held radios and used code names
so that Marcos' men couldn't identify them. Now Aquino was in
power, but the transition from dictatorship to democracy was
anything but smooth. Cronies that had enriched themselves during
the dictatorship were now trying to hide their riches or get away
with as much as possible. The new government was not yet
organized enough to stop them. Into this void stepped Aquino's
campaigners. Jokingly referring to themselves as the Office of
National Revenge, these vigilantes were not seeking vengeance.
Their purpose was to try and find the documents that were the
key to Marcos' hidden wealth before they could be spirited out of
the country. And they did it right. No premises was searched
without a warrant.

A good example was the raid led by Charlie Avila and Jose
Alcuaz. They received a tip in the morning that Marcos' daughter,
Imee, had kept a private office in the suburb of Mandaluyong, Metro
Manila, at 82 E. Delos Santos Boulevard. They couldn't get a
signature on the search warrant until late in the evening. Then
they rushed over to Camp Crame to pick up some soldiers. After
reviewing a plan they boarded four cars and drove to the premises,
arriving around midnight.

Soldiers scaled a fence and sealed off the area. Avila, Alcuaz,
and their men moved in and found documents in recently packed
cardboard boxes, desks, and filing cabinets. As they sorted through
thousands of pages gunfire could be heard outside, but it didn't
deter the search. Documents revealed the names of offshore
companies and overseas investments of Marcos and his cronies. It
was another link in the paper trail of hidden wealth. For several
months such raids would be repeated in private homes, aboard
yachts, and business establishments of known Marcos sympathizers.

Within hours after landing at Clark Air Base, Marcos and his
entourage were on an aircraft heading for exile in Hawaii. The plane

landed at an air base on Guam for refueling. While there they asked to be allowed to shop in the post exchange because they had not had time to pack any toiletries. They neglected to mention what they had packed, however. When they landed in Hawaii customs agents impounded 300 crates of luggage that had been sent on a separate aircraft. An inventory was later made public. Twenty-two crates contained ₱22,744,535 in newly minted currency, mostly ₱100 denominations, worth approximately $1.27 million. It was illegal for anyone to depart the Philippines carrying more than ₱500 in cash. In Marcos' defense, he had expected to be flown to Laoag, his home in the north, instead of exile in the states. But the pesos were just a drop in the proverbial bucket.

The inventory also included various certificates of deposit from Philippine banks worth approximately a million dollars, gold, jewelry, and art works valued at another five million, five handguns, 154 videotapes, seventeen cassette tapes, and 2,068 pages of documents. These documents, plus those found in the palace, the Mandaluyong offices, and elsewhere were the beginning of a paper trail of wealth that would lead all over the world, and reflected a greed obscene in its enormity. Most of all it gave the lie to the constant litany of denials that they owned no real estate in the United States and had no secret Swiss bank accounts. They not only had both, they had them on a scale difficult to comprehend. The Philippine government acted immediately. The Presidential Commission on Good Government was set up. The mission of the PCGG was to investigate and, where possible, bring lawsuits all over the world to prevent Marcos and his family from getting their hands on this vast accumulation of wealth. The hunt was on.

A few months later, in June 1986, former senator Raul Manglapus and Bonifacio "Boni" Gillego invited me to the Philippines to be the expert witness in a trial regarding the Marcos war medals. Both Raul and Boni would go on to greater prominence. Raul would again be elected to the Senate, and then resign to accept the president's appointment as minister of foreign affairs. Boni would be elected to Congress.

Marcos had always claimed to be the Philippines most decorated soldier of World War II. Indeed he was, but many doubted the veracity of the medals, including Boni. While Marcos was still in power Boni had written a series of articles for the *We Forum* newspaper questioning whether or not Marcos deserved the medals. This infuriated Marcos. As a result Boni had to leave the country abruptly or risk imprisonment or something worse. Greg Cendeña, Marcos' minister of public information, launched a propaganda campaign decrying the attack on Marcos the war hero. He even published a book which quoted dozens of eye-witnesses to Marcos' courageous exploits. At the same time Marcos initiated a libel suit against the *We Forum* for printing the articles.

I had also done some extensive research on the Marcos war medals while working on a book, and Marcos' wartime exploits, or lack thereof, had become part of *The Marcos File*. Ironically the libel suit was set for trial in June 1986. Marcos was no longer around but that wasn't going to stop Raul and Boni. The trial must go on. There must be an open and honest airing of Marcos' wartime exploits to determine the truth once and for all, they announced. Marcos' lawyers, however, didn't see it that way. They wanted to drop the suit. Now, it seemed, all those eye-witnesses to his bravery couldn't be found. A hearing was held in which I presented documents and evidence to show that his heroics were a complete fabrication. Afterward the Marcos lawyers said that they would not show up at any further hearings.

My testimony was finished so I made plans to head back home to San Francisco. Before departing I went by to see Boni, who was working with the PCGG. He showed me the list of items found in the 300 crates in Hawaii, and pointed to one. The contents of a briefcase was noted as "copies of old *Playboy* magazines." We laughed at the fact that Marcos had felt these were just as important as all the valuables he had packed. His reputation as a ladies' man was well known.

"You know about the gold in the other case?" Boni asked. I did not. "Oh yes. Customs allowed it to be brought in because it was embossed, 'To Ferdinand Marcos, from Imelda, on the Occasion of our 24th Wedding Anniversary.' Inside were twenty-four bars weighing one kilogram each." Marcos love of the yellow metal was no secret either, but how much he acquired remained a mystery.

"Your next project should be about his hidden wealth. Call me if you're interested," Boni said as I left.

Before leaving, I wrote an article for the forthcoming fourth of July issue of a local magazine. It was about the Hunter's Guerrillas, one of the illustrious forces that fought on in the dark days of the occupation, and one of their men, Tabo Ingles, who was captured and tortured in the dungeons of a 300 year old Spanish fort called Santiago.

Now, almost a half-century later, Tabo took me through the fort, from the stone steps leading to the top of the Bastion de San Lorenzo, to the torture chamber down below, to where his cell used to be. We walked slowly as he talked and pointed. Occasionally he stopped and quietly stared off into the distance, gazing backward over the years. He was trying to recall every agonizing detail as if its description could forever purge the terrible memory, but that could never be.

When the tour was over I turned to say goodbye and saw the expression in his eyes, of pain and grief. The nightmares would return tonight. We shook hands and I wished him well. Just before parting he said, "By the way, have you heard about the gold that Marcos found in the fort?"

There it was again. The mention of gold. First Boni, then Tabo. He went on to explain that Marcos believed the Japanese had buried a lot of treasure in the Philippines during the war. Part of his military did nothing but search for treasure, and Fort Santiago was one of those places.

"So now you're hooked," Boni said to me the next day as we sat in his living room.

"Not necessarily," I argued. I just wanted to find out what all this was about.

"Okay, go over to the PCGG and see this guy. Tell him I sent you," Boni said, scribbling a name on a piece of paper.

Cesar Parlade was the head of research. He was also an accountant with the quiet disposition and patience to deal with the formidable mountain of documentation and numbers. He was good at his job with a reputation for hard work and efficiency. He would soon be rewarded with a promotion to commissioner. The documents he provided painted an incredible picture of greed gone out of control. Now I could see why the *Guinness Book of Records* named Marcos the world's greatest thief. The documents also showed that Marcos was indeed interested in gold, but where did it come from?

CHAPTER TWO

The Central Bank

On 26 February 1986 Ferdinand Marcos arrived at Hickam Air Force Base in Hawaii. For security reasons he was housed on the base for almost a month. U.S. officials feared that he still might be assassinated, so enhanced security was provided by isolating him and his party on one part of the base guarded by military police. All incoming vehicles were placed under surveillance to preclude entrance of unauthorized persons. In addition to his own bodyguards, Marcos was protected by Secret Service agents and the Coast Guard patrolled the Pearl Harbor Channel. Only those closest to Marcos were allowed past this security to visit him.

On 19 March, Michael de Guzman flew into Honolulu and checked into the Ilikai Hotel. He called Irwin Ver, a friend and business associate. The PCGG had already linked Ver and de Guzman's bank to the ownership of a hotel in Los Angeles. After speaking with Irwin he asked to talk with his father, General Ver. De Guzman met with Ver and requested that a meeting be arranged with Marcos and Imelda. About 7:00 the following evening Irwin and a bodyguard picked up de Guzman and took him to Marcos' duplex on Hickam Air Base. There he met with Marcos, Imelda, and Ferdinand "Bong Bong" Marcos, Jr., their son, for several hours.

After the meeting Bong Bong and de Guzman drove to Honolulu International Airport where Bong Bong used a pay phone to call Ernst Scheller of Credit Suisse Bank in Zurich. They drove back to Hickam and told Marcos that it was arranged. Later, about 2:00 in the morning, Bong Bong made one more phone call to Zurich from de Guzman's hotel room to finalize the arrangements. At 2:00 that afternoon, 21 March, Bong Bong delivered the documents to de Guzman in his hotel room. More papers were delivered that evening. Then everything was set. The next morning de Guzman departed for Zurich. Accompanying him was a Lebanese businessman by the name of Dagher, who reputedly had substantial banking connections in Switzerland.

The reason for the meeting and the secret phone calls was money. De Guzman was given Marcos' and Imelda's letters of authority to meet Scheller in Zurich and have their deposits transferred to his bank, the Export Finanzierungsbank, in Vienna. In addition Imelda had given him $300,000 in travelers' checks for safekeeping, and Ver gave him a cashier's check for $150,000 with instructions to cash it and send him the money. In a portent of what was to come De Guzman cashed the travelers' checks and the cashier's check and kept the money.

De Guzman and Dagher flew to Zurich and on 24 March presented the two letters of authority to the bank to release the first batch of deposits which was in the form of cash, bonds, securities, real estate certificates, and gold deposit certificates. They amounted to approximately $213 million. The bank refused, however, because the Swiss government had frozen the accounts. De Guzman tried again on 7 May 1986, and was turned down a second time.

Only then did de Guzman turn to the Philippine government and offer to help them get the Marcos deposits in return for a 20 percent fee. He got their attention when he said that, in addition to the $213 million, he had identified eleven foundations set up by Marcos to hide his wealth. They held a total of $4.5 billion in deposits in nine different banks. De Guzman also claimed there was an additional $3 billion in precious metals and securities on deposit, but these were subject to final verification. That would bring the total to $7.5 billion. The amount of gold included in the precious metals was not identified. The government cooperated at first, but gradually that cooperation ceased.

There were too many gray areas. De Guzman had first tried to get the money without the help of the government. Then after seeking their help he was insistent in his demand that whatever was recovered be first transferred to his bank and then later to wherever the government requested. His bank had Marcos' former executive secretary, Alejandro Melchor, and crony Herminio Disini on its board. The government considered the situation. If the money were transferred to de Guzman's bank, then he could easily divert it to other destinations, and the money would be beyond their reach. That was enough to torpedo the deal.

The Philippine government proceeded through legal channels to demand the Marcos deposits. De Guzman never received any fee for his assistance. His bank declared bankruptcy on 7 April 1988. By the end of Aquino's presidential term the government still had not obtained the $213 million.

•

After Marcos declared martial law in 1972 something strange began to happen over at the Central Bank where the country's gold reserves were kept. They began to disappear. Or so it seemed because the level of reserves fluctuated so greatly on some occasions and not at all on others. Up to 1972 there had been a steady twenty-year rise in gold reserves. In 1972 they were reported at 1,857,000 ounces. In 1973, the first full year of martial law, they were 1,057,000 ounces, a drop of 800,000 ounces which was worth approximately $280 million. The Central Bank claimed that they didn't disappear, that they were sold.

For years 1974 through 1977 gold reserves stayed at exactly the same figure of 1,056,000 ounces. This would seem to be a statistical impossibility. The Central Bank's explanation was that up until April 1978 producers did not have to sell their primary gold to the Central Bank. They could sell directly to the international market, so it was possible for gold reserves to remain at the same level. But the fact is that they had never stayed at the same level before, not even for two years running.

Gold reserves began another steady annual rise in 1978. From then until 1980 they gradually increased to 1.9 million ounces. In 1981 they took a dip, to 1.65 million ounces. Some gold may have been sold during the financial crisis caused by Dewey Dee, a prominent member of the business community and friend of Marcos. In January 1981 he abruptly left the country leaving behind debts estimated at ₱635 million ($84.7 million).

Dee had borrowed most of the money using nothing more than his name as collateral. To date this was the largest financial scandal in Philippine history and it caused a severe crisis in the banking system. Credit was tightened. The automatic roll-over of loans was stopped. Those hardest hit were the cronies. Their positions allowed them easy access to funds with little or no collateral. As with Dee, most had borrowed way beyond their capacity to repay. When credit was halted they were in trouble. Over the next two years Marcos ordered the government financial institutions to provide ₱30 billion ($3 billion) in bail-out funds. Most of it went to his cronies and their companies.

This crisis was the catalyst for the gold leasing program begun in December 1981 to optimize the yield of its gold assets. The Central Bank began to ship gold to its accounts in London and New York and place it on deposit to earn interest. Occasionally, when the transaction was necessary, it would exchange good delivery bars in its vault for good delivery bars at a foreign financial institution. Called a location swap, a representative of that institution would accept delivery of the bars at the Central Bank and then be responsible for shipping them to London, New York, or wherever the financial institution was located. In return a swap fee would be paid to cover shipping, handling, and insurance costs.

About the same time the gold leasing program began, rumors began to fly about large quantities of gold being offered for sale. The first rumor began to circulate around the end of 1981. Someone in the Philippines was selling 525 tons of gold, worth about $5 billion. Adding to the deal's credibility was a prospectus on the letterhead of Mercantile Insurance Company in Manila. Its purpose was to arrange reinsurance of the cargo that was to be shipped to Hong Kong in January or February 1982. The company was owned by the wealthy Unson family who were known to be close to Marcos.

The rumor may have started because of the gold leasing program, but the amount was just too much to be believed.* The reserves that had been sold didn't amount to that much. Also, the Philippines' annual production averaged only about twenty tons, and the country's gold reserves were only about 1,659,000 ounces, or forty-seven tons, at the time.

* The total amount of gold mined since 3900 B.C. was 131,510 tons.

Another story came out of Hong Kong. In an interview with the *Far Eastern Economic Review* magazine Michael Young, a Tokyo-based businessman, said that a Hong Kong attorney, Tony Grant, had informed him that thirty-five 50-kilogram bars of gold were available in Hong Kong and another fifty bars were available in Manila. According to Grant, they were owned by "older generation people, marked AAA and stamped Sumatra Lloyd." The deal fell through when the sellers refused an inspection without a letter of intent to purchase. There might have been another problem even if it had gone through. There was no AAA or Sumatra Lloyd hallmark listed in the *Gold Ingot Hallmark Book*, which is the international bible of hallmarks.

Then the heavy breathers got into the act, spurring more rumors. The term heavy breather is used in the gold trade to signify someone that tries to convince a reputable dealer to issue a letter of intent to buy and then takes this letter to a legitimate seller and claims that he has a confirmed buying order. By bringing the two together he earned a small percentage which could be a lot of money. About the same time the rumors started about the 525 tons for sale, a Filipino-Chinese middleman in Manila claimed he had access to ten tons a week available through Singapore, Hong Kong, or London. An investigation revealed that he was just a heavy breather.

In 1982 General Ramon Cannu, chief legal council of the Presidential Security Command, met with an American, Ron Lusk, in Manila to arrange the confidential shipment of fifty tons of gold to Switzerland. Lusk had been recommended by Credit Suisse Bank. His reputation was well known in Asia and Europe. He could fly anything from a helicopter to a 747, and could smuggle anything, anywhere. What Cannu and Credit Suisse didn't know was that Lusk may not have been his real name. He was in the Federal Witness Protection Program. U.S. authorities at the Bureau of Customs and the Defense Criminal Investigation Service in the Pentagon thought highly of him. He was an informant for seven years and a key witness in the successful prosecution of many drug smugglers.

Cannu showed Lusk the gold. According to Lusk it was stored "underground, with a warehouse over the top of it, somewhere

outside of Manila." This could have been the summer palace at
Mariveles, a few hours drive from Manila overlooking the bay. Lusk
also said that some of the gold had Chinese or Japanese markings,
and some had none. It was stored in copper boxes. While making
the arrangements for the aircraft he was given another tour, this
time of a warehouse at Villamor Air Base. Inside was all kinds of
military equipment, made in the U.S.A. Lusk was told that it was
all for sale. If he could find a buyer he would earn a commission.

Lusk had made plans for two aircraft to fly the gold to
Switzerland but all of a sudden he was informed that his mission
was scrubbed. He was never told why. Two years later he was invited
back for the same purpose but again the plan was scrubbed. (After
the revolution the summer palace and its grounds were thoroughly
searched but no gold was found.)

On 12 August 1982 a telex was sent to Rolando Gapud,
Marcos' primary financial adviser. It stated in part:

> Further to conversation 130AM this date our
> time with your office the money has been placed in
> position by the Saudi National Bank in Madrid to
> purchase the first 6,000 tons metric of product
> discussed... Bill Erbe, President ITM

Whether or not this was related to the gold Lusk was supposed
to transport isn't known. The name Bill Erbe was probably an alias.
There was no further evidence to indicate what transpired.

The financial crisis caused by the Dewey Dee scandal gradually
subsided as gold reserves continued on their rise in 1982 to 1.866
million ounces. But in 1983 it happened again. Reserves dropped
to 289,000 ounces, a decrease of 1.577 million ounces, or 44.8 metric
tons, from the year before. This was twice the amount of 1972.
According to the Central Bank, there was a liquidity crisis at the
time and the gold was sold for badly needed foreign exchange. To
say there was a liquidity crisis was putting it mildly.

As Marcos tightened his control on the country he and his
cronies stole the country blind and salted away as many dollars
as they could get their hands on. At the Central Bank dollar
allocations needed by industry to purchase raw materials and
supplies from abroad became almost non-existent. Many major
manufacturers, whose very existence depended on raw materials

from abroad, could no longer obtain them. Factories began to close. The domino effect began. Other companies dependant on the manufacturers for business began to close. The unemployment rate skyrocketed. The economy was in a shambles. The numbers of the poor and starving began to increase by leaps and bounds.

The Catholic church played a large role in the lives of the Filipinos, especially the poor. They turned to the church for help and the church began to complain. Then businessmen and academics became more vocal in their own complaints. The press began to publicize these problems despite intimidation. In addition to all this Marcos had another problem at the time — his health. He had systemic discoid lupus, a debilitating disease that affects the body's internal organs. On 7 August he secretly underwent a transplant at the National Kidney Foundation in Manila to replace his failing kidneys. That was the situation when Senator Benigno S. "Ninoy" Aquino decided to come home. The country was in turmoil and Marcos was sick. Someone decided that Marcos didn't need another problem.

Ninoy was considered to be the only one that could beat Marcos in a fair election, so he was one of the first to be imprisoned when Marcos declared martial law. In 1977 he was sentenced to death for subversion. He was released in 1980 to go abroad for a heart by-pass operation. He could have stayed in the states, away from Marcos and the country's problems, but he heard Marcos was dying. The country would soon need a new leader, he decided, so it was time to return. On 21 August 1983 his brutal assassination on the tarmac at Manila International Airport shocked the world.

The international financial community reacted immediately. Banks began asking for full payment of their loans instead of allowing roll-overs. Marcos knew it was only a matter of time before the creditors, the World Bank, the International Monetary Fund (IMF), and indeed the whole world knew of their gargantuan financial problems.

In September 1983 Cesar Virata, minister of finance, announced that the foreign debt was $18.1 billion. Two weeks later he announced that it had risen to $19.1 billion. In early October all foreign creditors received telexes sent out by the government. They requested a moratorium on the principal payment of its foreign debt. This sent shock waves through the halls of international finance. On 17 October, Virata announced another surprise. Foreign debt wasn't $19.1 billion after all. It was $24.1 billion. He had neglected to include short-term debt.

The moratorium was granted and the Bank Advisory Committee, composed of the twelve largest banks representing the 483 commercial banks lending to the Philippines, sent an economic subcommittee to Manila to assist the IMF in an investigation. A preliminary audit revealed the Central Bank had exaggerated its international reserves by approximately $600 million. But that was only an initial finding. After the investigation was completed in 1984 the IMF reported that it had actually overstated its reserves by $135 million in 1981, $832 million in 1982, and $41 million in 1983.

According to the Central Bank the 44.8 tons of gold sold in 1983 was to help alleviate the liquidity crisis. At $423 an ounce, the average price of gold that year, that would be worth about $667 million, but reserves decreased much more than that in 1983. The publicity given to the IMF's report was bad enough, but it obscured another important fact. There was an actual decrease in reserves of $846 million in 1983, and $730 million in 1982, for a total of $1.576 billion for those two years. That could have been used to pay off a lot of foreign debt. Instead the government defaulted. In 1965, the year Marcos became president, foreign debt was $600 million. In 1982 it was $24.67 billion. Where did $24 billion go? Not for economic development. And if the sale of the gold was legitimate where did it wind up?

It is rather amusing that the Central Bank stated in a report earlier in the year that the Philippines was "the only country in the world that published accurate information about its foreign debt." The Central Bank governor at the time was Jaime C. Laya. He never was penalized for the reserves scandal. Instead he was relieved of his duties and later promoted to secretary of education.

There were still a lot of unanswered questions about the Central Bank's reserves, particularly its gold. Still this amount of gold didn't begin to reconcile with the huge amounts mentioned in the Mercantile Insurance Company prospectus or the 1982 telex to Gapud. And there was more.

In early 1983 a Luxembourg bank employee turned over to U.S. authorities photocopies of documents relating to a large transaction which the bank was involved in as correspondent. The documents included a sales agreement dated 2 February 1983. The agreement was between a "Secret Seller" and certain "Foreign Buyers," and involved three separate quantities of gold representing a total of 4,207,138 pieces, each weighing 12.5 kilograms, and hallmarked *Banco Central*. The agreement stated in part, "Whereas, to consummate these huge and secret deals, which is once in hundred years, and to prove to the 'secret seller' above, the financial capacities and capabilities of herein 'foreign buyers' represented by the undersigned to buy and purchase these 716,045 pieces of 12.5 kilos each bar, 24 carat and fineness 999.9%..." The value of the 716,045 pieces was quoted at $437 per ounce and the total amount involved was quoted at $125.7 billion. The 4,207,138 pieces totalled 52,589 metric tons. Its worth was over $800 billion.

The buyers had to buy the first batch before it could proceed with the other. This stipulation was also mentioned in a cover letter for an insurance agreement covering this transaction. It was dated 4 February 1983 and written on the letterhead of Mercantile Insurance Company of Manila, the same company that in 1981 was trying to arrange reinsurance for a 525-ton shipment of gold from Manila to Hong Kong.

The letter was addressed to "Foreign Buyers/Banks" through "The Engineering Construction Company, Ltd., 50 Shirley Street, Nassau, Bahamas," for the attention of "Mr. Daniel Swihart, attorney-in-fact, the foreign buyers," and "Mr. John Ramsingh, foreign representative-arranger/funders." It began, "Enclosed herewith are four (4) pages of the 'Memorandum of Agreement to Purchase Gold Bars,' numbering about 716,045 pieces at 12.5 kilos each bar..." The second paragraph referred to the "availability of these 230,400 pieces and 1,809,508 pieces and 2,167,230 pieces of 12.5 kgs. and for which all the buyers/banks abroad arranged by 'PN-1518254' are also acknowledged and the sales will be ready if their unconditional bank guarantees are all ready for verifications and acceptance before lifting of these gold bars." The PN-1518254 referred to the secret seller's representative.

Two other documents relating to the sale were written on Office of the President stationery. A "Memorandum of Strict

Instructions," was dated 28 April, a few months after the date of the sales agreement. It forbid the involvement of any embassy or Philippine government representative abroad, or the mention of Marcos, Imelda, or the Central Bank in the transaction, and warned that all contracts would be cancelled if this happened. The other document, also dated 28 April, had the heading "Below Matters Are Exclusive Prerogative of the President," and reiterated instructions already outlined in the sales agreement. The Memorandum was signed by Konsehala Candelaria V. Santiago, "Trusted woman of President & Secret-Seller." The signature block of the other document stated "By Authority of the President/Code One of the Philippines, by Candelaria V. Santiago, the President's Trusted Woman."

For such a large and important transaction the sales agreement and the documents signed by Santiago did not appear to be drawn up by a lawyer or someone with a good command of English grammar. Among the terms used were "secret-huge-transactions," "USBillion dollars loans," "USdlrs billion funding," "hard copies of several pieces of bank guarantees," "foreign representative-arranger/funders," and "this huge deal is once in hundred years."

Also, it stated that the hallmark was "Banco Central." That may have been the hallmark on those bars, but it wasn't the hallmark of the Central Bank. Its hallmark would have read "Central Bank of the Philippines, Gold Refinery and Mint."

There were several conditions attached to the agreement. The buyers had to pay a two million peso fee up front on signing of the agreement, and another $200,000 in advance for shipping charges. They also had to loan the government five to ten billion dollars at 8.5 percent interest for twenty years. Three percent of that amount went to various funders, agents, and middlemen. Even the selling price of $437 per ounce was broken down with $400 going to the government and $37 going to the same funders, agents, and middlemen.

An intriguing point was that Marcos' involvement was made very obvious. While referring to a "Secret Seller," the sales agreement stated "confidential documents otherwise known as 'notes for the president.' " And a few months later when Santiago began using Office of the President stationery it seemed that she wanted everyone to know that Marcos was behind this transaction. Despite the oddities of the agreement, Marcos apparently allowed Santiago to negotiate the deal on his stationery and even suggest he was a part of it. To do that without his permission in 1983 would be tantamount to suicide. Being a lawyer he had to be embarrassed at the wording of the documents, which also probably meant he never saw them.

The only other name that could be traced besides Santiago was Daniel Swihart, a shadowy American who claimed to be Ver's right hand man. Because the deal was never concluded it will never be known whether or not it was a scam.

The period following Ninoy's assassination was one of increasing instability. The murder touched off a powder keg of emotions. The people were mad and they weren't going to take it anymore. Despite intimidation and threats, businessmen in barongs demonstrated in the streets alongside taxi drivers in tee-shirts and society matrons in silk, all demanding that Marcos must go. All of this had to make him a little nervous.

Two weeks after the assassination, on 9 September 1983, 247 400-ounce gold bars were flown from Manila to London via Amsterdam on KLM flight 864. A KLM employee obtained a copy of the air waybill and made it available to the press. According to the waybill the gold was shipped in sixty-two crates and weighed 3,020 kilograms. Morgan Guaranty Trust Company of Manila was listed as the shipper, and Morgan Guaranty Trust Company of London as the consignee. The gold was purchased for $39 million and the proceeds deposited into the Central Bank accounts at Morgan Guaranty and Citicorp.

Also in September 1983 the local news in Manila reported that a Korean Airlines scheduled flight from Manila to Zurich via Bahrain failed to achieve lift-off and ran off the runway. Under a promise of secrecy the pilot later said that the plane's cargo had shifted and couldn't lift off "because of the weight of the gold." After Marcos fled the Philippines there was an investigation of this incident, but the control tower could not find the records of this flight. They had disappeared.

A month later, in October, a 707 from Amsterdam was chartered to carry "flowers" from Manila to Zurich via Hong Kong and Karachi. The plane had a diplomatic air waybill and also nearly crashed into the sea on takeoff because of the weight. Bong Bong, Marcos' son, was reported to be on this flight. The gold was supposedly strapped in individual seats to distribute the weight. The PCGG attempted to confirm this flight but these records had also disappeared from the airport.

On 24 November 1983 Northwest Airlines Flight 20 from Manila landed at the Seattle-Tacoma International Airport. On this flight was a Filipino attorney by the name of Jose Cruz-Cruzal. He was accompanied by his bodyguard, Clarence E. Decker, an American who carried a Philippine passport. Decker held dual citizenship because of his Philippine mother and American father.

At the customs area inspectors found a plastic bag which Cruz-Cruzal had tried to conceal in the small of his back. It contained documents which stated that Marcos wanted to borrow billions of dollars from banks through an American living in Alexandria, Virginia, by the name of Frank B. Higdon. The collateral to be used, according to the documents, was "four floors of gold" stored underneath a bank in Manila. Cruz-Cruzal carried an identification card showing he was an agent of the Presidential Security Command. He also carried a number of blank PSC I.D. cards for whatever purpose he would not divulge.

Cruz-Cruzal and Decker refused to answer any questions without consulting an attorney and both asked to call Higdon. When a customs agent did call Higdon, he asked that Cruz-Cruzal and Decker be allowed to depart without further delay, and asked that their documents not be photocopied. Cruz-Cruzal also carried some peso checks which amounted to about $40,000. These were seized but later returned when it was discovered that the checks had already been cleared through Cruz-Cruzal's Manila bank. All the documents were photocopied despite Higdon's request. Cruz-Cruzal and Decker's passports were taken and a case filed against them. The case was later broadened to include possible foreign corrupt practices violations and gold smuggling.

When a customs agent contacted Higdon again, he stated that Cruz-Cruzal's mission was sanctioned by U.S. government officials and that pursuit of the matter would prove detrimental to the government. Higdon hung up in the middle of the conversation because the agent was acting rude and unprofessional. Shortly afterward Higdon's lawyer called the agent back and told him that he would soon be contacted by a government official who would advise him to discontinue the investigation because national security was involved. No official called back, however.

Investigators found that Higdon, age sixty-seven, was a certified public accountant with possible connections to the CIA. He had tried before, through his lawyer, to arrange the shipment of a large quantity of gold from Manila to the states. Wells Fargo was the bank that was approached to handle the delivery. Discussions were ended when the bank advised them that it would not deliver to a private residence or non-financial institution.

Higdon's phone records were subpoenaed by a federal grand jury and it was revealed that he made a number of calls to Colonel Florentino Villacrusis, Jr. and his attorney, Jesus M. Capilli. Higdon accompanied Capilli and two other men on a trip to Hong Kong in 1983. They visited several banks. Brian Lendrum, head of American Express Private Bank in Hong Kong, recalled that several Filipinos had approached him about a large amount of gold for sale, but there was no transaction. He recalled that the name of Jaime Laya, the Central Bank governor, was mentioned but Laya wasn't there.

Higdon was also a friend of Villacrusis, who was known to be a member of the task force that Marcos had set up to search for the Yamashita treasure. Villacrusis was never connected in any way to the Central Bank. So were they trying to sell Central Bank gold or something else? Higdon's investigation was finally closed nine months later. There was no indictment. The charges against Cruz-Cruzal were also dropped.

That trip to Hong Kong coincided with information provided by an American from Las Vegas, Norman Lester "Tony" Dacus. He contacted U.S. Senator Chic Hecht of Nevada in April 1985 and claimed that he was involved with Marcos in selling gold. He showed Hecht two contracts, both dated 28 May 1983. The first was for 15,600 tons at $400 an ounce. The Seller guaranteed delivery of sixty tons a week, but reserved the right to deliver the entire volume within two years. The second contract was for 4,000 tons at $400 an ounce, with delivery of ten tons a week.

Dacus had lived in Hawaii at one time, and became friends with a neighbor, Joseph Zbin. Zbin confided that he needed financial help in a deal that was worth a lot of money. His phone bills were getting too expensive, and he couldn't afford to make a trip to Manila. Could Dacus go in his place?

Dacus flew to Manila in August 1983 before Ninoy Aquino's assassination. He met with Marcos on four occasions but dealt mainly with Ver. His only job was to protect his and Zbin's interest in the transactions. At these meetings he met an Australian, Michael O'Brien, whose company, Remington Limited, was the primary broker representing the buyers. Accompanying O'Brien was a man named Milne Juricich, a Yugoslav national.

According to Dacus, the gold for the first sale came from Hang Lung Bank in Hong Kong. The buyers were John Doel and Harry Elkins. Both contracts noted that their bank was Heritage Bank and Trust Company in Salt Lake City, Utah, and the correspondent bank was Mitsubishi Bank in Hong Kong. The seller's bank was Hang Lung Bank in Hong Kong, under the account of Pedro Laurel. The bank officer in charge of the transaction was Richard Yap, president and general manager.

The contracts also noted the agents to whom commissions were due. On the buyer's side, a 1 percent commission was paid to the following agents: Agent One was due 25 percent (of the 1 percent). No name was listed but this was Dacus and Zbin. Agent Two, listed as William H. Sener (two-thirds) and David A. Sayoc, Jnr. (one-third) was due 25 percent; Agent Three, listed as Bistre Limited, was due 25 percent; and Agent Four, listed as Remington Limited (Michael O'Brien) was due 25 percent.

On the seller's side, 1 percent was due to Domingo Clemente, and 1 percent to a group composed of Enrique Turaray, Rufino Barcelona, Rosauro Webb, Antera G. Clemente, and Yolanda Vidal. Dacus said that Pedro Laurel was the front man for Marcos in the deals. Clemente and Laurel sat in on all of Dacus' meetings.

The commissions of the buyers' agents were sent to Credit Swiss American Bank in Antigua; Hongkong Shanghai Bank, Bank of America, and Chartered Bank of Hong Kong, all in Hong Kong; and Chase Manhattan Bank in Nassau, the Bahamas. Dacus was paid a commission of ₱500,000 ($50,000), in pesos in Manila, when the first sixty tons, or 1,929,000 ounces, was sold in late 1983, and $45,000, in dollars in the states, when the second delivery was sold in early 1984.

Dacus said he saw gold bars on two occasions. The first time was at United Coconut Planters Bank in August 1983. He estimated that a hundred tons of gold was stored there. This could be the "four floors of gold" that Cruz-Cruzal referred to.

The second time was when he flew on a military helicopter with General Ver to Ilocos Norte in September or October 1983. There he met Bong Bong Marcos and was shown around an almost completed shrine of Marcos. He described it as a pyramid type building. When he walked in he saw a waterfall and a one-meter tall Buddha on a pedestal. It was shiny and looked like gold but he didn't know for sure. In the rear was a vault about ten meters wide and twenty-five meters deep. He estimated that 300 to 500 tons of gold was stored there. The bars were larger, about 25-kilograms, than those he saw in Manila.

They had flown to Ilocos Norte to discuss the logistics of moving the gold out of the shrine and taking it to Clark Air Base. From there it would be flown to Zurich via Hong Kong and London. Dacus claimed that's when he learned that CIA pilots were being used.

He returned home in April 1985 and turned over his documents to Senator Hecht before all deliveries were completed. He said that when he found out the CIA was involved he wanted no part of the deal even though he would have received $600 million in commissions if all deliveries in the first two contracts were completed. He also said there were supposed to be five more contracts. He doesn't know if these were ever completed.

Higdon returned to Manila in May 1985, and was asked to meet with an economics professor. They met in Higdon's room, 415, in the Manila Hotel. The man claimed to be in charge of disposing of Marcos' gold. They met two or three more times in the Bank of the Philippine Islands board room, with some men who claimed to be with the bank. Higdon refused to meet again after that because he thought they were phony. Among other things, they asked for a lot of money up front before the sale. "For a group who supposedly represented a gold seller, they were totally unprofessional," said Higdon.

Years later, the same economics professor told the *Daily Inquirer* newspaper in Manila a similar story, but asked that his name not be mentioned. He said Marcos asked him to meet with an American Mission sent by President Reagan. Supposedly this mission was composed of U.S. Secretary of the Treasury Donald Regan, Attorney General Edwin Meese, CIA Director William Casey, Professor Frank Higdon, economic adviser to the White House, Lawrence Kraeger, President Reagan's personal attorney, and the unmarried sister of Reagan. They met in room 415 of the Manila Hotel in May 1985. Their purpose was to ask Marcos to loan the American government 100,000 tons of gold. After the meeting all members of the mission departed except Higdon, who left in February. Before departing, Higdon said, "In two weeks Marcos will not be in Malacañang."

When Higdon read the story, his reply was, "I never met Edwin Meese, William Casey, Donald Regan, or any of the others. Nor was I an economic adviser to the White House. I'm an accountant. The only time I've ever been to the White House was as a tourist. And I certainly didn't predict that Marcos was going to be deposed."

Meese provided more information. "I've never been to the Philippines in my life," he said, and noted that Reagan never had a sister married or otherwise, nor did he have a personal attorney by the name of Lawrence Kraeger.

Higdon said he met a lot of people purporting to represent Marcos and his gold, but most of them were phony. In almost every case the phonies asked for money up front. When asked about his role, Higdon said he was a legitimate buyer, but he couldn't say who he represented. "That information has to remain secret for now. We are still involved over there," he said.

In October or November 1985 Interpol sent a cable from Manila. It began, "A Philippine national within (*sic*) direct access to the information reported herein who has reported reliably in the past..."

The cable went on to state that three suspicious shipments — one of gold and two of silver — had been made by the Central Bank in 1985. The informant speculated that the Marcos family diverted the precious metals to Switzerland and put them in their personal accounts. The only proof the informant had was a Bill of Lading from one shipment which showed that 244 silver bars, weighing 8,202 kilograms, were received by First United Transport, the broker in the Philippines, on 11 October 1985 and moved to the docks escorted by the Presidential Security Command. They were loaded onto the USS *President Kennedy* for shipment to Los Angeles, and then on to Drexel, Burnham, Lambert Trading Corporation in New York via Alba Forwarding Company of New York.

This information jibed with a secret U.S. Treasury report, which reported that in the fall of 1985 American President Lines, which owns the *President Kennedy* made three suspicious shipments of gold and silver bullion whose worth was estimated at between $12 and $36 million. The bill of lading for 244 bars of silver was also contained in this report. Drexel Burnham claimed the shipment was routine and that the proceeds were deposited in the Central Bank's account in the Federal Reserve Bank in New York.

Marcos fled the Philippines in February 1986. Computer printouts found in Malacañan Palace after he left showed that beginning on 3 December 1985, and continuing until he fled, there were twenty wire transfers totalling $94 million from the Central Bank's Federal Reserve account in New York to bank accounts in Switzerland and Luxembourg.

The default in 1983 coupled with the reserves scandal and the evidence about secret gold shipments did not sit well with the international financial community. Even more intriguing were the stories, of thousand-ton, billion-dollar gold deals. Were they real?

CHAPTER THREE

The Gold Deals

Orlando Dulay sat alone in his cell feeling dejected. When he first arrived at the prison he thought it would only be a matter of time before some of his old friends would intercede on his behalf and he would go free. That's the way it was in the Philippines. If you had powerful friends there were no laws that couldn't be broken, and in Marcos' time his friends were the most powerful. Now things were different but some of these people were still around. They would take care of him. He had been visited and assured of that many times. But as the months wore on he realized that nobody could help. He was on his own.

When Marcos first came to power Dulay was used as an enforcer to deal with his political enemies. Dulay operated with impunity and proved to be very good at his job. His reputation grew. As a reward for his services and loyalty he was appointed governor of Aurora province, the only military officer accorded such an honor. Unfortunately it was this skill at implementing Marcos' policies that proved to be his undoing. In 1987 he was found guilty of the murder of two of Marcos' political enemies and sentenced to life imprisonment.

Now, almost three years later, he considered his options. One, he could serve his sentence peacefully and remain in this rat hole until he died. That didn't sound too good. Two, he could probably escape but he would be hunted for the rest of his life. Naah. Then he got an idea. He called a trusted friend and asked her to come at once. He wanted a message delivered to a lawyer he knew, David

Castro. Castro wasn't just any lawyer. He was chairman of the PCGG, and he knew Dulay. Before, in the late seventies, he had served as his lawyer on another case.

After receiving the message Castro called Solicitor General Francisco Chavez. The following afternoon they visited Dulay in New Bilibid. The name of the prison was a misnomer. It was no longer new, and not much had been done to improve it since Tabo Ingles was incarcerated there by the Japanese forty-seven years before. Castro and Chavez listened politely at first, then more attentively, as Dulay explained. He had something they wanted so perhaps he could bargain. After he returned to his office Castro called a trusted attorney, Mario Ongkiko. "Can you come over?" he asked. "There is something important we need to discuss."

Mario drove over to the Philcomcen Building in Pasig, a suburb of Metro Manila, took the elevator to the sixth floor, and gave his name to the security guard. He was immediately ushered into Castro's office. They were old friends so there was little formality. Castro told him of the meeting with Dulay, and reiterated the fine points of their conversation. Then he asked "Orly is going to need a lawyer. Can you handle it?" Mario was just finishing his last job for President Aquino as prosecutor at the trial of her husband's murderers, so he said yes.

Now why would someone serving a life sentence for double murder all of a sudden need a lawyer like Mario Ongkiko? Mario's reaction was enough explanation. "If this is for real, then we could pay off our foreign debt," which was about $27 billion at the time. "What do you think?"

Castro replied, "Dulay was close to Marcos. He could be telling the truth. Let's check it out." What Dulay said was that Marcos had found the legendary Yamashita treasure, the gold buried in the Philippines by the Japanese during World War II. Marcos had already dug up half of it, worth about $40 billion, and shipped it out of the country. Dulay claimed to be one of three people who knew where the other half was buried. He wouldn't name the other two. He agreed to lead them to the site, but first he had to go to Japan to see someone involved with the treasure hunt. He was turned down.

"You have to deliver one gold bar to prove yourself first," Mario told him.

"Okay, but that'll take some time," Dulay said.

The gold bar has not yet been delivered. Was Dulay telling the truth? He had everything to gain and nothing to lose in making such claims. The Marcos stories about the treasure were nothing new. There was evidence that he did mount a task force to look for it, but whether or not he found anything was anybody's guess. If Dulay's claim proved to be true then it would be the first real proof that Marcos found a treasure.

.

In April 1986 Julie Amargo, columnist for the Malaya newspaper in Manila, obtained a duplicate copy of the KLM cargo airway bill dated 9 September 1983, and wrote an article about the mysterious shipment of gold that day. She asked the PCGG to investigate and pinpoint the persons behind the shipment. Two months later, in response to Amargo, the Central Bank published an article in its magazine, *Central Bank Review*. It stated that the shipment was a location swap that resulted in a sale, and was done to "beef up liquidity at a time when the Central Bank was having difficulty meeting its foreign exchange payments."

It provided the dates and quantities of all location swaps that had occurred during the Marcos era. There were twenty-seven. The first was on 21 December 1981 and the last was on 18 September 1985. (Marcos departed in February 1986.) A total of 5,390 pieces, amounting to 1,994,037.741 ounces, or 56.65 metric tons, was shipped out of the country. According to the article the swaps were done to earn interest, but some resulted in actual sales. The article did not specify which swaps ended in sales. The only sale known for sure was the 9 September 1983 shipment, and the press, not the Central Bank, reported that.

The title of the article was "CB's Gold and Silver Reserves Management: Clearing the Doubts." Somehow the title didn't fit with the information. When asked, the Central Bank admitted that, in addition to the location swaps, there were other gold shipments out of the country during Marcos' time but they wouldn't clear the doubts about those. They refused to provide further information. Only they knew how many more shipments were made, and where the money wound up.

After Marcos left, for some reason the mystery surrounding the final disposition of the Central Bank's gold and other reserves was never considered a priority issue. A lot of people thought it strange that President Aquino did not bother to replace the governor of the bank, who had been appointed by and served under Marcos. As the country struggled to correct the economic hardships brought on by Marcos the Central Bank's problems were all but forgotten.

The PCGG was hard at work following the paper trail of hidden wealth. More and more leads were developed as people began to talk freely. Reports started coming in about alleged treasure recoveries by a military task force led by Ver. Some locations were given: the train station at Paco in Manila in 1971 supposedly yielded eighty tons of gold. A church site at Agoo, La Union was richer, yielding 100 tons in early 1973. The fountain at the rotunda at Legarda in Manila yielded forty tons. Unfortunately such reports were almost impossible to verify.

On 16 March 1986 the *Los Angeles Times* reported that another seven tons of gold was unaccounted for in the Central Bank, but this story had a different tack. In 1978 Marcos signed a decree ordering all gold producers to sell their gold to the Central Bank which had set up its own refinery. This decree took effect on 17 April 1978. The Bureau of Mines had reported that 124,234 pounds of gold were refined between that time and the end of 1984, the last year for which statistics were available at that time. But the Central Bank reported receiving only 110,319 pounds during this same period. That left a difference of 13,915 pounds which couldn't be accounted for. At $390 per ounce (the average price of gold from 1978 to 1984) 222,630 ounces (13,915 pounds) of gold would be worth $86,825,700. The director of the Bureau of Mines refuted this claim, and stated that this gold was accounted for, that those figures were based on incomplete Central Bank data. True or not, with the findings about the Central Bank's creative accounting of its reserves, it was difficult to accept such statements at face value.

On 17 March 1986 the Archdiocese of San Francisco released a bulletin. It announced that they had:

> ... notified Filipino and U.S. authorities of a telex brought to its attention describing a transaction involving 5,000 metric tons of gold bullion allegedly connected to the government of deposed president Ferdinand Marcos.

The two-page telex was addressed "To: owner/seller, Manila Philippines, c/o Mrs. Alejandria Pineda Caldona," and called for the transfer of 160,750,000 troy ounces of gold bullion from a bank in Europe to a bank in Hong Kong. One of those involved, who requested anonymity, had contacted the Justice and Peace Commission of the Archdiocese of San Francisco and asked for help in advising the proper authorities because of the possible link to Marcos. Once again, the name given on the telex couldn't be traced and was probably an alias.

In April 1986 an Australian broker in Sydney told the *Sunday Telegraph* newspaper that a T.C.B. "Andrew" Tan had telexed him an offer to sell 2,000 tons of gold worth nearly $22 billion just before Marcos' downfall. Tan claimed to be a friend of Bong Bong Marcos. He said the gold was "24-carat, 999.95 percent pure gold, 12.5 kilograms per bar," and that it had previously been stashed in Hong Kong, London, U.S., Singapore, Switzerland, Panama, and the Netherlands Antilles. He also told the broker that the gold was part of the spoils of war taken by the Japanese in World War II. The broker couldn't handle the sale because of its size so he passed it on to an Arab consortium located in London. They were asked to deliver $1 billion to the Central Bank in the Philippines and exchange it for U.S. treasury notes. The treasury notes were then to be swapped for gold bars at a bank overseas. Negotiations on the deal had just started when Marcos was ousted.

A representative of the Great American Management Corporation from Houston, Texas, met in Hong Kong with someone from Manila to discuss the sale of "12,000 pieces" of gold. The size of the pieces were not clear as both 12.5-kilogram and 75-kilogram bars were mentioned. Negotiations for this sale began before the revolution and continued until May 1986. Those involved included various agents from Athens, Zurich, Capetown, and the U.S., but no deal was ever concluded.

In Tokyo an estimated twenty tons of gold, worth about $330 million, was sold on the black market beginning in the spring of 1986 shortly after Marcos' overthrow, according to the English-language daily newspaper *Yomiuri Shimbun*. It said its investigation revealed that the bullion was sold in Tokyo at unregistered precious metal stores for cash where records were not kept. Japanese traders and mining company sources claimed that before the gold was sold in those places, people who identified themselves as Marcos aides approached them and offered to sell the same amount. They refused, so it entered the black market.

On 28 August 1986 an informant for the National Bureau of Investigation by the name of Christina Concepcion Ismael, posing as a buyer, saw ninety 75-kilogram gold bars (about 7.5 tons) worth about $96 million, in an apartment building in Quezon City, the large metropolis bordering Metro Manila. The building was owned by Jonathan Dela Cruz, a friend of Bong Bong Marcos. Ismael was given a polygraph test a few days later and passed. The building was heavily guarded by a private security force owned by Roque Ablan. During the Marcos era he had been a congressman in Marcos' home province of Ilocos Norte and had also served as vice-governor. The governor was Bong Bong. Whether or not the building was ever searched isn't known. The NBI refused to comment. The head of the NBI at the time was still a Marcos appointee.

Meanwhile, in Honolulu, Marcos should have been content to sit back and enjoy his retirement in paradise. But no, that wasn't his style. He had to wheel and deal. And just now he had other things on his mind, like a coup.

In the pre-dawn hours of Tuesday, 27 January 1987, 500 heavily armed rebel soldiers still loyal to Marcos fanned out over Metro Manila. Headed by a general and seventeen officers, the soldiers intended to take over three key military facilities and two television stations, and then announce over the airways that Marcos had returned. Unfortunately things didn't quite work out that way. Of the five targets the rebels were routed at four within hours: the Channel Four television station; the Operations Center at Villamor Air Base; Sangley Point in Cavite, base of the Fifteenth Strike Wing; and Camp Aguinaldo, headquarters of the National Defense Ministry. The attack on the Channel Seven television station took a little longer to repulse. There a colonel and 150 soldiers took some hostages when they saw their efforts were futile, but released them and surrendered two days later. Just as the siege was ending rumors swept the country that Marcos had just returned to the Philippines and landed in Ilocos Norte, his home province.

While this was going on it was reported that the mother of Marcos, *Doña* Josepha, disappeared from her hospital room at the Philippine Heart Center just before the rebel soldiers began their attacks. In Honolulu, Marcos left his home and also couldn't be found for about twelve hours, fueling the rumors of his return to the Philippines. Tomas "Buddy" Gomez III, then Philippine consul general in Hawaii and later President Aquino's press secretary, announced that Marcos had not returned to the Philippines, that he was still in Hawaii although that wasn't where he wanted to be.

Gomez explained that he and his intrepid band of "Marcos-watchers," a volunteer group of Filipinos loyal to President Aquino who kept a close watch on Marcos and Imelda, had uncovered a plan by Marcos to secretly fly back to the Philippines and land on Bugsuk Island off Palawan. He had chartered a Boeing 707 from an aviation company in Miami headed by a Lebanese arms dealer close to Adnan Kashoggi, the billionaire disco-partner of Imelda. Kashoggi was a frequent visitor to the Marcos home in Hawaii. He once admitted that Marcos promised him 10 percent of a shipload of gold if he could find a safe port for the vessel, preferably an Arab country. Kashoggi never saw the ship or the gold, and later Marcos told him he had made other arrangements.

Gomez reported Marcos' plan to fly to the Philippines to the U.S. State Department, and told them that the aircraft was parked at a private airfield near the Honolulu International Airport ready for takeoff. State Department representatives had in turn visited Marcos and told him that they knew about the 707 waiting on the runway. They politely advised him that he could not leave the country. As usual he denied all knowledge of the incident and, as soon as the agents were gone, proceeded to hatch another scheme.

On 9 July 1987 Marcos' latest plot was made known to the public. Representative Stephen Solarz, chairman of the House Foreign Affairs Subcommittee on Asia and the Pacific, convened hearings in Washington, D.C. Two people, Richard Hirschfield and Robert Chastain, testified that Marcos had planned to return to the Philippines in late June 1987 and link up with a 10,000 man army to retake the Philippines. Their testimony was based on three and a half hours of tapes which were played at the subcommittee hearings. They had secretly recorded their conversations with

Marcos using a voice-activated tape recorder hidden in a briefcase. On the tape Marcos was quoted as saying he would try to take President Aquino hostage, by force if necessary. In Marcos' own words, "This is a go-for-broke deal."

Richard Hirschfield was a Charlottesville, Virginia, attorney who claimed to have as clients Muhammad Ali and a billionaire Saudi Arabian businessman by the name of Mohamad Al Fassi, known for his penchant for painting the private parts of the nude statues that adorned the walls of his Beverly Hills mansion.

Hirschfield called Marcos in the fall of 1986 and wangled an appointment. He flew there on 10 September with an associate, Robert Chastain. They met with Marcos and attended his birthday party the next day. They cultivated this friendship and promised to help him obtain citizenship in another country. In early 1987 Marcos asked if they knew anyone that could supply him with weapons and ammunition.

Although they were not in that line of business Hirschfield and Chastain decided to play Marcos along. Chastain claimed to have contacts with some arms dealers so discussions began. Marcos suggested that they use code names when communicating with each other. Marcos chose the name Charlie, and Chastain chose Andrew. In one conversation, which took place on 21 May, Marcos placed an order to equip his army that included tanks, Huey helicopters, armored personnel carriers, recoilless rifles, rocket launchers, machine guns, 8,000 M-16's, of which a thousand would be equipped with grenade-launchers, and three months' supply of ammunition.

When the method of payment was discussed Marcos asked for $18 million in financing. He added that he had $500 million in bank accounts in Switzerland and $14 billion in gold secretly buried in several different places in the Philippines which could be used as collateral.

When Hirschfield questioned him about the gold Marcos was somewhat vague. At first he inferred that he got it from the Central Bank through collusion with a former Central Bank governor now deceased. In his words: "It is my money but it, I borrowed it from these people who were buy, who were buying the gold..." (This scheme of using gold bullion still in the Philippines to borrow large sums of money was also mentioned in papers confiscated from Jose

Cruz-Cruzal when he was arrested at the Seattle-Tacoma International Airport in November 1983.)

Marcos then abruptly changed his story and claimed that the gold came from World War II veterans who had been guerrillas in his outfit. Wherever it came from, throughout the taped interview Marcos was adamant about two points. He would never admit having the gold and he didn't want to sell it. "We must never lose the gold. We can lose everything but the gold," he said, and went on to add that Imelda didn't know about the gold because "she panics." He said that Bong Bong, his son, knew where it was.

After the tapes were made on 21 May copies were turned over to the FBI and Philippine government. Hirschfield claimed that the copies were edited to delete some remarks made by Marcos who claimed to still have influence over several high-ranking U.S. officials.

Hirschfield also claimed to know the location of about one billion dollars worth of the gold Marcos had mentioned. As a result the PCGG entered into an agreement with him on 4 June, which entitled him to "5 percent of the value of gold or other precious metals within ninety days of recovery." He never divulged his information about the location and no gold was ever recovered. (A few years later Hirschfield ran afoul of the law himself, and was sent to prison.)

The State Department was informed about Marcos' latest fiasco. Once again they warned him about such activities. In addition, the Justice Department wrote and advised him that he must apply in writing forty-eight hours in advance for permission to leave the island of Oahu, which included Honolulu.

As the PCGG went about the task of attempting to locate and recover the hidden wealth of Marcos, they waded through mountains of documents and interviewed hundreds of people. In the different investigations involving gold holdings a pattern began to emerge. Marcos was suspected of having gold deposited in banks in the U.S, Hong Kong, Singapore, Switzerland, and several other European countries. When interviewing people about an account it would be mentioned that the vault or deposit box holding the gold could not be opened unless all trustees to that particular account were present. The number of trustees was usually three.

There was also mention of an organization known as Umbrella, which Marcos had set up. The apparent intention was to have each account controlled by a separate group of trustees. Marcos and Bong Bong were the only two people who knew the entire Umbrella structure. It was suspected that after Marcos died Bong Bong finally told Imelda about this, and they quietly went about trying to dismantle this organization because there was dissension in the ranks. The problem was that the people in each of these groups were loyal to Marcos, not Imelda or Bong Bong, and now they were out to protect their own interests.

Other gold deals continued to surface. In March 1990 the PCGG subpoenaed Geoffrey Greenlees, a British national living in the Philippines, who had just returned from Munich. They claimed that a member of the U.S. consulate in Munich reported to Washington that a sale involving 2,000 tons of gold was being arranged by the Hongkong Shanghai Bank there. Washington informed the PCGG lawyers in Los Angeles, who informed the PCGG in Manila. They ordered an investigation. That's when Greenlees' name surfaced, according to the PCGG.

Greenlees was somewhat skeptical. He had just returned from Munich, but how did they know he was back in Manila and staying in the Philippine Plaza hotel? He confirmed that he was arranging a purchase of gold, but he claimed that the sale was legitimate, and his being in Munich had nothing to do with it. Greenlees was an attorney. He had gone there for a client regarding legal matters. The PCGG stuck to their story, but Greenlees suspected that someone in Manila who knew about his gold deal had reported it to the PCGG in the hope of getting a finder's fee if the gold were recovered by the PCGG.

Greenlees confirmed that the gold deal was initiated in Manila when a lady whom he knew as Margaret Tucker introduced him to a Filipino attorney, Victor Santos, who represented the sellers. Greenlees contacted a consortium of buyers led by Credit Lyonnais Bank and the deal was arranged. The contract stated that 1,000 to 19,000 tons, not 2,000 tons, was being offered for sale. No price was specified, but the first sale would be for five tons. The sale was to take place in Singapore, not Munich. Greenlees flew to Singapore a few days later. He waited six weeks but the other parties failed to show up. Greenlees claimed he had not seen Santos or Tucker since he returned to Manila, nor did he know how to contact them.

The PCGG said that was the first time that those two names, Margaret Tucker and Victor Santos, had surfaced in any of the gold deals. They speculated that Tucker might be an alias for Edna Camcam, the girlfriend of Ver. Others thought she might be Candelaria V. Santiago.

The post-Marcos era in the Philippines was generally one of open and honest government, but there was still a cloud of doubt hanging over the Central Bank. Besides the confusing and misleading magazine article, the only information they officially released — the international reserves data to the IMF — was found to be fraudulent. The Central Bank remained the only Philippine government institution not examined by the PCGG. But the PCGG claimed that it could not investigate unless requested by the Central Bank. In military parlance this is known as Catch 22. Some congressmen publicly demanded an investigation into these matters but nothing happened.

So people were meeting all over the world to discuss gold deals emanating from Manila. But something wasn't right. The bars that Tony Grant had said were available were marked Sumatra Lloyd, definitely not the Central Bank's hallmark. And the fifty tons that Lusk saw had Chinese or Japanese markings. Also Philippine gold reserves only totalled forty-seven tons in 1981, but some of the amounts being negotiated were mind boggling: the 525 tons for sale in 1981 was worth about $5 billion at the time; the 6,000 tons mentioned in the telex to Gapud would be worth about $63 billion; and the 19,600 tons that Dacus mentioned would be worth about $205 billion. Then there was the 5,000 tons reported by the Archdiocese in San Francisco, the 2,000 tons reported by the broker in Australia, the 19,000 ton deal of Greenlees, and the agreement in Luxembourg which alluded to an initial sale totalling $125.7 billion followed by an even bigger deal worth over $800 billion. In addition Marcos told Hirschfield he had $14 billion stashed in the Philippines.

The amounts were almost laughable. Almost. Any discussion with a government official about Marcos and his gold usually brought the same reaction. "Impossible," someone would say when the amounts were mentioned, but with a curious look that said, "I wish it were true."

The PCGG was already getting plenty of reports about treasure recoveries. It was not surprising that the rumors started that Marcos' gold came from the Yamashita treasure buried in the Philippines during World War II. Those stories had been around a long time. Some people even believed that Marcos invented them to cover up his looting of the national treasury. Others contended that the stories were real, that there was a treasure and that it rivalled all other treasures known to man throughout history.

Now that kind of statement will get your attention. How big? And why the Philippines? And who was this General Yamashita anyway?

CHAPTER FOUR

The Legend

Before the war Los Baños had been a sleepy little village on the shore of Laguna de Bay. It was better known for the University of the Philippines College of Agriculture located just outside of town. Then the Japanese came, closed the school, and turned it into a prisoner of war camp for civilians, mostly American. It had been a hell hole for over three years but on 23 February 1945 the prisoners had been liberated in a daring raid as General MacArthur fulfilled his pledge to return. Tabo Ingles had escaped from New Bilibid Prison, and his guerrilla group took part in this mission.

Now, one year later, the war was over and life was returning to normal in the Philippines. But things were anything but normal for the villagers of Los Baños right now. They sensed that something serious was going on but nobody knew what. All day Friday there had been more military police than usual and security had been tightened around the Philippine Detention and Rehabilitation Center, located on the edge of town near the school. Military trucks, jeeps, and staff cars had been driving back and forth. As the sun set the hustle and bustle of the little village quieted down. Soon it was dark and peaceful.

Up the road, in the town of Muntinlupa outside Manila, people were wide awake at 1:30 in the morning. A U.S. Army convoy, under cover of darkness and escorted by military police, quietly drove out of New Bilibid Prison and sped south along the shores of Laguna de Bay. An hour later it entered Los Baños, drove through the village, continued on for about a kilometer, and turned left into the main gate of the Detention Center. After that all was quiet again.

A few hours later, before dawn while the village was still sleeping, the camp came to life. The main gate opened and the convoy drove out. Instead of turning right toward Manila they turned left, drove a few kilometers, slowed down as they came to a security checkpoint, turned right onto a dirt track heading up a hill, proceeded several hundred meters up this bumpy road, and stopped at their destination: a twelve meter square fenced off area lit up as bright as day by huge searchlights, and surrounded by a small army. There were no newsmen present and no cameras were allowed.

The fence was seven and a half meters high and covered with camouflage material so no one could see inside. All the doors of the staff car seemed to open at once as soldiers scurried to their assigned duties. Then the center of attention, the reason for all the bother, stepped from the car. For a moment everyone seemed to find an excuse to stop what they were doing and stare. The Japanese prisoner, shackled and clad in GI's fatigues and cap because he was "unfit to wear a military uniform," according to General MacArthur, got out and stood up. He was tall for a Japanese, over 1.8 meters, and somewhat portly, but he carried himself like the legendary figure that he was, with a military bearing that even simple fatigues couldn't hide.

The gate to the fence opened briefly as he was led inside the enclosed area. After blinking his eyes to adjust to the brightness the first thing he must have noticed were the three large mango trees. And the second thing, under the largest tree, was the gallows painted black. It was time. He slowly climbed the thirteen steps. He did so with the dignity that he had shown all through his trial. When he reached the top he turned to one of his guards and asked in which direction was Tokyo. The sergeant pointed in one direction with his finger. Later he would admit that he didn't know whether he pointed north, south, or toward China. He had no idea where Tokyo was. The general faced in that direction, bowed, and said, "I will pray for the Emperor's long life and his prosperity forever."

Then the noose was placed around his neck and adjusted. At 3:02 on Saturday morning, 23 February 1946, the first anniversary

of the liberation of the prisoners at U.P. Los Baños, Lieutenant
Charles Rexroad, the executioner, gave the signal. The trap door
was sprung and the Tiger of Malaya, Major General Tomoyuki
Yamashita, joined his ancestors.

Soon afterwards two others met the same fate. Colonel Seichi
Ohta, head of the dreaded *Kempei Tai* secret police, climbed the
same thirteen steps and was hung at 3:41. Takuma Higashiji, a
civilian interpreter convicted of torturing and killing Filipino
civilians, was hung at 4:17. The three bodies were wrapped in army
blankets and buried in an unnamed but numbered grave in the
Japanese cemetery at the prisoner of war camp nearby.

On 8 November 1941 Lieutenant General Tomoyuki
Yamashita celebrated his fifty-sixth birthday. He also received an
unexpected present — command of the Japanese Twenty-fifth Army.
It wasn't really a present. He had always been a good soldier, ever
since he graduated from the Military Academy of Japan on 26 June
1906. Japan had been victorious the year before in the Russo-
Japanese war of 1904-05. Now the country was going to war again
and it was his turn to carry on that proud military tradition. He
wound up his assignment as military minister to Germany and Italy
and hurried back to Japan to take over his command.

One month later Pearl Harbor was attacked. Now the world
was at war. General Yamashita and his army of 30,000 landed in
Malaya and charged down the peninsula. His orders were to invade
and occupy. He estimated this would take at least three months.
To everyone's surprise, including his own, eight weeks after he
started Yamashita found himself at the end of the peninsula looking
across Johore Strait. A twenty meter wide causeway separated them
from the island of Singapore. The island was forty-two kilometers
(26 miles) wide and twenty-three kilometers (14 miles) long. Most
of it was rubber plantations and jungle with a few scattered
settlements. The town of Singapore was located at the southern
tip of the island.

Facing Yamashita across the strait was Lieutenant General A.
E. Percival and his 80,000 man army. Yamashita's army stormed
across the strait and was on the outskirts of Singapore within a
few days. Hoping that Percival was not aware of his own numbers

Yamashita massed his troops outside the town in a show of strength and sent a message to Percival calling for a conference. The meeting took place at a bank in the early afternoon of 15 February. The scene was witnessed by dozens of newspaper reporters and observers. In the wire enclosure of a cashier's cage Yamashita and Percival met to decide the fate of the city. Yamashita put on his best poker face and immediately went on the offensive. He offered to spare the city but demanded that Percival surrender at once and order a cease fire effective at six o'clock.

Percival was still reeling from shock and surprise. A Japanese army had just showed up at the back door of a supposedly impregnable fortress whose big guns were pointing the other way out to sea after having stormed down the impassable Malay peninsula.

Trying to buy some time he countered that a cease fire could not possibly be effected that day, that it would have to be at eight the next morning. That frightened Yamashita for he knew that if his numerical weakness was discovered then he could be done for. He started shaking his head and jabbing his finger at Percival. "Did he agree to six o'clock, yes or no?" Yamashita's verbal barrage was relentless. "Yes or no. Yes or no?"

Percival capitulated. Reporters scribbled furiously in their notebooks. One described Yamashita as a ferocious conqueror and coined a new phrase — the "Tiger of Malaya." The mild-mannered Yamashita was surprised. He had been called many things but never ferocious, and certainly not a tiger. Later, in recalling the meeting with Percival, he would smile and say "It was a bluff, a bluff that worked."

In Japan, Yamashita was declared a hero and his popularity spread. That did not please the prime minister, General Hideki Tojo. A dozen years before as a colonel, Yamashita had supported a move to reduce the size of the army, and ever since he had not gotten along with the military clique in power in Tokyo. Now his popularity threatened to eclipse Tojo's and that could not be.

Yamashita was serving as supreme commander in Malaya when he received his new orders. Instead of an important position due a victorious general he was transferred to an obscure post in northern Manchuria thousands of kilometers away from the fighting. He was not even allowed to stop by Tokyo to receive the accolades due him.

He remained in that backwater until October 1944, when once again his talents were called for. By then the tide had turned. Now the Americans moved by leaps and bounds across the vast Pacific, retaking island after island. Every atoll had its terrible price in lives but Japan was losing the war and there was very little their high command could do about it.

When Saipan fell to the Americans in July 1944 Tojo and his cabinet resigned. A new government was formed. A few months later, out of desperation, the Tiger of Malaya was called on again. This time he was ordered to go to the Philippines and replace Lieutenant General Shigenori Kuroda, whose notorious predilection for wine, women, and song had contributed nothing toward the war effort.

Now Yamashita was allowed to stop in Tokyo on the way to his new assignment. He saw his family for a few hours, and exchanged his winter uniforms for tropical ones. At the briefing he realized that he was being asked to perform a miracle. The Americans had to be stopped at all cost, he was told, or Japan would be their next landing.

He arrived in Manila on 7 October 1944 and immediately assumed command of the Fourteenth Area Army. Things were not looking good. The Americans had already achieved air superiority and intelligence showed that an invasion force was on the way. His new Chief of Staff, Lieutenant General Akira Muto, did not arrive until thirteen days later, on 20 October, from Sumatra. On arrival Muto was informed that the Americans had just landed at Leyte in the southern Philippines. "Very interesting," he replied, "but where is Leyte?"

That was the almost impossible situation confronting Yamashita. Handicapped from the beginning he set about doing the best he could with what he had. In December he gave the order to abandon Manila after deciding that it couldn't be defended. The troop pullout began. At first the 16,000 naval forces under Rear Admiral Sanji Iwabuchi pulled back to Fort McKinley. Then he changed his mind and ordered his forces back to Manila. They linked up with 3,750 army security personnel, and within twenty-four hours they were cut off. They only had two choices. Surrender to the Americans or fight to the finish.

History has recorded what happened. After Yamashita's forces left Manila there was a lull in the fighting before the American troops arrived. Iwabuchi's troops began pillaging the city. They broke into the warehouses along the waterfront. One was filled with whisky. That was the fuel that sparked one of the worst murderous rampages of the war. Iwabuchi's demoralized, disorganized, and now drunk soldiers set out with a vengeance, raping the women and slaughtering everyone, even babies and children. When the Americans arrived they had to retake the city building by building, block by block. When it was over Manila was the second most devastated city of the war, behind Warsaw.

Yamashita pulled out of Fort McKinley, his headquarters in Manila, on 22 December and headed for Ipo, located forty kilometers (25 miles) north in Bulacan province. There he set up a temporary headquarters. On 3 January he went back to Fort McKinley for a conference with one of his commanders, Lieutenant General Yokoyama. He departed the next day and headed for the mountain resort of Baguio. The city was 250 kilometers (155 miles) north of Manila, high in the mountains at 1,372 meters. The weather was untropically cool and the scenery magnificent. The city, and the road to it, was built by Americans around 1913 after the American governor of the Philippines, William Howard Taft, made the trek there to cure his dysentery. The U.S. Army had set up a recuperative post, Camp John Hay, situated on a ridge with a panoramic view of the mountains. Now that would be Yamashita's base of operations. From there he attempted to coordinate his defense against insurmountable difficulties. Gradually his troops were overwhelmed in the mountain vastness of northern Luzon. As the American troops closed in Yamashita retreated northward.

He was forced to withdraw from Baguio on the night of 16 April 1945, and retreated westward to Bambang where he set up a new headquarters on 19 April. A month later, on 20 May, he had to withdraw again. Once again using the cover of darkness he slipped out of Bambang, passed through Bagabag, and headed north to Kiangan where he set up his headquarters about 121 kilometers (75 miles) north of Baguio. On 18 June advancing

American troops forced him further north into the mountains. Then the world's first atomic bomb was dropped on Hiroshima on 6 August 1945 and a second bomb was dropped on Nagasaki three days later. Emperor Hirohito ordered an end to the hostilities on 15 August.

Yamashita dutifully received his orders to surrender from the Emperor and on 2 September he and his surrender party, totalling twenty-one persons, made their way back to Kiangan where they had arranged to meet Major General William H. Gill, commander of the Thirty-second Infantry Division, and a special detachment of Company I, Second Battalion, 128th Infantry. From there an armed convoy took them to an airstrip near Bagabag where they boarded a C-47 aircraft. They were flown to La Luna by the Pacific Ocean in La Union province. Another convoy met them and they were taken to Baguio where they arrived at 2:30 in the afternoon.

The official surrender ceremony took place at noon the next day in the drawing room of the American High Commissioner's residence. Afterwards they were taken back to La Luna and flown to Manila. After landing at Nielsen Field at 6:17 in the evening, they were driven directly to New Bilibid prison thirty-two kilometers (20 miles) outside Manila.

Yamashita went on trial in Manila the next month. On 7 December, exactly four years after Pearl Harbor and one month after his sixtieth birthday, he was convicted of war crimes, including the rape of Manila and the slaughter of thousands of innocent men, women, and children in February 1945. It didn't matter to the court that he was over 250 kilometers to the north, that the evidence showed that the atrocities were carried out against his orders, and that he knew nothing about them until they were over. The responsibility was his, they ruled, and he died. It was an ignominious end for the Tiger of Malaya. Ironically all his brave deeds on the battlefield, for which he dedicated his entire professional life, were quickly forgotten only to be replaced by a myth.

After he died stories about Yamashita quickly spread. He had secretly possessed one of the greatest treasures known to man, but the secret of its location died with him on the scaffold, so the stories went. Treasure hunts were the order of the day especially in the mountains around Baguio. It seemed that everyone knew somebody that had seen a treasure buried. A lot of digging was going on. Most of it turned up old Japanese garbage pits and latrines. The rumors ebbed and flowed along with the digging over the years.

It took a long time for the Filipinos to get over the war. The people had been brutalized by the Japanese forces and they weren't going to forget it anytime soon. Not until December 1951 did the government officially allow a Japanese back into their country. Reverend Goto Mitsuzo, a Protestant minister, was allowed to attend the conference of the Far East Council of Christian Churches held in Manila. There were protests but the visit came off without any serious incidents. Ever so slowly the two governments groped toward an understanding as war reparations were worked out and the number of Japanese visitors gradually increased.

Eight years after the war, in 1953, President Elpidio Quirino announced that some Japanese soldiers, who were still in prison in the Philippines for crimes committed during the war, would be released. In exchange Japan would cooperate in an official inquiry to determine once and for all if Yamashita did leave behind a treasure worth billions of dollars as so many people now believed. If there was such a treasure then every attempt would be made to locate and recover it. The investigation was to be headed by Minoru Fukumitsu.

An American of Japanese descent, Fukumitsu's background was as much a mystery as the treasure itself. He claimed that he was born in Salt Lake City, Utah, on 28 March 1918. When the war came he taught Japanese at a U.S. Navy officer's school in Boulder, Colorado. For some reason he was not interned like all other Japanese when the "Yellow Peril" hysteria swept the U.S. at the start of the war. After the war he somehow wound up in Tokyo where he was assigned to work as one of the investigators of the Allied War Crimes Tribunal. His bilingual ability surely helped him get the job, but what qualifications he possessed as an investigator are unknown.

Fukumitsu never explained why or how he was chosen for this task but he obviously had connections somewhere. After being appointed he threw himself into his work. From Manila to Tokyo to Washington, he crisscrossed the globe in his search. He was given access to confidential documents in Japan, and he sifted through the voluminous documentation in the National Archives in Washington, D.C. More than 300 witnesses were interviewed including former members of Yamashita's staff that had survived the war. After researching the matter and talking to every possible lead, an expedition was planned to search for the treasure. It was led by Fukumitsu. Accompanying him was Major Mikiyo Matsonogo, one of Yamashita's staff officers during the war.

The expedition began in Baguio and retraced the route of withdrawal of Yamashita and his troops. The group spread out and methodically combed the areas where the soldiers had encamped. In addition they explored the countryside around each encampment and excavated potential burial sites. All they found, according to Fukumitsu when he returned to Manila nine months later, were a few old coins. There was no evidence to show that the treasure ever existed, he claimed. Then he departed the Philippines.

Over the years he became a consultant to various Japanese firms, and also a friend to then President Marcos. It seemed that whenever the question of the treasure's existence arose he would appear to refute the possibility with messianic zeal.

In 1977 after rumors began to fly again of a vast treasure he flew into Manila and held a press conference, proclaiming that there was no such treasure. "I don't want people to waste their time and effort looking for something which never existed," he said, and brandished a few documents and old clippings showing that the gold and silver belonging to the Philippine treasury had been shipped out before the Japanese arrived so there was no Yamashita treasure.

Again in 1978, when the *Philippine News* in the states exposed the Leber Group treasure hunt set up by Marcos, Fukumitsu surfaced to testify that such a claim was ridiculous. Ten years later, in 1988, the Philippine Congress was holding similar hearings after it was discovered that Americans had been permitted to dig for treasure at Fort Santiago. Fukumitsu appeared once again in Manila and held a press conference. No treasure existed and the diggings at Fort Santiago were for naught, he announced. When questioned he would not say who sent him to Manila, nor could he explain why he had made 600 trips to the Philippines since 1951. But he did admit that he was a friend of Marcos.

An interesting footnote to the Fukumitsu investigation is that, in addition to one of Yamashita's staff officers, there was also a

Filipino that assisted him who had been an officer in the army during
World War II and had served in that area. Venancio Duque had
been a lieutenant and the adjutant of the Fourteenth Infantry
Regiment, the same guerrilla outfit that Marcos joined in the latter
stages of World War II. After Marcos joined the Fourteenth an order
came down from higher headquarters to execute him for
collaboration. Duque had been one of the signers of a petition
attesting to Marcos' loyalty. The petition was then taken to his
uncle, Colonel Calixto Duque, the operations officer at
headquarters. As a result the order was rescinded. Marcos' life was
spared. Duque and Marcos went on to become friends.

Why Duque was chosen to assist in the search for the treasure
or what interest he had isn't known. The fact is that Marcos was
an influential second-term congressman in 1953. After he was elected
president, Duque was appointed by him to head the commission
on elections, a very important post in the Marcos era of voter-fraud
and stuffed ballot boxes.

Two years after Fukumitsu's expedition, in June 1955, another
joint operation of the Philippine and Japanese governments was
begun. This time it was maritime. A total of 269 sunken vessels
sunk during the war were to be salvaged by Japan. Their estimated
aggregate tonnage was 561,200. Of these, 124 vessels were located
in Manila Bay and the other 145 were in other parts of the
Philippines. According to the agreement, the Philippines would be
provided with the "services of the Japanese people including the
necessary equipment and supplies" for the project. In other words,
the Japanese would provide everything, the people, the equipment,
and the financing.

The Japanese had been pushing this project for years and
appeared anxious to start salvaging their own vessels. As soon as
the operation was begun rumors began to fly that some of these
vessels were hiding places for treasure, that they were filled with
gold bullion and then scuttled on purpose at designated spots for
retrieval at some later time. None of the rumors could be
substantiated, however.

Numerous privately funded treasure expeditions were
attempted after the Fukumitsu search but they ended in failure.
The yellowed pages of old Philippine newspapers and magazines

are a testament to their exploits. Some lost their money, others lost their lives in their quest for the vast riches of the legendary treasure. Finally in 1970, in the mountains around Baguio, Rogelio Roxas discovered a golden Buddha, and once again the treasure hunters trekked into the mountains to find their fortune. This time Fukumitsu did not make an appearance or give any comment.

Interest in the Yamashita treasure was renewed but there were still nonbelievers. Roxas was just lucky. There was no big treasure, they claimed. As further proof they pointed to the fact that several books had been written about Yamashita. Some of the authors had interviewed him and others examined his papers rather extensively. None mentioned a treasure. So what, the believers countered. That didn't prove that the treasure didn't exist. After all, if he took the trouble to hide it would he really want to tell anyone about it?

The arguments went back and forth. More convincing proof that Yamashita had little or nothing to do with the burial of a treasure is the historical record. He arrived in October 1944 and was only in Manila eleven weeks. During that time he was busy organizing his defenses, fighting the Americans who landed at Leyte a few weeks later, planning the evacuation of Manila, and withdrawing his troops into the mountains. But it is still possible that he possessed some war booty.

In the American army every soldier strived to collect a personal memento or two of the war, perhaps some Japanese yen, a rifle, or a bayonet. The luckiest might find a Samurai sword. Some of these men found out in a ghastly way that the Japanese didn't really appreciate this. If they found any of their items on a captured American soldier it was assumed that this soldier killed a Japanese to get it. And that would be the death knell for that soldier. There were dozens of reported cases like this on the Bataan Death March.

When the Japanese attacked in December 1941, General MacArthur ordered a withdrawal to the Bataan Peninsular. There they held out for over three months, but disease, starvation, and the battle finally took its toll. The surrender of these men and their forced march to a prisoner of war camp resulted in one of the cruelest episodes of the war, the Bataan Death March. During the march the Japanese searched every American and Filipino for anything of value such as a canteen, a watch, or cigarette lighter. If any

Japanese items were found the soldier was taken out of the column, beaten to a pulp, beheaded right on the roadside, and left there for all to see. These heads and headless bodies were a far too common scene indelibly burned into the memories of the survivors who could still recall the grisly sight with anguish almost half a century later.

In the Japanese army it was a little different. They lived off the land, and they pillaged more. It was an unwritten rule that officers had a right to a certain amount of booty. And every general officer had a right to even more than that. So it wasn't uncommon for the higher ranks to have their own private stash, maybe even a truckload or two. But just how big could all these stashes·be?

It's quite possible that Yamashita possessed his own stash, perhaps a few artifacts and some gold bars, or even a gold statuette of Buddha. And if Yamashita buried anything for safekeeping it was probably in the mountains around Baguio, where Roxas discovered his Buddha. But it is rather ironic that the few items Yamashita may have buried in those mountains started this whole thing. When he was executed the secret of the treasure supposedly died on the scaffold with him. That was part of the myth, told and retold, and reenforced in the telling over the years.

CHAPTER FIVE

The Evidence

It was 1 April 1945 and the war in the Pacific was less than six months away from its atomic conclusion. The Americans were winning the war in the Pacific but the Japanese would not give up. Every battle was a fight to the bitter finish. Out in the South China Sea it was business as usual. A U.S. submarine patrolled the Formosa Strait looking for Japanese vessels about 650 kilometers (400 miles) north of the Philippines.

Around 10:00 in the evening Commander Charles E. Loughlin saw the familiar low silhouette of a Japanese destroyer on his radar scope. After an hour of maneuvering the U.S. submarine *Queenfish* fired four torpedoes. Cheers of congratulations echoed through the sub as all four found their mark. The *Awa Maru* lit up the evening sky as it exploded and sank in less than three minutes twenty-three kilometers (14 miles) off the Chinese mainland.

Soon enough Loughlin found out that he was the victim of a cruel April Fool's joke. The vessel that he sunk was a hospital ship painted with giant white crosses, and had been guaranteed safe passage by the U.S. It was to deliver Red Cross packages to allied prisoners of war in Hong Kong, Saigon, Singapore, Djakarta in the Dutch East Indies (Indonesia), and Sumatra, and then pick up wounded Japanese soldiers and bring them home. The 11,600 ton vessel was on the return trip to Japan when it was sunk. Of the 2,009 aboard ship only one, a steward picked up by the *Queenfish*, survived. The crew testified that after the vessel went down the *Queenfish* surfaced and lifelines were thrown to those in the water. Strangely no one grabbed hold except the steward.

Japan demanded indemnities for damages from the U.S. government. Loughlin was court-martialed. At his trial he claimed that he couldn't see the white crosses because of the dense fog, and because the ship was so low in the water it looked like a destroyer or destroyer escort. But the lost lives weighed heavily against him. He was found guilty of negligence in obeying orders, the least severe of the charges against him, and given a letter of reprimand. The incident did not diminish Loughlin's career, however. He was subsequently promoted to the rank of rear admiral.

Later it was discovered that the Japanese had taken advantage of its safe passage guarantee and loaded the ship to the gills with a cargo which it felt was more important than their wounded soldiers. When the ship went down it carried with it forty tons of gold, twelve tons of platinum, 2,000 tons of tungsten, 3,000 tons of tin, 3,000 tons of rubber in bales, 2,000 tons of lead, 800 tons of titanium, 500 tons of brass and bronze, two tons of quicksilver, 150,000 karats of diamonds, forty cases of jewelry, five cases of ivory, an unknown quantity of silver, several large bales of paper currency, and numerous crates of art, all plundered by the Japanese occupation forces.

There were very few wounded soldiers on board, but there were a lot of passengers, mostly Japanese VIPs trying to get back to their homeland. Passage during that time was only available to those with the best connections in government, or those with enough money.

The ship was so overloaded that it sat very low in the water looking, unfortunately, like something else. The estimated value of the cargo ranged from $241 million to $5 billion, making it one of the most valuable sunken treasures in history.

This was a violation of the accords set forth by the Geneva Convention, a dirty trick of the lowest order. The usual protests were filed through diplomatic channels, and then nothing more was heard of the incident. Japanese archives do not have any record of an investigation into the matter. In this case their silence on the matter was deafening. For a ship flying the flag of the Japanese Imperial Navy to be able to carry off an international crime of this magnitude would require approval at the highest level of the military, and possibly even a higher level than that. So who was giving the orders?

Minoru Fukumitsu, he of the first Yamashita treasure hunt, took enough time off from denying there was a treasure to write a book about the *Awa Maru*. Even with his contacts, when he queried the Japanese government he was told there were no documents relating to the case. He thought this was strange, and persisted. Finally he was told that even if there were he could not see them.

In 1976 Loughlin, John E. Bennett, the *Queenfish* navigator in 1945, John Lindbergh, the son of famed aviation pioneer Charles Lindbergh, and former astronaut Scott Carpenter applied to the Republic of China for permission to salvage the sunken vessel. Permission was denied. Fukumitsu also applied and was turned down. One can only wonder. How many other times had the Japanese disguised ships carrying valuable cargo? And how much total wealth was taken from these defeated countries?

.

In 1940 travel brochures touted the Philippines as the Pearl of the Orient. Visitors docking at Pier 7 in Manila unloaded at the "longest and finest covered pier under the American flag," according to Ripley's Believe It or Not. The heat might be stifling but they could stay in the Manila Hotel nearby, one of the few hotels in Asia to have that new-fangled invention called air conditioning. It was located on the bay across the boulevard from Intramuros and Fort Santiago. Cocktails on the veranda at sunset were a must. It was difficult to describe the brilliance and the beauty of the setting sun on the bay.

The first impression of Manila was of big white government buildings contrasting with the older Spanish architecture that still dominated the town as a subtle reminder of another time. It was a neat, clean city, but it had an ugly side hidden away. Within a few kilometers of the Manila Hotel, on the other side of Intramuros, were the slums of Tondo. They were easy to find. Just follow the smell of feces. The closer you got the more overpowering the smell became. Very few visitors looked for Tondo.

For an American living in the Philippines, the way of life wasn't too bad. The work day was from 8:00 until 5:00, with a two hour lunch break, from noon until 2:00. At 5:00 friends met for *merienda* or cocktails. Dinner was usually served around 8:00 in the evening.

And it really was served, by servants plodding around in their bare
feet. That's the way it was done back then. In the most sophisticated
households the house maids were always barefooted.

Even the lowest American civil servant posted overseas lived
well, with at least two or three servants. There were usually a maid,
a cook, a gardener, and perhaps a driver. Depending on one's station
there might be two or three, or four or five, of each. Such vestiges
of power harkened back to colonial times, which weren't really that
far back anyway.

On the weekends everybody was off to their favorite club for
polo, swimming, tennis, badminton, bowling, or whatever struck
their fancy. The Manila Polo Club was the choice for the so-called
white aristocracy. No Filipinos were allowed. The Los Tamaraos
was the Spanish polo club. Filipinos were allowed there. The Wack
Wack Golf and Country Club was the most cosmopolitan. Japanese,
Chinese, Filipino, Spanish, and American mingled together. The
other two prominent clubs were the University and the Army-Navy.
Except for Wack Wack they were all located on the bay. From the
beach on a clear day you could see the island of Corregidor, forty-
two kilometers (twenty-six miles) away, and the South China
Sea beyond.

For shopping downtown, everybody went to Heacock's
Department Store, also air conditioned. Inside it was as if a piece
of Americana had been transported from the states and dropped
in the middle of Manila. All the latest dry goods from the U.S.
were for sale, from Hershey chocolate bars to cotton shirts and
bathtubs. Because the Philippines was a U.S. protectorate everything
was duty-free.

There were other social rituals depending on one's status.
Formal attire was expected at the Manila Hotel for the dinner dance
on Saturday evenings. There was less formal dancing over at the
Sta. Anna Cabaret on Tejeran Street which sported the world's
largest dance floor. And some just preferred to go drinking with
friends from bar to bar around town and then end up at Tom's
Dixie Kitchen on Plaza Goiti at 6:00 in the morning for breakfast.
It was run by an American Negro.

Francis B. Sayre had just moved into the newly built High
Commissioner's residence, which cost the U.S. government the huge

sum of $500,000. It was a beautiful building located just down the road from the Manila Hotel. But the most imposing structure in Manila was the Malacañan Palace. Located just a few kilometers away on the Pasig River in the district of San Miguel, it was the home of President Manuel Quezon.

There were 8,500 Americans, 5,700 Spanish, 29,000 Japanese, 117,000 Chinese, and 16 million Filipinos in the country at the time. The Chinese had integrated themselves into the population a long time ago. But only recently, over the last decade, had the Japanese arrived. Some ran shops. Others had menial jobs such as gardener or driver. Many were fishermen. They controlled the deep-sea fishing industry and knew the coastal waters as well as the local fishermen. About 18,000 lived around Davao on Mindanao, the large island about 1,000 kilometers (620 miles) south of Manila.

There was ominous gossip going around about the Japanese. War was coming. Probably not soon, but it was coming. And probably not the Philippines, since General MacArthur was preparing the defenses for Quezon. Everyday MacArthur could be seen leaving his palatial suite on the top floor of the Manila Hotel and driving over to his "office in the wall" at One Calle Victoria in Intramuros. As long as he was here the Japanese would think twice about taking on this country. That was the talk back then. As the sun set on those halcyon days, the Japanese Rising Sun slowly enveloped the horizon. Pearl Harbor was attacked, and soon afterwards the Philippines.

In December 1941 and early 1942 the Japanese Imperial Forces rolled through Asia conquering all in its path. One of the main reasons for all this conquering was to systematically pillage each country of its raw materials and ship them to Japan to further their war effort. Japan had zilch for raw materials and could not consider ruling their half of the planet without tin from Malaya, oil and rubber from Dutch East Indies (Indonesia), rice from Thailand, cotton from India, iron from Indochina (Vietnam), and the mineral resources of the Philippines, rich in iron, chromium, manganese, and copper. As each country fell before the Yellow Peril, the Greater East Asia Co-Prosperity Sphere came closer to reality.

Of course, in addition to raw materials there were other items worthy of the soldier's consideration. All banks, treasuries, and other depositories of wealth were looted. Even the bodies of enemy dead were violated. Gold teeth were ripped out and fingers with rings cut off. This macabre booty added considerably to the spoils of war. But that wasn't enough. Museums, temples, and churches were also looted, along with the temples of vice.

Centuries before World War II started, in addition to the normal commerce of each Asian country, there was a thriving sub-economy worth billions. It consisted of the usual trades, gambling, prostitution, smuggling, narcotics, and money lending. When the *gweilos* (foreigners) came to colonize these countries they groped with these problems for awhile and sooner or later gave up. Then the heathen was left alone to his own devises, and these sub-economies continued on their thriving course.

The money involved in such activities was considerable and it created a black market where the currency of a transaction might be paper money, jewelry, gold, silver, or anything of value. The preferred currency of the Chinese, who usually ran the commerce and the black market in most of these countries, was either precious metals or gemstones.

When war visited the Far East, in almost every village in Asia there lived at least one or two Japanese employed in some menial position, such as gardener or driver. After the army was victorious they donned uniforms and marched through town pointing out the black-marketeers. Sometimes they were robbed on the spot or just taxed and retained to help run the local gambling, prostitution, or drug ring, until their usefulness ran out. Whatever the method, each country was methodically looted by the Japanese. Included in this was a considerable amount of so-called hidden wealth. A very large treasure could have existed.

What some people believe, and the eye-witnesses swear, is that there was a large and powerful Japanese organization behind the looting of these countries. This alleged treasure, which consisted of gold, silver, platinum, coins, jewels, and artifacts, came from Indochina, Hong Kong, Thailand, Malaya, Burma, Borneo, Singapore, the Dutch East Indies, and China.

One story that had been going around for years was that the British, fearing an eminent attack from Hitler in 1940, packed up all their gold bullion and other precious metals, and shipped it to

Singapore where they knew it would be safe in that impregnable fortress. A subsequent investigation proved this wasn't true. But it was a fact that Spain, fearing a similar attack in World War II, shipped all of its gold reserves to Russia for safekeeping. Guess who never saw their gold again?

At least the Philippine treasury was spared. While the Americans and Filipinos were holding off the Japanese at Bataan in February 1942, primarily because of the skipper's need for ballast, President Quezon had twenty tons of the Philippine treasury's gold bullion and silver pesos loaded on the submarine *Trout* and taken to Australia. Another 350 tons of silver pesos, worth ₱15,792,000 (almost $8 million), was dumped in the waters off southern Corregidor in May 1942, and several million dollars in paper currency was burned after the serial numbers were noted and radioed to Washington. During their occupation the Japanese spent a good deal of time looking for the dumped silver and did finally manage to retrieve about ₱2 million worth.*

It is almost impossible to estimate the total value of such a treasure. The gold bullion alone was estimated to be worth over $100 billion in 1978, according to state department documents examined by noted Washington columnist Jack Anderson. This estimate was based on the fact that in 1975 an eye-witness gave 172 Japanese maps of treasure site locations to a group of treasure hunters led by Marcos. The number written at the bottom of each of these maps was the value in Japanese yen of that particular site. For example, at the bottom of one map was the figure 777,000,000,000. The value of 777 billion yen in 1975 would have been approximately $8 billion. For some unexplained reason most of the maps contained triple numbers at the bottom, such as 555 and 777, followed by nine zeros.

If the "large and powerful organization" theory is correct, just exactly who was making the decisions regarding the movement and placement of such vast wealth is somewhat of a mystery. It had to be someone or some group who had enough power to control

---

* After the war the U.S. Navy recovered another ₱5 million worth of the silver pesos, and the Philippine government ₱6.5 million more, but all this still amounted to only 75 percent of what was dumped. The rest is still down there.

naval transport like the *Awa Maru,* and large groups of military
personnel, preferably army engineers, to secrete the booty. With
at least two branches of the military involved the authority had
to come from a very high level. There are stories that a relative
of the Emperor devised this grand scheme, along with Field Marshal
Hisaichi Terauchi, commander of the Southern Command in the
Pacific. The Fourteenth Army in the Philippines was a part of this
command. Terauchi was made a Count for his efforts during the
war. There is no evidence, however, linking Terauchi or an imperial
relative to such a scheme. The purpose was also unclear. Some with
noble thoughts believe that all this wealth was being amassed
for presentation to the Emperor. Others believe greed was the
primary motivator.

Supposedly the gold, silver, coins, and jewels were sorted and
crated at the country of origin before being shipped. This valuable
cargo was either destined for the Philippines or for Japan via the
Philippines since the sea route usually included a stop there. Most
of the treasure was transported there first, and for whatever reason
most of it never left there.

Armchair historians proffer several schools of thought for why
it could have remained. One is that Japan was certain that even
if it lost the war it could still retain the Philippines in a negotiated
settlement and afterward recover the treasure. (They didn't know
the U.S. possessed the atomic bomb.) Another was that the Japanese
in the quest to carve out their Greater East Asia Co-Prosperity
Sphere had chosen the Philippines to be its financial capital and
all this gold would serve as the standard for its currency.

All that may be true, but in the end the main reason it may
have stayed in the Philippines was that there was very little choice
after about the middle of 1942. That was when the tide of battle
began to turn. The Japanese forces' invincibility was dealt a shattering
blow with the victorious Battle of Midway in June, followed by
American victories at New Guinea and Guadalcanal. As a result the
Japanese war effort was stepped up and troop and materiel movements
had to take priority over other shipping. It was conceivable that if
there were any planned movement of treasure back to Japan these
plans would have been changed. It may have been considered an
interim measure at first, but later as victory slipped from their

grasp the powers that be could have made the decision. They would get very few opportunities like the *Awa Maru* to ship their plunder home, so what was already in the Philippines would stay there.

But is that what really happened, or was this story the result of too many old and fertile imaginations? As the evidence was probed there was no lack of data or people willing to talk. There were dozens of small treasure hunting groups around, some making a less than valiant attempt to operate secretly while everybody in the neighborhood knew what they were doing.

Some had copies of old maps or sketches. There were scores of others who had been involved one way or another with a treasure hunt, including alleged eye-witnesses to treasure burials. A lot of this data proved to be misleading or false, but some eye-witnesses claimed that there was a plan to bury some treasure in the Philippines, and that a group of Japanese officers were implementing this plan as early as the middle of 1942 assisted by a special engineer brigade.

Their method of operation supposedly went something like this. They would go to the nearest town and ask the mayor for laborers to help in building some fortifications nearby. Almost always these would include a tunnel complex. After the work was finished the local workers were sent home. Occasionally the Matagumi Kaisha, the Japanese civilian construction corp, would assist in preparing the fortifications but they were always supervised by the army engineers. They knew nothing about a treasure either, and would also depart before its arrival.

Some of these fortifications were selected in advance as treasure sites. On arrival of the treasure, another group of workers came in. Sometimes they were a civilian Chinese work force from Formosa; sometimes they were *makapilis* (Filipinos who collaborated with the Japanese); and occasionally they were prisoners of war — Filipino, Australian, and American. That group prepared the site for the treasure and carried out the actual burial in absolute secrecy. Sometimes all workers at a site would be killed to insure that no one talked. Some alleged eye-witness told of such occurrences.

Most of the fortified sites were very sophisticated and required months of excavation with elaborate tunnel systems. That the Japanese built tunnel complexes in and under their fortifications was no surprise. In every major battle with the Japanese, where they had time to prepare for the American forces, major tunnel complexes were found. The entire atoll of Iwo Jima was honey-combed with tunnels. Biak, in the Mariannas, had five-story caves. The Japanese defense of Okinawa was directed from a vast tunnel complex thirty meters below Shuri Castle. Saipan had its own network of tunnels as did the Philippines. But there may have been one difference in the Philippines. Some of the tunnel systems may not have been fortifications. They may have held the immense bounty of Asia.

According to the eye-witnesses, all the big sites were at least twenty to thirty meters below ground and a few were even deeper. A few of the larger sites had tunnel complexes large enough to hold trucks. Sites holding five or more tons of gold were always located below the water table. But how, one may ask, did they dig a hole thirty meters deep, if the water table was at ten meters? And then how did they fix it so that it filled back up if the wrong person started snooping around?

The answer to the first question was simple. The source of the water was dammed up or kept out with water pumps. Keep in mind the Japanese built the first underwater tunnel from Kyushu, furthest south of the four major islands, to Honshu, the largest island, in 1942. They had the technology. The answer to the second question may be found 17,700 kilometers (11,000 miles) to the northeast, at Oak Island in Mahone Bay, Nova Scotia.

One summer day in 1795 Daniel McGinnis rowed out there from the mainland to spend the day exploring. The island was covered in oak trees, hence its name. McGinnis came across a clearing covered with rotting stumps and one oak tree standing in the center. One limb of the tree had been sawed off. Directly under this was a circular depression in the ground indicating something had been buried. That was enough to whet his curiosity. He spent the rest of the summer there digging with his friends and wondering what they would find at the bottom. Now, almost 200 years later, the answer to what lay at the bottom of the Money Pit, so called because of the millions spent, was still unknown.

What the boys found was a shaft four meters in diameter that had been filled in. As they dug down, every three meters they encountered log platforms placed across the shaft. At the twenty-seven meter level there was another platform, but atop this was a rock slab bearing an inscription in a language no one could decipher. When they removed this platform along with the rock slab, water gradually began to fill up the shaft. It rose to within nine meters of the surface which was the water level of the island. Despite bailing the water remained at this level.

News of the mystery shaft at Oak Island soon spread and people came from all over to try and solve the water problem. Everyone was convinced that some immense treasure lay just beyond their grasp, but they all went away empty-handed.

In 1850 one part of the mystery was solved when some rock walled tunnels were found beneath the beach at Smith's Cove. On inspection these tunnels turned out to be an ancient drainage system which led from the islands interior to a point just past the low-tide mark of the cove. This remarkable system was composed of alternating layers of rock, eel grass, and some kind of brown fiber. Somehow this combination prevented silt from clogging the drains. Analysis of the brown fiber proved it to be coir, or coconut fiber. The nearest coconut tree was over 2,400 kilometers (1,488 miles) away.

The drainage system was ingenious in more ways than one. On close inspection it appears that it also served as a booby-trap. The log platforms apparently acted as a sort of hydraulic seal. When they were removed the seal was broken and the shaft flooded. Efforts in the past twenty years have uncovered more flooded tunnels and chambers, some more than sixty meters deep.

Core samples have yielded pieces of wood, charcoal, cement, iron, brass, china, and hand-worked clay. The wood has been carbon-dated to 1575, plus or minus eighty-five years. The cement-like material was of a type used in the sixteenth and seventeenth centuries. The metal was smelted before 1800. What all this means is that about 300 years ago somebody came to this island with a serious intent to either bury something or to create one of the world's greatest puzzles. Triton Alliance, Ltd., a Canadian group, has been formed to find out what's down there. They are prepared to spend up to $10 million to solve the mystery once and for all.

There were reports of treasure hunters in the Philippines encountering a smelly, brownish-green, tar-like substance while tunnelling. Once this was removed water began to seep into the tunnel. Whether or not this was related to the booby-trap technology of the Money Pit was anybody's guess. Only one thing was certain. There were plenty of coconut trees, and coconut fiber, in the Philippines.

According to eye-witness accounts, the way the treasure was buried at the large sites was almost as ingenious as Oak Island's drainage system. Once a site was chosen the engineers were brought in to dam up any water source and dig the tunnels. There were at least two tunnels for each site, usually at opposite ends of the site. They didn't just dig a deep hole, shove it in, and cover it up. They were more sophisticated than that. Besides, each site was supposed to look like a fortification of some sort.

The configuration would depend on the surrounding topography (mountains, jungle, church, fort), but a treasure burial supposedly went something like this. A spot was chosen for the air vent which would be directly over the target. An exact distance was marked off. From that point a tunnel was dug at a prescribed angle and for a certain distance. This tunnel would wind up at a point exactly twenty or thirty meters below the air vent, depending on the depth chosen for the target. At least one other tunnel, but sometimes two or three, would start from the opposite end or wherever the topography dictated, and wind up at the same spot. In this manner there would never be a tell-tale depression in the earth. Why at least two tunnels? Because one was for the workers and the treasure, and the other for the officers. The Japanese were very picky about things like that. There might be more than one air vent but all were artfully concealed using rocks, trees, or some kind of natural foliage. The main one directly over the target could always be located by a specific marker.

After this was done all those not assigned to the actual treasure burial had to leave. The second group of workers was brought in and phase two of the operation was then begun. At the target a chamber just large enough to hold the material was prepared and lined with either concrete or stout logs. Sometimes railroad ties were used. After the treasure was secreted, the entrances to the chamber were booby-trapped, using explosives, poison gas, or a combination of the two. Then the water source was booby-trapped in whatever fashion they deemed necessary, and the tunnels and air vents were either backfilled or blown up to prevent future access.

The key to a recovery was to locate the markers placed in the vicinity. A marker was a stone or other object, and could be buried or on the surface. There were different kinds. One could point to the exact location; another could mean you were on the right track; still another could spell danger.

With a coded map the first marker could be located. It usually indicated the location of the air vent, which was the only safe way to excavate the site. The air vent was also backfilled but in a special way. Every few meters, in addition to the dirt and rocks, a layer of something would be added to show they were on the right track. These layers might be composed of charcoal, green glass, bamboo, or even human bones. This route was the only safe way down. On the way other markers might indicate the presence of a booby-trap. There was one last clever touch. A sucker deposit, consisting of a few gold bars or some jewels, was usually placed about halfway down the air vent so that anyone persistent and lucky enough to get that far would think that was the treasure, and hopefully stop excavating, thereby leaving the bigger deposit alone.

Another simple and expedient method of treasure burial was the water site. It was easy to load a ship, take it to a designated spot, and drop the material off the fantail or scuttle the ship in water at least thirty meters deep.

While a site was being prepared its measurements were taken and a general sketch of the area was made. After the treasure was secreted this information was used to draw a coded map which was then turned over to a superior. Toward the end of 1944, as the Americans approached, the sites became less and less sophisticated. Simple holes were dug or caves were used. By then the main trove had been secreted.

The accounts of treasure burials were told to me by the eye-witnesses. All the publicity about there being only 172 maps is wrong, according to one of them. He should know. He provided the maps that Marcos used. In addition to the map sites, there were many smaller sites of individuals who had collected their own booty and had to hide it hastily as they retreated and the Americans advanced. The number of these smaller sites has been estimated at anywhere from several hundred to over a thousand. So who were these eye-witnesses, and could they be believed?

CHAPTER SIX

The Eye-Witnesses

Pedro, Pol, and Ben. Sounds like a Mexican rock group. But music isn't their forte. Treasure is, supposedly. They're all Filipino senior citizens, either pushing seventy or easing past it, and they all claim to have been there when this treasure worth a billion dollars or so was put into the ground. They didn't act in concert. They hardly knew each other at the time but they all claim to have been there at different stages of the operation.

All three are as different from each other as Filipinos can be. When the war came Pedro, from Laguna province near Manila, was studying engineering at the University of the Philippines. He joined the army and a few months later became a prisoner of war after surviving that terrible Bataan Death March. Pol, from Sorsogon in the south, was working at a logging camp when events turned him into a lieutenant in the Japanese army. And Ben was the teenage son of a simple farmer working in the north when a Japanese officer adopted him. One is proud of what he did; another is almost too ashamed to talk about it. All three claim to have gazed upon treasures that are only written about in fairy tales. Yet none of the three are well off and could even be considered poor.

Therein lies the paradox. How could this be if they are telling the truth? One 75-kilogram bar is worth over a million dollars and they saw thousands buried. In forty-five years they couldn't find just one? These men have made a living for the past quarter century by helping others *look* for treasure. Why haven't they found anything?

When Pedro, Pol, and Ben surfaced one at a time and told their stories they were greeted with a mixture of hope and skepticism. People wanted to believe them. There were bits and pieces of proof, like the maps which Ben had been given and the pencilled sketches that Pedro supposedly made almost fifty years ago. But was it all a hoax? Bigger preparations have been made for smaller con jobs.

They do have excuses. They claim that they were warned by their Japanese masters not to look for the treasure for twenty years. All three were young, naive, and impressionable back then. And Filipinos are exceptionally superstitious. Maybe that explains it. Maybe not. Also, for a long time after the war it just wasn't healthy to admit that you had helped the Japanese do anything. It was a good idea to just keep your mouth shut, go about your business, and wait for the right moment. That right moment never came because by 1965 Marcos was president and his treasure hunting task force dominated treasure hunting for the next twenty years.

In addition, Pedro, Pol, and Ben supposedly knew how well these treasures were buried, how deep and complicated each site was even if they could locate it, which presented another problem. Twenty years is a long time to remember where you put something no matter how valuable. Even with coded maps it wasn't easy. They were almost impossible to decipher if the codes weren't known. They were counting on being able to find the general location of each site, and quickly found out that wasn't so easy either. In the Philippines a jungle or mountainous area changed a lot from one rainy season to the next. In twenty years the area could be totally unrecognizable.

Even if they located a site they also knew that to find and successfully excavate it would require men, equipment, and financing. During the Marcos era if you went looking for financing to excavate a treasure site the talk would get around and soon enough one of Marcos' men would be banging on your door. If you were asked to help you usually did because most of these men weren't nice.

They're all older now. Pol still has all his hair but it's white and thinning. He could still pass for a Japanese if he wanted with those chinky eyes. Barrel-chested and muscular, he is still as strong as an ox. Pedro is slender. He hasn't gained or lost two pounds in forty-five years. His face is fuller, and he wears glasses, but he still wears his thinning gray hair in a crewcut. Age hasn't been kind to Ben. The wrinkles are beginning to show, and the hairline is receding. When he smiles, and he smiles a lot, the front teeth are missing. There is nothing outstanding about the three. They are typical of the common people who were caught up in an uncommon time almost a half-century ago and survived, except for the fact that they may know where billions of dollars in gold was buried.

.

Almost a quarter century after the war ended Colonel Florentino R. Villacrusis, Jr. had a most unusual job in the Philippine army. He worked for Secretary of Defense Ismael Mata and was in charge of granting government permits to search for treasure that may have been buried by the Japanese. Experience had taught him that most of these treasure hunts were based on fake maps or eye-witness accounts of old men who could recall just about anything for the right monetary inducement. But he was instructed to issue the permits anyway and stay on the lookout for anything unusual or exceptional. In 1968 the unusual and exceptional occurred.

Villacrusis had his own treasure-hunting group, called The Professionals, who devoted their weekends to this pursuit. One of the members was Romulo Sison. Sometimes when Villacrusis would stray as far north as Nueva Vizcaya in his search he would spend the night in Bambang at the home of Romulo's relative, Ben Valmores. Ben was a simple farmer, uneducated but hard working. Villacrusis was the apotheosis of the career military officer, urbane and intelligent. One might think the two would have trouble getting along but that wasn't the case at all. Ben described Villacrusis as quiet, nice, and kind, not arrogant at all. He liked the man and looked forward to his visits. One weekend, after several visits, Ben decided he could trust Villacrusis enough to show him something he had kept hidden for twenty-three years.

He left the room and came back dragging a dirty, musty leather satchel about sixty centimeters square, twenty-five centimeters thick, and secured by a leather strap. Opening it, he and Villacrusis stared at the contents. There appeared to be hundreds of maps, all the same size — about twenty by twenty-five centimeters — on what

appeared to be parchment paper waxed on both sides. In addition
there were other items in the bag — another parchment containing
deciphered codes and symbols, and some sticks that appeared to
be some kind of measuring device. Ben said he didn't know what
to make of them but he recognized some of the maps as the sites
where he had been before.

"What do you mean, Ben? Where have you been?" Villacrusis
asked. And Ben told his story.

Benjamin Valmores was only sixteen when war came to his
part of the country. His father was a farmer. The family lived in
a small hut in Dulao, a tiny barrio in the northern province of
Nueva Vizcaya. One day in November 1942 he was cutting sugar
cane in the fields and stacking it by the side of the road when all
of a sudden he was surrounded by Japanese soldiers pointing guns
at him. One of them stepped forward and motioned for Ben to put
down the bolo, the long knife he was using to cut the cane. He
dropped it on the ground and raised his arms.

"San Antonio?" the soldier that seemed to be the leader asked.

Ben assumed he wanted to know where the town was. He
pointed in the right direction and told them, "Four kilometers
that way."

"No," the soldier said in English, "You." The implication was
clear. They wanted Ben to take them there.

"I cannot," Ben replied. "My father told me to finish cutting
the sugar cane today so I can't leave."

In recounting the story Ben said he wasn't trying to be brave.
He was just more afraid of his father than the Japanese. Surprisingly
the soldier agreed to talk to Ben's father first. So they went back
to his hut and, in Ilocano, the soldier asked the father if Ben could
lead them to San Antonio. The father agreed, and off they went.
About halfway there the soldier halted his group and told Ben that
he had changed his mind, that instead they were going to San
Fernando, another village about three kilometers from Dulao.

Another argument ensued. "I cannot," Ben pleaded. "I must
take you to San Antonio and then get back home to finish my
work. That's what I promised my father."

So everyone marched back to Ben's house. Another discussion
ended with another permission, and off they went to San Fernando.

Upon arrival Ben was surprised to see a Japanese army camp and a lot of soldiers. He was ordered to stay with them and warned that he would be punished if he tried to run away. So he stayed. Ben eventually learned that the name of the Japanese officer that had spoken English to him and Ilocano to his father was Hadachi, who became his friend.

The days turned into weeks and the weeks into months. Ben didn't try to run away. He just obeyed them as his father had ordered but sometimes he couldn't help but refuse their commands, like the time they tried to get him to fire a rifle. He said he could not. Then they threatened him and told him to shoot a water buffalo. When handed the rifle he pointed it in the general direction of the buffalo but looked away, grimaced, and pulled the trigger. He was only two meters away and couldn't miss, but he did. When a soldier would order Ben to fetch his gun Ben would grab it by the barrel and hold it at arms length as if it might bite him while toting it over to the soldier. Gradually the kid who was afraid of guns became a friend to the soldiers. Sometimes he was a cook, sometimes he was a bottle washer, but mostly he was just their mascot.

At the camp Ben noticed that there was one Japanese who stood out from the others and was obviously the leader. He was a captain in the Imperial Navy by the name of Kawabata. Ben never knew his first name. He always called him by his nickname, Kawa.

"Kawa developed a particular fondness for me. He watched over me and treated me like a son," Ben remembered.

One day about two months after arriving in San Fernando, Ben was in a field herding water buffalo and Kawabata came up. Apparently Ben looked depressed. Kawabata spoke excellent English but for some reason he had trouble with Ben's name. He pronounced it Ben-ha-meen.

"Ben-ha-meen, what is wrong?" he asked.

There were tears in Ben's eyes when he said "I miss my parents."

Kawabata grunted and walked off. Later he sent word to Ben to pick the best water buffalo out of the herd and bring it to the camp. Ben did this thinking it was for the evening meal, but on arrival Kawabata ordered his men to hook up the water buffalo to a cart and load some boxes on it. Then Kawabata said, "Come, Ben-ha-meen, we are going home."

Ben boarded the cart and they headed for his home in Dulao, a few kilometers away. There was a lot of excitement when Ben arrived. Kawabata had brought them food and some sake wine was produced. And there was one more surprise. Kawabata asked Ben's parents for permission to adopt him. If the parents would agree then he would take care of Ben and give him a good life. Also in return he offered them the water buffalo, the cart, a Singer sewing machine, one sack of rice, and one rice bag full of money. Ben's parents were poor farmers. All these gifts were like a fortune to them. It was an offer they couldn't refuse.

Ben left the countryside that day and began an adventure that lasted for over two years but it would affect the rest of his life. He travelled all over Luzon, the main island, and sometimes even flew to Cebu or Bicol in the south.

Kawabata told him that he was an engineer assigned to inspect fortifications and bury war materials. There were three other Japanese officers, apparently aides to Kawabata, who befriended Ben — Hadachi, Kabarugi, and Tasaki. Ben doesn't remember their first names. He always called them by their last.

He could only recall the first name of one person — Kinsu Morakusi — who always seemed to show up whenever there was a burial of war materials. His manner and his dress indicated that he was obviously of higher rank. Ben didn't know if the man were army, navy, or what, but his uniform was better than Kawabata's. He was tall, handsome, and had a cultured voice. He called himself Kinsu Morakusi but apparently that was some sort of inside joke since *kin* was the Japanese word for gold. Kinsu, like Kawabata and his aides, became attached to Ben and also looked out for him.

During his travels the only thing that struck Ben as strange was that the boxes they buried were so heavy. Most of the time it took six men to carry a box about sixty centimeters square. Ben was always told to wait nearby. He was never allowed near the fortifications. This went on until the end of 1944. By then everyone knew that the Americans were coming. There was talk of fighting to the death which frightened Ben.

In January 1945 they were in San Francisco Del Monte, which was part of Quezon City near Manila. Kawabata received an urgent message to proceed to Baguio. By now American planes were flying overhead all day, constantly strafing and bombing the roads, so the convoy could only travel after dark. It took them most of the night to travel the 250 kilometers (155 miles) to Baguio.

After they arrived they were ordered to go to Tabuk in Cagayan province, about 140 kilometers (85 miles) further north. Ben noticed that many horses and carts loaded with heavy boxes were added to their convoy for this trip. The strafing and bombing was so bad it took them two nights of travel to get there. Just outside Tabuk all the boxes were offloaded and buried in holes blasted in the side of a mountain.

From there they were ordered to Kiangan nearby, where they remained waiting for further orders. There seemed to be more American planes dominating the skies. One day Kawabata and Kinsu took Ben aside and told him to gather his belongings, that he was going home. That evening at sundown, Ben and all his friends — Kawa, Kinsu, Kabarugi, Hadachi, and Tasaki — boarded a car and drove to Dulao. The family was happy to see Ben. "We thought you were dead," his mother said as she cried and hugged him.

Kawabata said that the Americans would come soon and that there would be a lot of killing so "Ben-ha-meen" should stay and protect his family. Kawabata then handed him a leather satchel with a strap and told Ben to keep it for him until he returned. He said it may be twenty years but he knew he could trust Ben because he was like a son to him. They all said goodbye and left. At first Ben buried the bag. Then he dug it up and hid it in the house. He told Villacrusis he never opened it.

The war ended soon after that. Ben started farming in Bambang, a few kilometers away. He married a few years later. Then one day his cousin showed up with Villacrusis.

When Ben finished his story Villacrusis said, "Ben, I think the maps are very important. Hide them and don't show them to anybody. I have to leave now but I'll be back in a few days."

Villacrusis left but returned two nights later. He asked Ben to come with him and bring the maps, that they were being summoned by Marcos. They left that night and flew to Manila on a private aircraft.

As soon as they arrived they went to the home of General Onofre Ramos. Ramos was one of those assigned by Marcos to track down leads regarding the Yamashita treasure. Ben told his story again and showed Ramos the maps. They counted them. There were 172. Villacrusis looked at Ramos and said, "We should tell him."

Ramos nodded and turned to Ben. "These maps probably show the locations of treasure buried by your friends."

Ben only nodded and said, "Oh." He wasn't that surprised. He always suspected that's what they were. That's why he had taken the precaution of taking some of the maps out of the satchel and hiding them before showing them to Villacrusis.

It was late so they spent the night at Ramos' house. The next morning they went to the office of Secretary of Defense Mata. Once again Ben told his story and showed the maps. Ben never did meet Marcos but Mata, Ramos, and Villacrusis asked him to keep quiet about the maps and to help them locate those sites. The maps were left with Ramos.

Some time later it was decided that Ramos and Villacrusis should go to Japan to try and locate Captain Kawabata. They departed along with two other colonels and several assistants. The presidential mission was received in Japan and every courtesy accorded them. Ramos discreetly informed his Japanese guests that his mission was top-secret and proceeded to ask about Kawabata and the treasure.

Through the assistance of a local Catholic priest they were able to locate him through the War Ministry. Shortly afterward Kawabata was brought to the visiting dignitaries and introduced. At first he denied any knowledge of the treasure but when they mentioned the name of Ben Valmores his demeanor changed completely. He asked if it would be possible for them to contact "Ben-ha-meen."

Ramos said that he could, and they called Ben in Manila. He was staying in the house of a friend, Tony Pratts, at the time. Soon they had Ben on the line and handed Kawabata the phone. After a few minutes of exchanging pleasantries it was obvious to Ramos and Villacrusis that Kawabata and Ben were indeed close friends. Then Kawabata told Ben, "Please, no soldiers, no Americans, no Filipinos, and no Japanese must know about the maps. I just come back. Wait for me." This surprised them but it was of no consequence. They had their confirmation, they had an eye-witness, and they had the maps. They hurried back to the Philippines to tell Marcos.

One day in 1969 Villacrusis was in Nueva Vizcaya working at one of the treasure sites which Ben's maps had pinpointed when he heard that someone else was also working on a treasure site in the same province and had uncovered some interesting markers. Villacrusis located the site and met a man by the name of Pol Giga (pronounced Heega). Pol told him that he worked for Colgate Palmolive in Manila and was just a weekend treasure hunter. They talked for awhile and it became obvious to Villacrusis that this man knew a lot more than the average weekend hole-digger. It was also obvious that the man was wary of strangers so Villacrusis didn't impose too much that first meeting. Over the next few months they began to meet more often and gradually they became friends. Villacrusis came to be called Vill and Giga, Pol. They began to share more information about their mutual interest, and one day Pol shared the ultimate piece of information. He told Vill who he really was.

Leopoldo "Pol" Giga was born 27 June 1923 in the province of Sorsogon in the south. In 1939 at the age of sixteen he went to work for the Cadwaladen Lumber Company in Camarines Del Sur. That same year it burned down. His boss, Wesley Schlager, found a job in another lumber company in Camarines del Norte owned by Atlantic Gulf and Pacific and also found a job for Pol. He was still working for Schlager when the war broke out. All the American civilians in the area decided it would be better to go to Manila to surrender.

They were placed in an internment camp at the University of Santo Tomas. Pol knew this and came to Manila to try and find Schlager. He finally located him at UST. Schlager had lost a lot of weight, so Pol contacted the National Women's Federation. They were helping to feed the prisoners at UST, and Pol volunteered to assist. He made several trips to the camp daily, bringing food and cigarettes. One day a lady at the NWF asked him on his next trip to the camp to find a Mr. Smith and give him a pack of cigarettes. This time he was searched at the camp entrance. They

found a message in the pack of cigarettes and arrested him. This
was September 1942.

Pol was turned over to the *Kempei Tai*, the Japanese military
police unit known for its brutal torture and execution of prisoners.
He was taken to Fort Santiago and imprisoned in the dungeon.
A few paces away was the Bastion de San Lorenzo. Before it had
been a Spanish powder magazine. Now it was used for something
more sinister. Several of its chambers were used as solitary
confinement cells. The largest room was used as an execution
chamber. The room adjoining it was the torture chamber.

The first two days Pol was there he was taken to the torture
chamber for interrogation. They wanted to know who he worked
for and what guerrilla outfit he belonged to, but they couldn't get
any information out of him because he had none to give. He wasn't
working for anyone or any organization other than the National
Women's Federation, he kept repeating. Pol said that by the third
day he just couldn't take any more of the beatings. He admitted
he was a spy. His interrogators grunted in satisfaction and they took
him back to the dungeon.

On the fourth day they didn't come for him until noon, but
instead of taking him to the torture chamber he was taken out to
the middle of the fort and tied to the flagpole. He asked what was
going on and they told him that he would be executed at two
o'clock. He remembered laying on the ground, sweating under the
hot sun, and thinking that he had screwed up by talking. The
situation was hopeless. He was tied so tightly that the ropes chafed
his skin.

After about an hour some soldiers walked up and asked if his
name was Giga. He nodded. They untied him but, instead of taking
him toward the Bastion, they led him the other way, out the front
entrance of the fort and over to the row of buildings that housed
the *Kempei Tai* headquarters. He was taken inside one of them to
an office and told to sit.

A Japanese naval office by the name of Captain Naboru
Ichihara appeared and for the next hour he was questioned but
this time there were no beatings and no threats, just questions about
his family and his name. He never found out why the sudden change
in plans but he was informed that he would be released if he would
agree to serve as the valet of Ichihara.

After about six months, in which he displayed a certain amount of loyalty to the captain that had saved his life, he was sent to Kyoto, Japan, in December 1942. There he met a Japanese governor by the name of Giga. Now he understood. Ichihara thought that he might be a relative of the governor. After all he did look a little like a Japanese.

Pol went through a six-week orientation course, part of which taught him how to prepare fortifications. Tunnelling was included in this instruction. While there he also was taught how to read and write Japanese. He said he was taught the *katagana*, the simplest method of writing. (There is *hirgana*, more difficult than *katagana*, and *kanji*, the oldest method of written Japanese and the most difficult.)

Before leaving he was commissioned as a second lieutenant in the Japanese army. On returning to the Philippines he was again assigned to Captain Ichihara along with three other Japanese lieutenants who were engineers. According to Pol their names were Morita, Matsuda, and Hadachi. After a few weeks all of them were told to prepare for a trip to Germany. They were sent to Cologne, accompanied by a German naval officer by the name of Von Dauden. There they studied other tunneling techniques for about a month and then returned to the Philippines. This officer, according to Pol, was an admiral and one of those in charge of the treasure burials and the only non-Japanese involved at that high level.

On returning to the Philippines they began to travel all over the countryside, visiting fortifications and taking inventory of war materials being deposited at each of the sites. At first Pol and the other lieutenants were not aware of their real purpose. They just counted the number of boxes buried in each place. One day they saw a truck pull up to one of their sites and a box fell off the rear. It cracked open, and precious stones spilled on the ground. It was then that Ichihara told them that some of the tunnels were being used for burial of treasure. They were ordered to keep quiet or else. From then on they attended staff meetings that planned the treasure burials. At one of the meetings Pol met the head of the entire operation, a relative of the Emperor by the name of Lord Ichivarra.

The job of Pol and the other three lieutenants didn't change. They still counted boxes but now they knew they were inventorying treasure. One at a time they would enter the site and conduct their inventory and then turn it over to Ichihara. If all four of their inventories did not tally they were slapped and cursed.

Pol did this work from May 1943 until November 1944. The Americans were coming so he and the other Japanese officers involved in the treasure burial were then ordered to head north to Bambang, Nueva Vizcaya, for a meeting. When Pol arrived he found out that all the Japanese officers he had seen at the various fortification sites were also there. They had all been called to the meeting. The conference was to take place the following evening at Tunnel Number Eight. (All the tunnels in the area were numbered. Each tunnel had a purpose. Tunnel Eight was a storage tunnel for grenades and rifle and small-arms ammunition.)

There were a total of thirty-three officers, including Pol, who had knowledge of the treasure. The next evening they all gathered at Tunnel Eight. At the tunnel several of the officers confided in Pol that they knew they couldn't defeat the Americans. Some of them gave Pol maps and sketches of treasure sites, saying that if they survived the war then perhaps they could return to see Pol some day. They thought he would survive since he was Filipino. In addition to the maps Pol was given a Japanese flag signed by all the officers present as a memento.

After all the officers had sat down at a conference table Pol was called out of the tunnel by Ichihara. A few minutes later a huge explosion collapsed the roof and destroyed the tunnel killing all the officers. Pol said that Morita, Matsuda, and Hadachi were also killed in this explosion.

Ichihara had known in advance about this and had requested that he be allowed to execute Pol. He took Pol aside, pulled out his German Lugar pistol, and told him of the plan. But he couldn't bring himself to kill Pol because now they were like brothers. Instead he fired three shots in the air and told Pol to get away. Before they parted Ichihara gave Pol his code book, which deciphered all the codes and symbols on the treasure maps. Ichihara said that he hoped this would help Pol some day but do not attempt any search for at least twenty years.

Pol escaped that night and made his way to Sorsogon, his home province. That was in March 1945. There he joined the Bicol

Brigade, a guerrilla outfit, and fought side by side with another townmate, Boni Gillego, in an around his hometown of Bulan. After the war the Bicol Brigade won U.S. Army recognition as an outstanding guerrilla force.

After the surrender Pol enlisted in the Philippine army in January 1946 and was sent to Pampanga for training. There he decided to make the army a career. He became friends with his platoon leader, Captain Thomas Hogan. One day he handed Hogan the code book which Ichihara had given him. Hogan asked what it was. Pol replied that it was an intelligence code that the Japanese had used during the war and that perhaps the army may be able to use it in some way. Pol said it was his way of burning the last bridge to the treasure and starting a new life.

Pol was sent to Japan in 1947 for one year of occupation duty. While there he visited with the parents of Captain Ichihara and was told that Ichihara never returned from the war so he must have been killed. After his tour in Japan he was assigned to the U.S. Army Tenth General Hospital in what is now Fort Bonifacio.

His job was to requisition food for the hospital. While assigned there he met G.H. Carpenter, a vice president of Colgate Palmolive. He had been interned at UST during the war and was convalescing at the hospital. They became friends. Pol got out of the army in January 1948. When he went looking for work he remembered his friend at Colgate Palmolive. He contacted Carpenter and was hired. He started work on 16 July 1950.

Pol kept quiet for a long time about his past. He knew what could happen to collaborators. He could be tried for war crimes, so his past remained a deep dark secret. But treasure hunting was a big weekend avocation in the Philippines, so gradually, and carefully, he became interested again. He spent weekends like many other part-time treasure hunters. He was digging at his first site in Nueva Vizcaya when he met Villacrusis.

In 1968 Pedro Lim was at Fort Bonifacio in Manila to fill out some paperwork about his military pension. A man approached him and said that a Japanese war veteran was looking for him and wanted his help in locating something of value. Pedro said he didn't know any Japanese and started to leave. He wondered how this man knew who he was. Another walked up and identified himself as Colonel Mario Lachica. Pedro had never met Lachica before either but knew that he was a confidant of Marcos assigned to the Presidential Security Command and involved in treasure hunting. Lachica wanted to know if he would be interested in helping him on a treasure hunt. From Lachica's demeanor Pedro decided that he had better cooperate this time.

Since the late 1950s he had been approached periodically by friends that knew and by the occasional Japanese that he had worked with during the war but thus far he had always managed to refuse their overtures. Pedro wasn't stupid. His desire for wealth was no different than the next person's, but something held him back. To some people he was a collaborator. And he still remembered Yugurra's words of warning. He had avoided them as long as he could. Now it was inevitable. He knew that what Marcos wanted Marcos usually got, one way or another.

Pedro Lim was attending the University of the Philippines when the war broke out in December 1941. He was supposed to graduate in engineering in March 1942 but he never did. He had taken ROTC while in college so when he joined the army he was commissioned a third lieutenant and assigned as a security officer to the S-2 section of Company C, Twenty-first Infantry Division (the same unit as Ferdinand Marcos). The Twenty-first was on Bataan when it was overrun in May 1942. He survived the Death March and was imprisoned at Camp Odonnell in Capas, Tarlac.

He had been there about two weeks when a Colonel Yugurra showed up one day and asked him some questions about his background and schooling. Afterward he was released into Yugurra's charge. They went to the Jai Alai Club in Manila and billeted there for about a week. Then they proceeded to Muntinlupa on the outskirts of Manila and stayed for about ten days. From there their journey took them to Canlubang on Laguna De Bay where they remained a few days. Then they proceeded to the University of the Philippines campus at Los Baños, to the foot of Mount Makiling.

The animal husbandry school there had been converted into a concentration camp. That was Pedro's home until the Americans liberated the camp in 1945. Unlike the others imprisoned there, however, he would do a lot of travelling while a prisoner of war. Pedro recalled that he was only at the camp about thirty or forty days during the entire Japanese occupation, and while there they were kept away from the other prisoners.

Pedro learned that Yugurra had been a professor of finance at a university in Japan but he never mentioned which one. Now for some reason he was engaged in construction engineering. His primary occupation during the war was the burial of treasure. He employed about thirty *makipilis* who assisted his own engineers. Pedro could still recall the names of the Japanese engineers whom he worked with — Fukumicho, Matsushita, Fukuroda, and Miyori. His recollection of Yugurra was of a mild-mannered man who disliked giving orders. Everyone that worked with him liked and respected the professor.

Pedro was unaware of what he was really doing at first. He just followed orders. Nobody ever came out and said the word treasure but it slowly dawned on him why everything was so heavy. It depressed him at first. The Japanese would surely kill him after they have buried everything, he thought. He decided to get close to Yugurra, who might help him at the right time. So Pedro became his orderly, preparing his food and washing his laundry. And he was right. This devotion would pay off later.

Pedro's group was always assigned the first phase on an excavation site, which was to dig ten meters down; then a second group took over and dug ten more meters: and a third group if the excavation were deeper. He said that all the excavations he worked on were twenty or thirty meters in depth. At the end of a shift each group had to submit a report on their digging.

Pedro's work shift consisted of about thirty Filipinos, which included himself and two Japanese. After the shaft had been dug, wooden and steel boxes, and sometimes safes, were brought in. And again Pedro's shift was responsible for taking it down the first ten meters. The boxes were so heavy that each had to be carried by several men. The Japanese claimed to be experts at what he called "underground engineering" and in "sinking and sliding" techniques. They could analyze the composition of the earth in a shaft and determine how far an object of a certain weight would settle or slide over a period of years. They always discussed such matters during the burials.

Pedro was sent to various places to dig — Baguio in the north, Alabang near Manila, and San Pablo in Laguna among others. In

1943 and 1944 he was sent to Fort Santiago several times to work
on a large excavation. After they finished there they were taken
to Fort McKinley and worked in three places burying treasure. The
biggest site, he recalled, was near a drainage area that flowed into
the Pasig River.

The reason Pedro was able to recall such detail is that he had
obtained a small notebook. When he worked on a site he would
make an entry that night about what he had done that day, usually
a sketch along with the dates he worked there, and an added
comment about the materials he unloaded and the work he was
engaged in. Maybe, he thought, these sketches might come in handy
some day, if he could survive the war without getting killed.

They were at Fort McKinley a week and were in a hurry
because everyone knew the Americans were close. Afterward they
were taken back to Laguna and helped to repair the railway line
from Santa Cruz to Santa Maria along Laguna de Bay. This took
about a week. Then they were delayed in Santa Maria ten to twelve
days because the Japanese were engaged in a big battle with the
Americans near Mount Banahaw.

After the battle they were told to report to Colonel Yugurra
at a camp on Mount Makiling about sixty kilometers (37 miles) away.
They did so and were there about a week when they heard that
the prisoners at U.P. Los Baños had been rescued. Yugurra then
ordered Pedro and the other *makipilis*, along with nine prisoners
of war that were with them, to withdraw to the top of Mount
Makiling.

They arrived at the top about 9:00 in the evening, ate some
rice, and went to sleep. About midnight Yugurra woke him up and
told him to take the nine POWs and leave immediately, that
something bad was going to happen to the others in the morning.
Pedro recalled that Yugurra told him, "Look at me. Swear to me
in the name of Shinto, that you will not reveal the secret of the
treasure. I'll be back in twenty years. If not you may reveal it. But
if you do, then study the men one by one, even your own father
or brother. They may turn against you. So be careful. If you are
successful use it for humanitarian reasons."

At midnight Pedro and the POWs slipped out of the camp
and made their way down the mountain to Santa Rosa about twenty

kilometers (12.4 miles) away. From Santa Rosa they headed for Zapote on Manila Bay where they linked up with the U.S. Army Eleventh Airborne Brigade. He was hospitalized with scurvy for a week at the Ninety-sixth Evacuation Hospital. There he learned about the massacre in Calamba, his home town.

On 11, 12, and 13 February the Japanese garrison in Calamba rounded up all the inhabitants they could find, took them to a sugar mill outside town, and slaughtered them. More than 5,000 men, women, and children were killed by gunshot, bayonetting, and beheading. It was one of the largest massacres of the war in the Philippines. There were others. An estimated 8,000 people were killed in Manila in January and February as the Americans approached. In the town of Lipa 20,000 persons were executed between 16 February and 19 March 1945. And many more. Hundreds of such massacres took place all over the country.

The news of the Calamba massacre shocked Pedro. He then joined the Eleventh Airborne Brigade and remained with them until the war ended. He had no qualms about killing Japanese soldiers after that. There was more bad news. Pedro later found out that the thirty *makipilis* that remained with Yugurra were executed the next morning.

Pedro stayed in the army after the war. He kept his word with Colonel Yugurra and never discussed his exploits with anyone. It would not have been healthy to do so anyway. For a long time after the war there was bitter resentment toward collaborators and his exposure could have meant the end of his military career. He retired in 1953 and devoted most of his time to running a bakery in Calamba.

Those were the stories of the eye-witnesses as told to me by themselves. They didn't just sit down and tell me these stories from beginning to end. In addition to numerous one-on-one interviews of each eye-witness, they came from dozens of conversations over a period of several years, beginning about the middle of 1988. They had told other people the same stories, or at least stories similar enough to be believable. The stories didn't appear to be memorized. There was the occasional mistake. Pol said that he saw the Japanese cruiser *Nachi* sunk in Manila Bay in 1943. It could not have been because it was at Surigao Strait in 1944 and was later sunk on 5 November 1944. When a mistake like that occurred it was passed off as a lapse in memory. But was it? Were these men what they claimed to be? How could it be determined if they were telling the truth?

CHAPTER SEVEN

Father Bulatao

The first time I met Father Bulatao in 1988 he asked me for a ride to the hospital because he had no car. He wasn't sick. He was going there to help children who are in pain by utilizing his talent. This time it was a young girl who had been badly burned in a fire. Through hypnosis he would help her forget a lot of the pain that comes with the healing process. This was not his first patient. He has helped many, but this kind of devotion to God's duty was only a small part of the man's character.

The Psychology Department at the prestigious Ateneo de Manila University was where Bulatao called home. He headed the department from 1960 to 1971 and then turned it over to others in order to concentrate on his teaching and research. His credentials included a Ph.D. in Clinical Psychology from Fordham. The best way to describe the man was to recall a story told by a colleague.

In 1987 Father Bu, as he was affectionately called by students and academics alike, and another teacher from Ateneo visited China as exchange professors. On their return they were asked to tell about their experiences. The first teacher told of the difference in life styles of the two countries and described the hardships she had endured on her trip. She was correct in her assessment of the situation as she saw it. China was a rough place for those unaccustomed to its culture and way of life.

Then it was Bulatao's turn. He could hardly contain his excitement as he ebulliently described a bus trip he took with some Chinese kids, the fun he had in the classroom with another group, and various other encounters. The reaction of this sixty-five year old string-bean of a man was not unlike the reaction a ten-year old might have on his first trip to Disneyland. The laughter and excitement that always seems to surround Bulatao are infectious. To be around the man was to be alive.

This love of life and its mysteries was what Bulatao was about. Especially its mysteries. For most of his life he has studied the paranormal, trying to find an explanation for things that are not scientifically explainable. Things like ghosts and spirits. When asked if he believed in ghosts he replied, with a look of mischief, "Yes, I do, but I'm not sure what they are. Are they part of a person's deep unconscious, or are they real little entities with sheets on them?"

He explained that he believed there are phenomena related to ghost-experiences which the conscious human mind cannot understand. His chosen field of expertise was the altered state. He has earned quite a reputation in this area. A number of students in his classes have demonstrated remarkable extra-sensory perception (ESP) ability. He has worked with them to help expand their talents to an extraordinary degree.

As an example, in 1988 Elvira Manahan, a popular television star in the Philippines, was murdered in her home. The solicitor general contacted Bulatao and asked if his group could recall the crime in order to try and see if there were details his investigators had missed. Even though none of them had ever visited the scene of the crime they did so with incredible accuracy and were helpful.

Then there was his use of regression, or hypnotizing people to help them remember. A good example of his work in this area is the case of the man who had inherited his mothers house. In it was a safe containing some valuable papers but no one knew the combination. The woman had died without telling anyone. The man did remember that as a child forty years ago his mother sometimes let him open the safe. She would call out the numbers one by one and he would twist the dial until it clicked. It was a game for him back then and he had never thought to memorize these numbers. Someone heard his story and suggested that perhaps Bulatao could help. He did. Under hypnosis the man was regressed back to that time forty years before and vividly recalled the scene.

But this time as the man repeated the numbers his mother called out Bulatao was there to write them down.

A person undergoing regression, if properly guided, could recall the most minute detail of any experience. No matter how far back in memory, the subconscious still had it stored. One other interesting point was that, with the proper technique, it would be very difficult for the subject undergoing regression to lie about past experiences.

•

Father Gabriel "Gabe" Casal was head of the National Museum in Manila. He issued the permits to look for Spanish galleons and other antiquities. The museum also helped with the technical aspects of other treasures. It might assist in identifying recovered artifacts or help determine the age of an old document. Gabe was an exceptional person, generous with his time and possessed of a boundless curiosity which certainly helped in his profession.

One day in January 1989 we were having lunch at the Manila Hotel and discussing the Filipinos' avid belief in superstition. According to the eye-witnesses, at each treasure site the Japanese executed several people and buried them with the treasure to serve as guardians throughout eternity. I wondered aloud if this had affected Pedro, Pol, and Ben's ability to locate the treasure. Perhaps deep down they didn't want to disturb those spirits. This was assuming they were telling the truth of course. It had occurred to me that their recall of these events might just be a figment of a vivid imagination set to work on aging minds. Gabe mentioned that he might know someone who could help me.

A week later Pedro Lim and I headed for Ateneo University and an appointment with Father Bulatao. Pedro was chosen as the first subject simply because he was available. Pol said he was too busy — he still worked for Colgate Palmolive as a consultant — and Ben had gone back to his home province in Nueva Vizcaya for a few days.

On arrival we were greeted by Susan, Bulatao's secretary and girl Friday, and ushered into his office. That was my first surprise. In a room about three meters square there was the usual desk, chairs, and some bookshelves. But that was all that was usual about it. The entire room was covered with stacks of books, papers, and assorted psychologist's paraphernalia. The desk, chairs, and floor were hardly visible because of the clutter so we stepped carefully as we walked in.

Bulatao greeted us warmly and ushered us into this inner sanctum of seeming disorder. He removed the books and papers from some chairs and asked us to sit. While we were talking I couldn't help but notice his eyes. They seemed to twinkle behind thick wire-rimmed spectacles. This enlarged the gaze he bestowed, or the stare he inflicted — which one depended on whether or not you were lying, and believe me he knew — on the subject seated before him.

We talked about the problem for awhile, about the eye-witnesses and their stories and the uncertainties. Then Bulatao turned his attention to Pedro. The questions were general at first, about family and home life. Then the war was mentioned and soon Pedro was telling about his experiences. After awhile Bulatao asked Pedro if he were willing to be put to sleep so he could remember it in greater detail. Pedro agreed. We chose a particular site so that Bulatao could regress him to the date he was working there. I asked if I should leave the room. Bulatao said no, to stay and observe. Then it began.

There was no pendulum, no watch on a chain swinging back and forth. Just the calm, soothing voice of Bulatao as he told Pedro, "Get comfortable in your chair, put your hands on your knees, close your eyes, and breathe deeply. At first your finger tips will start to tingle and then your hands will start to rise up in the air, but don't worry. This is normal during a regression. Just relax . . . breathe deeply . . . now you feel yourself rising up out of the chair and flying back in time . . ."

As Bulatao talked he kept observing Pedro's eyes. Later he told me he could determine how deep in sleep his subject was by watching the blinking of his eyes, called rems or rapid eye movements. Soon Pedro began to raise his hands and arms. Gradually he raised them up and over his head. They remained in that position during the entire regression.

The disarray around me dissolved as Bulatao worked his wonderful magic, if it could be called that. Back in time went Pedro to a treasure site he had worked on forty-five years ago. He described the sights and sounds around him. At the same time I scribbled furiously while trying to concentrate. (I would bring a tape-recorder to all the subsequent sessions but this one I didn't. I forgot. How's that for memory.)

When Pedro spoke the first thing he said was, "Where do I put this. It is very heavy."

The rest of the session is documented below from the notes taken that evening. It has been edited. P is Pedro and FB is Father Bulatao:

Then P said, "I can see the big hole. It's about twelve meters from the bridge. But I can't go near it. It's guarded. There is a soldier manning a machine gun in the middle of that abutment over there and it's pointed at the big hole. And over there, near the big tree, there is another hole. There is a sentry under that tree guarding that hole also. We bring all our boxes over there and they're lowered into the hole. Oh, Morakusi is coming, and there is Pol behind him. I must bow."

P leaned forward in the chair, attempted to bow, and began singing something unintelligible, like Banzai, Banzai. FB leaned over close to P and, in a soft voice, began to sing with him. After about a minute the singing stopped, and P straightened up in his chair. P spoke again: "Oh, Commander Makami is coming. Hurry. Down, down. . ."

(Pedro told me that Makami was the commander at the Bridge site. He was a brutal man who always carried a big whip, and he was following P down into the hole. He also said that when Morakusi arrived he had to bow his head and sing some Japanese song showing reverence to Morakusi. FB sang along with him. I then learned that FB spoke and read Japanese fluently.)

P said, "Sgt. Kamuchai is coming. Now we are ordered to go to the barge. Now we are on the barge ready to sail but Pol is still inside the hole with Morakusi. On the barge with me are other prisoners

of war — eleven Filipinos, two Negroes, and four white
Americans. Wait. I will ask Kamuchai what we are
putting down in that hole that is so heavy."

(Pedro asked and then paused for a few moments.)
"He doesn't answer. He only glares at me. Kamuchai
is the smallest of the guards but he is very strict and
sometimes brutal." (Pedro told me that normally
Morakusi and Pol would show up together about 2:00
in the afternoon and go down in the hole. They would
still be down there when he left at 5:00.)

P spoke: "Oh, here comes Lieutenant Hitachi. He
is a good Japanese soldier. I can talk to him." (Pedro
asked Hitachi.) "Hitachi said that there were riches and
gold brought from Corregidor for burial here... Now
we are approaching the bridge at Escolta. Soon we will
dock at *Sunog Apog* (a poor district of Manila on the
bay). The smell is from burning sea shells which are
turned into lime. Tomorrow we will go back again. Now
we are resting and guarded by Japanese Marine sentries.
While we are resting I am making my daily record and
putting it in my pocket."

The information in parenthesis was given later in an interview
with Pedro after the regression. Pedro said they worked at that site
for about thirty days, and everyday they boarded the barge, went
to work there, and came back in the evening.

After about thirty minutes Bulatao told Pedro that was enough
and that he could wake up now. He always limited the sessions
to about that time period. Pedro's hands then came back down to
rest on his knees and in a few seconds he woke up. He looked at
us a little surprised and asked, "What did I say?"

We told him. He was obviously excited about what he had
just experienced. He talked on and on, "I remember floating up
out of the room and through the roof and then coming back down
at the Bridge site. How did I do that? I felt like I was twenty-two
again. It was a great feeling. I wouldn't mine going back again just
to feel young again."

After the session Bulatao asked for a ride to the hospital for
his appointment. We talked along the way. I asked him if it were

possible for Pedro to lie while under regression and he said no. But, he explained, if a person convinced himself that what he said was real, then it might be possible to repeat the fantasy under regression.

Bulatao seemed to be interested in the treasure, and asked a lot of questions. I always carried a small picture of Yamashita. It was actually a picture I took of a picture exhibited at his shrine on the spot where he was executed. While we were talking I showed it to Bulatao.

Part of an inscription could be seen above the picture. The numbers "19.7.17" were showing. He explained that the numbers were a date, 17 July 1944, that the 19 was Showa 19, the nineteenth year of the Emperor's rule which began in 1926. That was the first of many lessons about the Japanese which Bulatao would pass on. When we parted he said to contact him anytime if he could be of service. He probably regretted saying that. I bothered him a lot.

Pedro was brought back several times. Bulatao was convinced that Pedro was telling the truth, that he had been at the treasure sites he talked about. He also confirmed the story he had told about his experiences with Colonel Yugurra.

Ben was the next eye-witness to be brought to Bulatao. I had already interviewed him six times before his first regression, and had briefed Bulatao on the information I wanted confirmed. Ben's sessions were different. He didn't go under like Pedro. Instead he would lean over and put his head in his hands, close his eyes, and doze off within a few minutes. Then he would start talking about what we had discussed just before he went under.

According to Bulatao he was in a deeper sleep than Pedro so we couldn't ask him questions. We had to discuss the details of his regression in advance. One time, when Ben was under, he started singing a song in Japanese to the tune of "Lily Marlene," a popular World War II ballad. Bulatao sang along with him. Afterwards he explained that it was a song that the Japanese sang at supper as a sort of prayer to the Emperor. Eventually we got enough information to convince Bulatao that Ben told the truth. Pol, however, was a problem.

Pol Giga was a quiet and reserved gentlemen, dignified in his own way. He had a quirky side to his character though which drove me up the wall sometimes, like the time he introduced me to the Spiritualist and the Third Eye.

One day Pol asked if I wanted to meet the spiritualist who had helped Marcos find several treasure sites. Pol claimed he was present in 1976 when this spiritualist went to a site at Laor in the province of Nueva Vizcaya and helped Marcos' men find a treasure. According to Pol, she dug a hole about a meter deep and a meter in diameter and poured something called essence into it. Then she asked everyone to go away while she prayed. A few hours later she called everyone together. Some small gold bars had appeared in the hole. Pol said he was there and was a witness to this amazing event. He also said that the essence could only be brewed by the spiritualist, and it cost ₱50,000 (about $2,500) to fill one hole. I told Pol I wasn't sure about buying any essence but he agreed to bring her around anyway.

The following evening Pol brought them to the house and I met Laura and Craig. Pol explained that Craig was the one with the Third Eye. Supposedly he could see into the ground and spot the treasure. Craig told me that presently he was helping another group but he was willing to help me now since Pol was my friend. I told him I appreciated that, and asked if he had ever recovered anything.

He didn't answer. Instead he turned to Laura and, as if on cue, she pulled out a red cloth and unwrapped it. Inside was a piece of gold-looking metal, about five centimeters wide by eight centimeters long, and two centimeters thick. He said that this was part of the treasure Laura had found at Laor. I examined it. It wasn't gold. It only weighed about 240 grams. A piece of gold that size would have weighed at least two kilograms. When this was mentioned Laura responded by talking about the spirits that guarded all the treasures. She said she knew the head spirit so she could communicate with him. Also, she said, the reason she decided to help me was because I had the right aura.

At this point it dawned on me that Laura and Craig were not on my wave length, but what the hay. Since the start of my search I had spoken to quite a few faith healers, spiritualists, and funny people with strange machines (or was it strange people with funny machines?) and these two were not a bad sort. They were also friends of Pol. So I thanked both of them for coming over and agreed to let them visit a treasure site nearby that I knew about so that both could provide a free demonstration of their talents. They agreed to go with me the next day but they never showed up. Instead Pol called me and said they changed their mind. I believe my aura burst when I used the word free.

Later I found out that Pol had introduced Laura and Craig to two American treasure hunters and they paid the ₱50,000. The hole was dug, the essence was poured, and up floated a jewel wrapped in an oil cloth. They took it to a jeweler who identified it as a piece of green glass. They reported this to Pol, who told Laura what the jeweler said. Unfazed, Laura explained that this jewel was so rare that even jewelers couldn't identify it properly. Rare or not the Americans were out ₱50,000 and no treasure. Pol didn't mention Laura and Craig again.

Now I know what you're thinking. Pol was a first class con artist with a second rate act. But I'm not sure about that. Judging from Pol's humble surroundings he wasn't well off. When he was paid for services he occasionally rendered he would say that this money was being saved for Leo's education. (All of Pol's children were grown except for one, Leo, who was four. When Pol's first wife passed away he remarried and, at the age of sixty-one, sired a son.) I never observed any evidence of an ostentatious lifestyle. Pol just didn't have the dubious motives one normally associates with con men, and he wasn't a hustler. The fact is that, for whatever reason, he believed in these people.

In defense of Pol, there was a widespread belief and acceptance of spiritualists, faith healers, and the like in the cultural milieu in which he was raised, so it wasn't a big deal. On more than one occasion I had seen normal, rational, well educated people sacrifice two white chickens when the moon was full. Sometimes it was difficult to reconcile such maddening inconsistencies unless some effort was made to understand the Filipino.

After Pedro's first session with Bulatao I called Pol, told him what happened, and asked if he would attend our next session. He said he was busy. Pedro was told about Pol's seeming reluctance and he suggested a plan. By then Pedro was completely sold on the idea and he wanted his friend, Pol, to share the experience. So one day we were all together and Pedro started telling Pol about Bulatao and the wonderful experience he was having. It just so happened that we were going over to Ateneo in a little while and would Pol tag along?

Pol sat in on Pedro's regression. His reaction was both of amazement and amusement. In this session Pedro recalled details about a site we had been on that day. Afterwards Pedro asked Pol if Bulatao could ask him just a few questions pertaining to that particular site. Bulatao joined in. His manner was persuasive. Besides he had already been briefed on Pol and our strategy. Pol finally agreed. The following is culled from my notes of that session.

FB began the session. Pol closed his eyes and gradually relaxed as his breathing became deeper. But his hands never rose from his knees. FB talked to him every few minutes and examined his eyes to see if he was awake. He was satisfied that Pol was under, but his regression was different. His facial expression was a grimace and his jaw was set as if he were determined not to talk. His hands firmly grasped his knees. He appeared to be under a lot of stress.

FB would occasionally ask him a question or make a comment and Pol remained the same. After about ten minutes FB asked him what he saw and Pol finally replied, "I see a light focussing on my forehead, a very bright light."

FB pursued this line of questioning. "Can you go around it?" He couldn't. "Can you turn around and go the other way?" No, because the light is still in front of him.

The entire session was taken up with how to deal with the bright light. Afterwards Bulatao explained to Pol what happened. Sometimes the stress of the first session prevented a subject from relaxing. Now that he knew what it was like maybe he would like to try again next time. A week later we used the same strategy just to be certain Pol wouldn't back out. We didn't tell him we were going there until the last minute so he tagged along. Pedro had his session and came out of it chattering away as usual. "I feel young again," he joked with Pol.

Pol's session was a near repeat of his first session. The bright light was still there. After about fifteen minutes Bulatao decided to try another approach. Here are the edited notes of that session:

FB asked, "Is Pedro your friend?" Pol said something under his breath that we couldn't understand so FB said, "He's not?"

Pol answered "Yes," in a very forceful manner.

FB asked, "Did you give him food?"

Pol: "Yes."

FB: "Let's go back to the tunnel."

Pol: "Okay."

FB spoke to Pol in Japanese. Pol snapped to attention in a sitting position in the chair and then bowed reverently. (FB told Pol that his commander asked that he take us through the tunnel.) For the next ten minutes we listened as Pol described the prisoners digging in the main tunnel of that site. Sometimes his whole demeanor changed and he spoke in Japanese loudly and forcefully. FB said he was cursing the prisoners. Pol was obviously a tough man to work for back then.

Somehow Bulatao's mention of Pedro had gotten Pol past the bright light. But because it took so long to get Pol fully regressed Bulatao had to bring him back after about ten minutes. When he did it was obvious that Pol's reaction to regression was different from Pedro's. There were tears streaming down his face and he looked very old and upset. All the way back home that evening he kept saying over and over, "That Father Bulatao is an amazing man...amazing."

We had hoped that Pol's regression signified a breakthrough, that we could now get past the bright light and find out more about him and the treasure sites, but it wasn't to be. Pol refused outright to attend the next session, and never went back.

Before the sessions with Bulatao, on several occasions Pol had talked about his experiences during the war, and his story was pieced together. But he talked of those times with great difficulty. Sometimes tears came to his eyes. Perhaps the memories were too painful. Perhaps he didn't wish to recall too much. Only one thing was certain. Pol's story as told by himself wasn't true, at least not in every detail. This was disheartening. He was so believable despite his problems with regression.

As Pol told his story I went to work trying to check the details. This time the regressions were of no use. Father Bulatao said that Pol's recall of events may not be correct since he was under so much stress and since he was obviously not cooperating. It took over a year to inquire through the various official agencies and a few unofficial channels about the various segments of Pol's story.

Slowly the replies trickled in. There was no Lord Ichivarra or Ichibarra in the royal family. Nor was there a governor of Kyoto Prefecture called Giga or Higa. The National Institute for Defense Studies in Japan reported that they didn't show a Captain Naboru Ichihara or a Lieutenant Leopoldo Giga as ever having served in World War II. The three lieutenants — Morita, Matsuda, and Hadachi — could not be traced because Pol could only recall their last names.*

The German War Ministry reported that they had no record of a naval officer by the name of Von Dauden. And the Register in the U.S. Army Library in Washington, D.C. had no record of a Captain Thomas Hogan ever serving in the army in the Philippines or anywhere else in World War II. There was a G.H. Carpenter who served as General Manager of Colgate Palmolive from 1941 to 1953. There was a Cadwaladen Lumber Company run by an American before the war, but no one could recall the name of Wesley Schlager.

Boni Gillego did confirm part of Pol's story. Pol did fight with the Bicol Brigade in 1945 in the area of Bulan, Sorsogon, his hometown. After the war Boni said that he and Pol made the trip to Manila together with Pol carrying Boni's youngest child in his arms most of the way. In Manila, Boni stood as Pol's sponsor when he got married in 1946. Pol does understand and speak the Japanese language fairly well. He was either taught or he picked it up during the war. So there was Pol's story, an intricate pattern of truths and non-truths interwoven to conceal...what?

*This holds true for Ben's three friends who were aides of Kawabata — Kabarugi, Tasaki, and Hadachi. Also, judging from the interviews, the Hadachi that Ben spoke of is of no relation to the Hadachi mentioned by Pol. Ben's friend, Kawabata, and Pedro's friend, Yugurra, also could not be traced for lack of first names. Even under regression Ben and Pedro couldn't recall their first names because neither had ever used them.

Pol came to my house one evening and I told him about the results of my research. I suggested that perhaps after forty or fifty years his memory wasn't as sharp as it used to be. I asked him if he would go back and talk to Bulatao just one more time to see if he could recall the correct names. He said he would but just now he was very busy and perhaps in a few weeks he could find time. But he never did.

Pedro claimed that Pol served in the Japanese army, possibly as a lieutenant, but that isn't known for certain. Pol did wear a Japanese uniform and he was an aide to an officer. Pedro recalled how they met the first time. It was in 1943 at a rest and recuperation area on a lake a few hours drive northeast of Manila. The Japanese referred to it as Little Tokyo because it had all the comforts of home, but its Philippine name was Montalban.

Pedro had accompanied Yugurra there as his driver. He was standing by the car in the rain waiting for him when a stern looking Japanese walked up and asked his name. Pedro replied. To his surprise, the man pulled an ear of corn out of his knapsack, handed it to Pedro, and told him, in fluent Tagalog, to get out of the rain and eat the corn. From the accent and the language Pedro knew the man in the Japanese uniform wasn't Japanese after all but a Filipino. They talked for awhile and Pedro met Pol Giga for the first time. Over the next two years their paths occasionally crossed at various treasure sites and Pol always had an ear of corn, a camote (sweet potato), or something to offer Pedro. There was never enough to eat during those desperate times. Pedro would never forget Pol Giga and his acts of kindness.

On the other hand, Ben doesn't remember Pedro or Pol during the war. That doesn't seem odd considering the circumstances. Pedro and Pol were involved in the actual burial of treasure and Ben wasn't. He was around but was not allowed near the actual fortifications and tunnels so it is conceivable that he didn't pay any attention to the workers at the sites. Pedro and Pol, however, did notice the young Filipino friend of the Japanese officers and wondered who he was. It would be a long time before they found out.

On different occasions I have been with one, two, or all three of them at treasure sites. I have seen that thousand-yard stare as they looked back forty odd years and recalled how it was. It would be difficult to fake the casual repartee that they engaged in when they were together. They recalled landmarks that didn't exist anymore. On checking I would find out the landmarks did exist back then. They also recalled particularly amusing (never sad for some reason) incidents that occurred back then.

One incident occurred at a site located in what is now Green Hills in Metro Manila. Pol, Pedro, and I were at the home of someone who believed that a treasure was buried beneath their house. We were discussing the details when out of the blue Pol turned to Pedro and yelled, "Hey, Roco!" and they both started laughing.

Pol explained to me who Roco was. It seems that Pedro talked a lot back then (a trait he has not lost over the years). He would babble on about anything just to keep himself entertained. The Japanese sergeant in charge of this site nicknamed him Loco (crazy) but, being Japanese, he pronounced the *L* like an *R*, and it came out Roco. That became his nickname. I witnessed dozens of such conversations. If such spontaneity could be rehearsed then the men deserved an Oscar for acting.

Pedro and Pol usually provided most of the recollection about a site with Ben adding only an occasional comment. Pedro also provided hand-drawn sketches of the different sites which he claimed were made back then. He seemed to produce a sketch of every site we investigated. Pol surprised us on two or three occasions with notes about sites he worked on. The sketches and notes were usually on note paper yellowed with age and appeared to be authentic. We had samples tested at the National Museum. The paper was the right age but since all were done in pencil and not ink a more precise date could not be determined. It is rather ironic that Ben never made any sketches but he was given the maps.

At a later session with Bulatao, Pedro and Ben talked about Pol. They suspected that Pol had a deep dark secret that he wouldn't talk about. Pol's position back then required him to be stern and tough. The Japanese military were sadistic by nature. They were brutal to their own men, slapping and cursing them in the name of discipline. And that discipline was legendary. American GIs in the Pacific spoke with awe of their fighting spirit. When they were surrounded they would almost always either fight to the death or commit *hara kiri* (suicide). If they were brutal to themselves they were even more so to the vanquished. During the occupation the atrocities visited upon the population were horrendous. Brutality and savagery were a way of life. And therein may lie Pol's secret.

In my earlier interviews Pol had confided that on three occasions he had been ordered to behead some prisoners. He was not proud of what he did. To the contrary he was defensive and apologetic. He swore that each time the death sentence was meted out it was justifiable. He told of one instance at a treasure site in Teresa, Rizal. The tunnels being dug there were quite large and required several hundred laborers. The work force was made up of Filipino, Australian, and American prisoners of war. One of the Americans was caught stealing. He was beaten severely and warned that the next time he would be executed. Sure enough he was caught again.

Pol was ordered to carry out the execution while everyone watched. The sword swished in the air and the head came off cleanly. It hit the ground, rolled over, and came to rest against a stone marker next to Pol's feet. It was facing upward and the eyes were open looking at him. Pol swore that as he walked away the eyes followed him. He couldn't get that picture of the disembodied head and the eyes out of his mind. He said he still had nightmares about it.

Maybe this was just another of Pol's stories that he made up. But if it were true, then perhaps that had something to do with that light in his subconscious that blocked his path to the past. Perhaps the way to the truth was through that light.

Even without regression, of the three eye-witnesses Pol seemed to have played the biggest role in the treasure burials. Pedro had a smaller role and Ben was an observer. They claimed to have been part of a group or groups that included engineers, *makapilis*, civilian work forces, and thousands of wartime prisoners, whose job was to bury treasure over a period of two or three years. Ben's friend that carried out this work was a captain in the navy and Pedro worked for a colonel in the army so this does imply someone of high rank giving the orders across both military services. Pol also claimed to have worked for a naval captain but the name he gave proved to be false.

Only Kawabata was ever actually located. The trip to Japan in 1968 to find him was confirmed by three different sources: Reverend Simeon Lepasana, who worked with Colonel Villacrusis on one project; Johnny Wilson, an actor and city councilman who served informally as the historian for Marcos' treasure hunting task force; and Tabo Ingles, who was a friend and classmate — Philippine Military Academy, Class of 1945 — of Villacrusis.

Pol claimed to have known Lord Ichivarra, a relative of the Emperor and the leader of the organization, but there was no such relative. Ben recalled Kinsu Morakusi, who showed up at all the burials. He thought Morakusi was of higher rank than Kawabata, but not of royal blood. No proof of Morakusi could be found. It was probably an alias. In one regression, Ben mentioned that he was present when Prince Chichibu and General Yamashita met Kawabata at San Agustin Church in Intramuros in November 1944, but that was the only time he recalled the prince being there. A Japanese Embassy official in Manila denied this, however. Chichibu was the oldest of the Emperor's brothers. He was in the army and graduated from the Military Academy in 1923.

The idea of a royal relative controlling the organization may be just a romantic touch to their stories. Or it may have been a well-placed rumor to give official sanction to the organized thievery. Whether there was one group or several acting in concert, its leader or leaders may never be known.

The eye-witness interviews and regressions, and the maps and sketches they provided are the only evidence that a treasure existed and was buried in the Philippines. The data on the *Awa Maru*, suggests that a large and powerful organization could have been behind the collection and disposition of large amounts of gold and other items, but there is no proof, other than the eye-witnesses testimony, that an organization was behind the burial of any treasure in the Philippines.

A lot of people could have been involved in the treasure burials, and some could have been killed at the treasure sites while others died during the fighting when the Americans returned. And if Pol is to be believed the ring-leaders were blown up in a tunnel in February 1945. Still there would have to be some survivors. This could be how the secret of the treasure eventually leaked out. Or it could all be an elaborate hoax started by rumors, which began as soon as soon as the war ended.

The treasure hunting began in earnest shortly afterward. If the stories were real, the treasure was buried deep and buried well. And if anyone did know about it they were not about to admit anything yet. Filipinos that had openly collaborated with the enemy were not well thought of. Put another way, a child rapist had a better chance in court. As a result most of the initial treasure hunting was done by amateurs and their efforts ended in failure because they were disorganized or underfinanced.

It wasn't until about twenty years later when a young senator from Ilocos Norte by the name of Marcos was elected president. He took the stories of the eye-witnesses and their evidence seriously, and put together a task force that carried out a concerted, well organized campaign to find this treasure.

Some former members of this task force were contacted, but most would not talk about it, perhaps because they were still loyal, or afraid, or both. Those that would talk swear that Marcos was successful but they offered no physical proof, and none displayed any visible signs of exceptional wealth. That is intriguing. If Marcos were successful why wouldn't he share some of the wealth?

The eye-witnesses also swear that Marcos was successful. Ben said that he could have been witness to one possible recovery but he isn't certain. He said that during the time he and Villacrusis were together they actually only worked at three or four sites, and on every site but one Villacrusis ran out of money. That one site was in Bamban, Tarlac in the seventies. He worked with Villacrusis and Lieutenant Colonel Porfirio Gemoto. They found a large concrete vault but it was never opened. A crane picked it up, placed it on a truck, and the truck drove away. Whatever was inside, Ben was never rewarded and he doesn't think Villacrusis was either.

Pol said he was successful at the Laor site already mentioned but his claim couldn't be verified. Pedro claimed he was successful at two sites — at Cabuyao, Laguna, in 1974 and Palanan, Isabella, in 1976 — but admits that he never saw any gold either. He was taken from the site before the actual recovery. None of the three were ever given anything for their efforts and they don't display any signs of wealth.

Up until about 1980 there were a few other eye-witnesses still around. Pol claimed that there were two more Filipinos assigned to the third level of work but they were dead now. Pedro recalled that there was another Filipino in Yugurra's group by the name of Jose Castillo but he disappeared. Pedro and Pol recalled that Julio De Guzman, the favorite cook of a Colonel Itoh, was an eye-witness, and another Filipino-Japanese by the name of Okusura worked at the staff level, but they couldn't be found either. There were a few who claimed to have been witness to a single site near their home or farm. And there were some Japanese eye-witnesses mentioned but no names could be obtained, just a lot of whispered rumors of the aide to this Japanese admiral or that general which were virtually untraceable.

Pedro, Pol, and Ben were the only ones left that may have seen it all buried, but there was still that lingering doubt. Why, after almost half a century, couldn't they prove that they found something, at least a bar of gold or silver, or a few diamonds and jewels? It would have added considerable credibility to their stories.

The only man who could provide physical proof that he actually found a treasure was Rogelio Roxas in 1970. And he wasn't an eye-witness or part of a task force. What Marcos did when he found out about that will help develop some insight into the character of the world's greatest thief.

Since the war only three efforts to locate this treasure were well-publicized: Fukumitsu in 1953; Leber Group in 1975; and the Nippon Star group in 1986-87. General John K. Singlaub, who led the Nippon Star group, admitted that he believed in the treasure, but Fukumitsu repeatedly denied its existence. Marcos denied his association with the Leber Group in 1975 despite overwhelming evidence to the contrary. But before that, in 1971, he called a press conference to make a curious announcement.

CHAPTER EIGHT

The Treasure Hunts

Ferdinand Marcos sat in his study at Malacañan Palace in January 1970 contemplating his latest problem. He was about to begin his second term as president which gave him four more years of power and time to plan his next move. Although the Constitution didn't allow a president to serve more than two terms he had no intention of ever leaving office. He had visions of a Marcos dynasty that would last forever. But first there were a few details to take care of, a few problems to solve. The press was still calling him the most corrupt and ruthless leader the Philippines ever had. That didn't bother him too much. In fact it was kind of a back-handed compliment. Just how the hell did people think he got where he was? By being Mister Nice Guy? And they were calling the recent election the most corrupt ever held. Big deal. Who was sitting in the palace now? No, that didn't bother him too much either. After all the screaming and shouting died down he would still be president.

It was the other, very specific charge that worried him, the one about him being the richest man in Asia. That kind of talk could hurt, especially in the U.S. when it came time to ask for another loan. How much did those idiot journalists really know? Probably very little since the rumors about his wealth had started even before he opened his Swiss accounts. No, the bank accounts were not it. He knew the problem, and he also knew that he would never be able to do anything about it. In all the Philippines right now there was one thing that sometimes hurt him the most which he would never control and that was Imelda's spending habits.

That woman could spend more money in less time than
anybody he knew. That recent Christmas shopping spree of hers
was bad timing. Be that as it may, he had to counter these charges
somehow. That's when he came up with the idea. On New Years
Day he announced to the nation that he was giving up all his worldly
wealth. The Ferdinand E. Marcos Foundation was already set up
and his possessions being inventoried for donation to the Filipino
people. This was in gratitude for electing him to a second term
thereby becoming the only president ever to be reelected, he proudly
proclaimed.

It was a brilliant idea. So why did it bomb? At first the
announcement raised a few eyebrows but that was it. Then the
reporters started in again. Instead of an outpouring of thanks they
just wanted to know what he was up to. By then they had him
pegged and he knew it. His reputation was of a man devoid of
scruples who would use any means at his disposal to accomplish
his end. They knew that the announcement would change nothing,
that the corruption would continue.

A few days later, after a round of golf, Marcos met with
reporters. It wasn't long before his ill- gotten gains were brought
up again. "That's unfair," he complained again.

They braced themselves for the usual lecture. Then, out of
the blue, he did something totally uncharacteristic. He admitted
he was rich. This was amazing because Marcos never admitted
anything. He always denied everything he had ever been accused
of. Everything.

Marcos continued while the reporters leaned forward and
scribbled furiously, hanging on every word. They had a headline
here and, who knows, maybe a raise. Then came the blockbuster.
"You know how I made my pile? I discovered Yamashita's treasure."

They stopped scribbling. This was a joke. Marcos was a bit
of a wit sometimes. They waited for the punch line. None came.
They stifled a collective yawn, put away their note pads, looked
at their watches and said, almost in unison, "Would you look at
the time," and started edging toward the door, mentally discounting
the raise they earned a few moments ago, and wondering once again
what he was up to this time.

The Yamashita treasure story was old hat by then. Too many
front-page stories had announced that so-and-so had found the

treasure, only to announce later that the story was a mistake or a hoax. And now Marcos. What a shabby excuse. It wasn't even original. Or was it? Had Marcos discovered something that, even by his standards of wealth, was incredible? Had he momentarily lost his composure in the excitement of the moment and blurted out the truth? Probably.

.

In 1968 Ferdinand Marcos had been in power three years. He did not yet have the complete control which would characterize his later years in power. His political career was in serious jeopardy. He had done little to deliver his campaign promises of 1965 when he was first elected to the presidency. There was still widespread poverty and extensive unemployment. Graft and corruption still prevailed in government and business. And the enormous chasm between the lower and upper class had grown wider. The daily newspapers constantly reminded him of the lackluster performance of his regime. In February, Imelda competed with him for front page news when it was reported that she had been hospitalized. There were rumors that she was dying of some dreaded disease. Such pronouncements in a predominantly Catholic country where women are placed on a pedestal helped somewhat to deflect the most biting criticisms of corruption and inefficiency in the Marcos government.

If Imelda were sick she apparently didn't feel bad enough to cancel the appointment with her Swiss banker. In early March, Walter Fessler, an official of the Credit Suisse Bank in Zurich, came to Manila to see Marcos and Imelda. He was brought to the palace where forms were filled out and signatures appended. On his signature verification form Marcos wrote out "William Saunders (pseudonym)," an alias he had used in his World War II days, and underneath that name he wrote "Ferdinand Marcos (real name)." Imelda did the same thing, choosing Jane Ryan as her pseudonym. Four bank accounts were opened and four checks, totalling $950,000, were given for the deposit.

While the ink was drying on their deposit slips the blood of sixty-eight soldiers was drying on Corregidor. Soon enough the newspapers once again exposed another example of the Marcos presidency. On 21 March 1968 the *Manila Times* headline was

"CAMP MASSACRES BARED." It reported the massacre of sixty-eight soldiers on Corregidor. Marcos had secretly ordered the military to recruit and train a group of Filipino-Muslims on that island. When they found out their mission was to be sabotage and insurgency in Sabah they rebelled and were massacred. Only one survived.

The incident was a black-eye for the military and a political bombshell for Marcos. Once again Marcos was on the defensive and once again sickly Imelda came to the fore. One day the newspapers soberly announced that the First Lady had a miscarriage. She was out of danger and resting comfortably but was still depressed over the loss. True or not the story was a masterly political move and quieted one more storm of protest.

General Ramos and Colonel Villacrusis returned from Japan and reported to Secretary of Defense Mata the exciting news of their visit. Mata passed it on to Marcos. He ordered them to step up the search but be careful. Because of Corregidor the military had a big enough black eye already. They went their own way while Marcos continued to plot and scheme his political survival. Election year 1969 was just around the corner and once again his propaganda machine had to be cranked up to denounce graft, corruption, and anything else the people were against.

It was all a show of course. He didn't really care what they thought. His only purpose was to stay in power, amass wealth, and build a dynasty. Winning wasn't a problem. The important thing was that the election had to look good especially to the U.S., the IMF, and the World Bank. He could handle that if the press wouldn't meddle too much. Fat chance.

Marcos won a second term. The press called it the most corrupt election ever held in the Philippines, characterized by fraud, terrorism, vote-buying, and ballot-box stuffing. Once again a strategic move designed to relieve some of the pressure was needed. Apparently it was decided that Imelda just couldn't have another dreaded disease or miscarriage. So the Ferdinand E. Marcos Foundation was formed and Marcos announced that he was giving away all his wealth. The press didn't take the bait this time. Then all of a sudden he called another press conference and announced that he had found the Yamashita treasure. Had Mata delivered another message, perhaps of a treasure recovery?

The two announcements made back to back tended to confuse more than enlighten the issue of Marcos' wealth. But wealth wasn't that important an issue just then, according to the students. A few weeks later 40,000 of them stoned Marcos in front of the legislature building to show their disgust after he delivered his State of the Nation address. They presented him with a mock coffin to represent the death of democracy in the Philippines. In what is now known as the First Quarter Storm the protest turned violent and bloody when the military were ordered to quell the demonstration with their truncheons, water cannons, and guns. Four students died. While this was going on Marcos received word that someone had found a golden statue while treasure hunting in the mountains of northern Luzon.

Rogelio "Roger" Roxas was a locksmith in Baguio when he started treasure hunting in his spare time in 1962. He searched in the provinces of Nueva Vizcaya, Nueva Ecija, Cagayan, and the mountains around Clark Air Base but never found more than a few old coins and some Japanese weapons and ammunition. In May 1970, right after he got married at the age of twenty-seven, a Japanese, Albert Fushugami, gave Roger a sketch showing a treasure location. Fushugami claimed to have been with a group of engineers during the war that had buried some treasure during Yamashita's retreat. His sketch showed where ten truckloads of treasure had been buried in a tunnel complex in the mountains near Baguio. When asked, Roger could not explain why Fushugami gave him the sketch other than the fact that he was president of the Baguio chapter of the Treasure Hunters Association at the time, and he had just purchased a new metal detector. He was showing this off to his fellow treasure hunters when Fushugami came forward with the sketch.

Such maps and sketches were not uncommon. In treasure-hunting circles maps were not the problem. There were plenty to go around. The fact that they were all bogus was the problem. Perhaps it wasn't considered polite to ask why anyone would want to give away such a key to wealth, or maybe treasure hunters didn't really care just so long as they had a promise of riches beyond their wildest dreams. Roger had been brought up on stories about the

Yamashita treasure. He knew he wasn't the first to search for it in those mountains. Even the search by Fukumitsu in 1953 concentrated around that area. Thus when Roger and his intrepid band began their search in the same mountain vastness they had to know their chances were slim. But like the mountain climber who climbs "because it's there," they had a lead and so the hunt was on.

Because of the work required at this excavation, Roger decided more men were needed. In addition to his regular group of sixteen, he hired about a dozen Igorot tribesmen who lived in the mountains nearby. They found the mountain within a few days and began looking for an entrance. It wasn't going to be easy. The tunnel had been blasted shut twenty-five years ago. Now even if there was an entrance it would be covered in dense undergrowth.

After two weeks of sweaty, back-breaking work cutting away trees, bushes, vines, and thick undergrowth they finally spotted the debris of what looked like a collapsed cave. Then after a few days of removing boulders, rocks, and dirt, they broke through to a tunnel. Cautiously they groped their way inside hoping this was the one, but knowing that even if it was there could be booby-traps that would cause another cave-in.

About 100 meters inside there was another pile of debris which appeared to be the result of another attempt to blast the tunnel. Roger asked his surveyor to examine the old sketch and determine their location. Then they made a new shaft at a right angle to the tunnel, dug in that direction for a few meters, turned left again, and dug parallel to the old tunnel. They proceeded about thirty meters and made another left turn to tunnel back to the original shaft. It was still collapsed, so back they went to their tunnel, went another thirty meters, and tunnelled in again only to find another collapse. Their shaft now was about 100 meters long.

The surveyor checked again and told Roger the shaft wasn't level, so they started angling upward. About thirty meters further on, and at an elevation about fifteen meters higher, they finally broke into an open tunnel. They had been digging for four months. It was now September.

The air was musty but breathable. Roger stepped through the hole, took one look, and jumped right back out. Laying there in the open tunnel, against the wall in an eternal sleep was a soldier or rather a skeleton in the rags of a Japanese uniform.

In the tunnel they found all kinds of medical items — old dextrose bottles, syringes, and assorted instruments — indicating this may have been a first aid station. They also found something else — snakes. There were big ones and small ones of all kinds. Roger said that was the worst problem of all. After trying to kill a few they found out something. If they just left the snakes alone they didn't bother anybody. It was a tenuous standoff at best but they managed to concentrate on their digging.

Further on they found that the tunnel spiralled downward about twelve meters, like a spiral staircase, to another tunnel with laterals which contained old kitchen items. Using the surveyor's calculations they walked to the end of this tunnel and began digging. They had only dug about three meters when one of the shovels broke through to the outside. They were now on the other side of the mountain. The light poured in and a breeze flowed through. The ventilation cooled the men and propped up their sagging spirits.

In mid-November, Roger called a halt to the digging and told everyone to go home for a two-week rest. He didn't tell them he was almost out of money and supplies. But once again he managed to beg and borrow enough to resume, and they were back in operation by the first week of December.

Christmas 1970 was approaching and still Roger and his group had nothing to show for their efforts. Based on the old sketch, he figured the main tunnel was off to the left of where they were digging, so they started excavating in that direction. The work was hard, tedious, and slow but they continued on. The end of their rainbow was somewhere in this labyrinth.

December came and went. While his men were digging the new shaft Roger decided to systematically test the whole tunnel complex with his metal detector. From tunnel to tunnel, going into each lateral and out again he led his machine. Foot by foot, from side to side he swept the instrument, watching for snakes and watching the meter at the same time, listening for that tell-tale buzzing which would indicate metal below. Occasionally he would detect something but all he would find was old ammunition or scrap metal. Up and down those dark tunnels he went with his detector.

The stride he used made him appear to be skating on the dirt floor or doing some strange dance.

In late January his men were still digging toward the main shaft and he was still checking each tunnel for metal. He was back in the tunnel where the skeleton was found when the meter began to give off a loud buzzing. He called for a few of his men and they began digging. Two meters down they struck a heavy solid object. They couldn't budge it so they dug around it some more. Gradually a head was revealed. The excitement grew as they frantically dug around the object until it was uncovered. Then they all stood there, staring in disbelief at their find, at their rainbow's end. It was a gold statuette of Buddha, about seventy-one centimeters in height and too heavy to lift. Ecstatic over their find and fearful of another cave-in — they had experienced several during the dig — they decided that the Buddha was enough treasure for the time being. Using ropes and pulleys they drug it out of the tunnel. On further examination they found out that the head screwed off. Inside the small space were a few handfuls of diamonds. They borrowed a truck and brought the Buddha back to Roger's house in Baguio. It was 2:00 in the morning on 27 January 1971.

Some scales were found and the Buddha weighed in at almost one metric ton. Roger put it in a sturdy wooden case for display. Word of the locksmith's find quickly spread. Strangers began to show up at his house to have a look. A representative from the Treasure Hunters Association in Manila came to appraise the Buddha, and valued it at $5 million. Several offers were made but a price couldn't be agreed upon. Some ladies arrived from Manila claiming to be Blue Ladies, the personal attendants of Imelda Marcos. They made an offer of P3 million ($500,000) for the Buddha, but Roger had to bring it to Manila. He knew it was worth a lot more, so he declined. One day in early April a man came to the house. He claimed to represent Doña Josepha Edralin Marcos, the mother of Marcos. The Buddha was inspected and an offer was discussed but nothing was agreed upon.

On 5 April, Holy Monday in the Philippines, at 2:30 in the morning, Roger was awakened by persistent pounding on the front door. His brother and two cousins had been acting as makeshift security guards since the Buddha had arrived. When they opened it there stood about fifteen to twenty armed men. They couldn't count the exact number. Four of them barged inside. Three were in uniform. One of them handed Roger a piece of paper, claiming it was a search warrant. But when he started to read it the paper was snatched out of his hands. Then Roger's family was ordered into the kitchen and told to lie on the floor.

Four men stood guard on the family while others came in and proceeded to ransack the house. When Roger tried to intervene he was clubbed. His wife, who had given birth recently, started bleeding but despite the pleading of Roger she was forced to remain on the floor. The pillaging continued for about half an hour. A steel handcart was brought in. The men quickly loaded the Buddha and departed.

Roger took his wife to the hospital. Then he went to the police station and made a sworn statement. In it he claimed that, in addition to the Buddha, seventeen small gold bars,* a Samurai sword, a bag full of foreign coins, a boltless .22 calibre rifle, ₱500 in cash, and some personal photos were taken.

After the statement was completed he called Judge Pio Marcos. The judge was the uncle of President Marcos and had signed the search warrant. All he would say was that Roger should not have called the police — he seemed upset about that — and that the seizure was legal because Roger had violated a Central Bank regulation. In hindsight Roger suspected that the man who had claimed to be a representative of *Doña* Josepha Marcos was a spy, sent to check out the house, its security, and the location of the Buddha.

The newspapers heard what happened and took up the story, screaming government thievery. Three weeks later there was a court hearing. A Buddha was produced but Roxas said it was a fake. It was made of brass and its head wasn't detachable. Also produced at the hearing were fourteen bars of brass, the sword, and the rifle. The police chief, Victoriano Calano, admitted taking part in the raid but he denied taking any gold bars, foreign coins, ₱500 in cash,

---

* In the police report, Roger stated that the seventeen gold bars were found on another treasure hunting expedition. He did not mention the diamonds because they had already been sold.

or photos. (Later a Senate investigation could only establish that the Buddha, the rifle, the sword, and some metal bars were taken. Whether the bars were fourteen in number and made of brass or seventeen gold ones could never be ascertained.)

Once again the injustice was reported in the newspapers and this time several senators demanded a hearing. Roger testified and an investigation was ordered. The investigation followed but probably not in the way they envisioned. The authorities arrested Roger, not the thieves. They were not in uniform but Roger knew they were military. He was blindfolded and driven to a secret location. He thought it was a military camp in Pampanga province, outside Manila. There they questioned him repeatedly and tried to make him sign a statement stating that Marcos' people were not involved in the theft of the Buddha, and that he was paid a large sum of money by some people to implicate Marcos. He refused, so they tried more persuasive methods evocative of the Kempei Tai during the Japanese occupation in World War II. Only this wasn't war. This was a so-called democracy under Marcos and this was his method of getting what he wanted.

They beat him; they burned his arms with cigarettes; then somebody showed up with something that looked like a car battery. After gagging him so he couldn't scream, they hooked up some wires to his arms and tried the shock treatment. Roger finally fainted, both from the pain and the exhaustion of being questioned for twenty-four hours nonstop. When he woke up they started again, but he couldn't take it anymore. He signed their statement and they released him.

He went into hiding and, through his contacts, reported to some friendly congressmen what had happened. At the time a national election was coming up so Roger was invited to speak at a rally held by the opposition (Liberal Party) candidates to kick off their campaign on 21 August at Plaza Miranda. He was to address the crowd right before the principal speaker of the evening, Senator Ninoy Aquino. But it never happened. During the rally two grenades were hurled at the platform. The explosion killed nine people and injured many others. Marcos publicly decried the incident and ordered an investigation but the perpetrator was never caught.

By now it was obvious that Marcos controlled the military, the police, and the courts. It wasn't total control yet but it was enough for now. In June 1971 he convened a Constitutional Convention to rewrite the country's Constitution which had not been changed since 1935. On the surface the task seemed perfectly legitimate but with Marcos around nothing was ever as it seemed. He needed it rewritten so he could run again for president. He was in his second term and could not run again according to the present Constitution.

Marcos had a penchant for rewriting things. Before running for president he had his life story rewritten portraying himself as the Philippines' greatest hero of World War II. During the time the Constitution was being rewritten, in an interview with *Asia* magazine, he said that he had received the surrender of General Yamashita. This was absurd of course. Only years later would it be discovered that his heroic deeds were all fake.

Now he was having the Constitution rewritten. Next he would hire some historians to rewrite the history of the Philippines. Guess how he would be portrayed in this? For now a new Constitution would make things appear democratic, especially to the U.S., the IMF, and the World Bank. But what if it didn't work out the way he wanted? Well, there were other ways.

The Constitutional Convention was fast at work when one of the delegates exploded a bombshell. As president, Marcos was supposed to remain aloof and impartial to the proceedings, so he had Imelda do his bidding. At first she tried to use his influence to persuade the delegates. When that didn't work she resorted to outright bribery. Her weekly distribution of envelopes containing cash to delegates who might be receptive to her cause became an open secret and an embarrassment to the entire convention. Finally one delegate reported the bribes.

In what was known as the "Payola Exposé" Eduardo Quintero of Leyte exposed the corrupt practice and the reaction was swift and furious. The opposition newspapers had a field day criticizing Imelda. It was the most serious assault on the presidency since Marcos took over. Now he was angry. The top secret plans for Operation Sagittarius were finalized and put into effect. On 21 September 1972 martial law was declared to combat, according to

Marcos, the "awesome communist threat." The bombings in Manila and the recent ambush of Secretary of Defense Enrile's car proved that things were getting out of control. Later Enrile admitted it was staged.

The personal attacks on Roger did not let up. After the Plaza Miranda incident he went into hiding again. But after martial law was declared he was found, arrested, and charged with illegal arms possession. Roger said the only weapon he had was that boltless .22 calibre rifle but that was enough. He was tried and sentenced on 31 January 1973 to a year in prison. He served that year but they still wouldn't release him. They finally let him out on 19 November 1974. When he got home he found out that his wife was gone. When he tried to contact her he discovered that she had divorced him, married someone else, and left for the states. The Buddha disappeared.

In 1988 a Filipino engineer came to Fort Santiago, where I was working, and asked if I wanted to meet Roger Roxas. A secret meeting was arranged a few days later. Marcos had been out of power over two years but Roger was still in hiding and still afraid. He bore the physical as well as the psychological scars of his ordeal.

I couldn't understand why Marcos had done this. He used all the might of his office to steal from a poor locksmith from Baguio, harass and torture him, and then have him thrown in prison for almost two years. It didn't make sense. Why couldn't he have bought the Buddha from Roger and then offer to help him find the rest of the treasure? I soon realized there was no answer to this kind of question. I was trying to rationalize the acts of an irrational man.

Sometimes it helped to talk about it. Roger and I talked a lot over the next two years. How he could function in a normal manner after the terrible things they did to him was beyond me. It took a great deal of courage, and Roger had plenty of that. He was still an avid treasure hunter and he had plans for recovering the remaining ten truckloads as soon as the time was right. A friend of his in the states filed suit against Marcos and Imelda to recover the Buddha. The case was pending.

The Golden Buddha site did not appear to have been one of the sites worked on by Pedro, Pol, and Ben. The tunnels were obviously some sort of base of operations or underground medical facility. Whatever treasure was left there was probably buried hastily near the end.

On the positive side the Golden Buddha discovery proved that a treasure did exist and that anybody with perseverance had a chance, if they could avoid Marcos. The word got around about what happened to Roger and this put a damper on a lot of treasure hunting activities. The incident showed Marcos' true colors. After he became president he used, or rather misused, the full extent of his office to track down any and all treasure and heaven help anyone who got in the way.

While Marcos was running for his political life in 1969 Pedro Lim accepted Colonel Lachica's offer and accompanied him on the treasure hunt. They headed north for Laor, Nueva Vizcaya. With them were General Jose Marcos Lizardo, a relative of Marcos, and another eye-witness, Jose Castillo. He had been with Yugurra's group during the war and had acted as a sort of valet, being in charge of Yugurra's trunks when he travelled. Like Pedro, he had also survived the slaughter at Mount Makiling. During this dig Pedro overheard Lachica and the others talking about someone who had recovered a treasure below the flagpole at Camp Aguinaldo, the Defense Ministry. Was this the Yamashita treasure that Marcos announced he had found? (The flagpole has since been replaced by a statue of General Aguinaldo, the legendary Filipino who fought against the Spaniards and then the Americans in his quest for a free Philippines.)

As they dug deeper and deeper, and the group thought they were getting closer to the target, bickering broke out as to who was the leader and, therefore, who had the power to handle the disposition of the as yet unrecovered treasure. The power struggle turned nasty with Lizardo and Lachica threatening each other. Pedro said that he and Castillo were afraid for their lives during this time, and that they were virtual prisoners. One day the digging was halted and Pedro and Castillo were told to go home. They had been there two years, dug down to about seventy-three meters, and found nothing. The site was vacated. Pedro and Jose were allowed to leave but they were warned not to talk about their expedition. Pedro returned to Calamba and went back to his bakery. He claimed that Jose disappeared after this. He never saw or heard from him again. (This was the same site that, according to Pol, five years later he was with another group that brought Laura, the spiritualist, who poured her essence into a hole and produced some small gold bars.)

In 1974 a policeman came to Pedro's bakery and said that an elderly Japanese gentleman by the name of Yugurra was looking for him. Yugurra was now ninety years old and had made the trip with his sixty year old son and several other elderly Japanese officers. Pedro and Yugurra had an emotional reunion. They had not come to dig for treasure, Yugurra told him. That was no longer important. They had come to make peace with their ancestors and with the Filipinos. He told Pedro it was okay to search for the treasure now but he must still be careful of anyone he might get involved with. He said everyone would try to hurt him, and that greed brought out the worst in people. Pedro promised his friend that he would follow his advice.

After Yugurra's visit Colonel Lachica contacted Pedro again and asked if he wanted to go on another dig at Cabuyao, Laguna, near Calamba. Pedro agreed, and they worked there for about four months but found nothing. Pedro went back home again. Later, while working with another group at a site on nearby Mount Makiling, he received word through a priest from Cabuyao that Lachica had discovered a golden crocodile at that dig. Pedro tried to verify this, hoping for a share, but he never could.

While Roger Roxas was digging in the mountains of northern Luzon in 1970 there was another dig going on in Manila. Villacrusis had introduced Pol to a friend, Cesar Leyran, who was a dentist but whose first love was treasure hunting. They became friends and one day Cesar asked Pol to help him at a site located at Christ the King Church in Manila. Tony Pratts, a Spaniard and also an avid treasure hunter, was working with Cesar at the church. He had negotiated the agreement with the church officials and secured the permission to excavate. Also involved were a young senator by the name of Ninoy Aquino and his brother in law, the vice mayor of Quezon City, Charlie Albert.

Before Cesar asked Pol for help he had been drilling in various spots around the church for a few months hoping to hit something below ground that would pinpoint the tunnels. According to Cesar,

Pol arrived at the church, took a look around, and told him that he was drilling in the wrong place. He should drill under the stairs. Pol said that he had been there when the treasure was buried, and it brought back painful memories of a German priest named Baudenbrock who had been there when the treasure arrived at the church for burial. The priest was ordered to leave the church but he refused. Leave or die, they threatened, but he still refused, so he was bayonetted to death. (According to church records at Christ the King there was a priest named Baudenbrock who died in 1943, but there is no record of how he died.)

Cesar started drilling again, this time under the stairs. At twenty meters the drill bit broke through into an opening of some kind. There were congratulations all around. Equipment was brought in and they started tunnelling downward. Villacrusis wasn't involved but Cesar used one of his maps. When Pol saw the map he asked Cesar where he got it. Cesar told him it came from Villacrusis.

Pol began to tell Cesar about the codes and symbols on the map. This was not your typical treasure map showing a few identifiable landmarks along with the distance to the treasure where X marked the spot. It was a far cry from that. The map was useful only to someone who knew what the codes and symbols represented or who had a code book. He said that when a treasure was buried an engineer took all the important measurements and made a rough sketch of the site first. He remembered that one of the engineers was a Filipino.by the name of Santos. He also recalled that a Japanese by the name of Kesagi, whose office was in the Santa Mesa district of Manila, received this data, transcribed it into codes and symbols, and produced the final map elaborately drawn on rice paper which was then waxed.

Pol told Cesar what a few of the codes and symbols meant. There was something resembling a clock on each map. It usually had two, three, or four numbers showing on its face. The sum of these numbers indicated the degree of descent of the main tunnel. One code or symbol on the map designated the starting point and the direction in which to dig. Another code or symbol designated the distance from the starting point to the target. The clock on each map held several clues to the treasure location. Some clocks had one hand. Others had two. And some of the hands had one arrow while others had two. All this meant something.

A group of dashed lines on the clock face indicated a second tunnel, and the number of dashed lines in that group would indicate the angle of descent of that tunnel. If there were three groups of dashed lines that would mean there were three more tunnels. A dashed line on the map, outside the clock, denoted a tunnel. Other symbols and codes designated markers and booby-traps. There was a Japanese flag on a staff which wasn't there for decoration. Some of the data was easily recognizable such as the reference points. They were usually depicted as they actually were, possibly a tree with a nail in it, or some other recognizable marker. The value of the treasure was given in yen at the bottom of the map.

The type of treasure was noted by other symbols. A square with an *X* inside meant there was a box of diamonds; two squares with *X*s meant two boxes of diamonds, and so on. A square with a dot inside was a box of gold. There were also squares with crosses inside but these were not treasure. It meant that for every cross there was a bomb buried with the treasure. There was one more easily recognizable symbol on every map — the Japanese character for gold.

Each map was quite a work of art, exquisitely brush painted on a piece of paper which had the texture of parchment, twenty by twenty-five centimeters in size, and waxed over. But even with a map the exact location of the treasure could not be determined without someone who knew what each code and symbol stood for. Without knowing, it was almost impossible to decipher.

Pol told Cesar that he once had a code book but had given it to Captain Hogan, his commanding officer right after the war, and now even he couldn't decipher all the codes and symbols. There, it happened again. He provided all this incredible detail about the maps to Cesar and then he threw in a name that wasn't real. But Cesar wasn't wondering about Hogan just now. He wondered who Pol really was. Very few people knew about these maps, and Villacrusis obviously had not shown them to Pol.

They worked at Christ the King for over a year. Pol still had his job at Colgate Palmolive but after work and on the weekends he would come over and assist. At a depth of twenty meters they hit a small tunnel. Pol said it was an air shaft. The longer they worked there and the more Pol studied the map, the more he could remember. He recalled that this was a big site and the treasure was buried deep, so they continued digging. Then martial law was declared and shortly afterward Villacrusis told Cesar that they had to stop the excavation. The only explanation was that Marcos ordered the halt, so they shut down.

In early 1973 Cesar called Pol again. He had another site picked out, this time in the Green Hills subdivision between Manila and Quezon City, and he wanted Pol to help.

They met at the Coronado Bowling Lanes in Makati. This time Cesar was accompanied by Villacrusis and Johnny Wilson. There was also a fourth person there, someone that Pol hadn't seen in almost thirty years — Ben Valmores. Ben didn't remember Pol but soon they were talking about old times. Pol found out that Ben had provided the maps. He also discovered that Marcos had organized a task force which operated in total secrecy. Their mission was to gather intelligence about treasure and then recover it.

The task force leader was General Ver, head of the Presidential Security Command and Director General of the National Intelligence and Security Authority, the Orwellian intelligence apparatus designed more for intimidation of anybody considered an enemy of Marcos than for anything useful like fighting communism. NISA had control over all intelligence organizations in the country.

This showed how close Ver was to Marcos. They were related and were from the same town of Sarrat in Ilocos Norte province. In 1963 Captain Ver of the Philippine Constabulary was assigned to Marcos, who was president of the Senate. He was intensely loyal, a trait Marcos liked, especially if the loyalty were to him. Ver remained with him, rising in rank and prestige as Marcos rose in power. In 1981 he would be appointed armed forces Chief of Staff.

Ver picked a select group of loyal soldiers to assist him. The key members were mostly military, some retired and some still on active duty. Progress reports to the president about various treasure site diggings were found in the palace after the 1986 revolution. They were on stationery of the Presidential Security Command and signed by Colonel Mario Lachica and Brigadier General Santiago B. Barangan, commanding officer of the PSC.

General Ramos and Colonel Villacrusis had retired in 1971 but they were still part of the task force. Ramos was the liaison to Ver and Villacrusis was one of the operations officers. The head of the task force was originally Ramos but upon retirement he was replaced by Lieutenant Colonel Porfirio Gemoto who had been the chief of operations. Others involved were Brigadier Generals Ramon Cannu and Tomas D'impit, Colonel Renato Gemora, who worked with Cannu, Colonel Crlando Dulay, Major Barangan, brother of General Barangan, and Major Patrecio Dumlao. Besides Johnny Wilson, the group's historian, there was only one other civilian directly associated with them. His name was Venancio Duque, Marcos' old friend who had accompanied Minoru Fukumitsu on the 1953 treasure hunt.

There were other members of Ver's inner circle who were not officially part of the task force but who nevertheless wanted a piece of the treasure-hunting action. Ver did nothing to encourage or discourage them. Apparently Marcos told Ver to handle the big sites personally. He let his military friends excavate the minor sites, in exchange for a large percentage of course. Only when he found out that someone was digging at a major site which he had not sanctioned would he step in and stop the dig. This had happened at Christ the King. Cesar had Villacrusis' approval but he was still not recognized as part of the task force.

Ben and Pol said they were afraid for their lives at first. After all, they knew who they were working for and they knew the reputations of Marcos and Ver. But they realized that although the maps were the key to each site each of them had some invaluable expertise to offer. Ben could help recall the locations of the sites, and Pol could help with the interpretation of the maps. As long as there were sites they would be needed, and there were a lot of sites.

Ben and Pol only worked on a few sites together with Villacrusis but they came to like and respect him. This is reflected in one particular act. In the leather satchel which Ben had been given, in addition to the maps, there was a Japanese flag about the size of a bed sheet that had the symbols denoting the locations of all the treasure sites in the Philippines. Pol also had a Japanese flag signed by all the Japanese officers who had participated in this adventure. Both men gave their mementos to Villacrusis.

The first site that Ben and Pol worked on together was located on Ortigas Avenue in Green Hills. It was owned by patriarch Don Paquito Ortigas and called the Three Jars site because, according to the maps and the eye-witnesses, three large earthenware jars of diamonds stood at the entrance. Don Paquito's nephews, Joaquin Ramirez and Rafael Ortigas, had been approached by Villacrusis and they agreed to work with him in exchange for a percentage of the recovery. The excavation went on for almost two years until late March 1975. Then one day Ver dispatched some men to the site and ordered everyone off the property. The digging came to a halt. Villacrusis was surprised at Ver's move but later he found out why.

The reason for the abrupt halt dated back to 1968. During Marcos' first term as president, Don Paquito was called to the palace and asked to donate a sixteen hectare (about six and half acres) parcel of land in Green Hills. He refused but was finally intimidated into selling the property to Marcos below cost under terms and conditions dictated by Marcos. Six years later, in 1974, Marcos called Don Paquito to the palace again. At that time the subdivision streets were being laid out.

Marcos pointed out that there was a strip of land between the street and his property. He wanted this strip also. This time there were no niceties. After all it was martial law. He had this land, about two and a half hectares (one acre), added on to his other parcel without paying for it. A year later he heard about the treasure excavation being conducted on Don Paquito's property just a few meters away from his property. It must have angered him. He called Ver and the dig was halted immediately.

While Villacrusis, Ben, and Pol were digging at the Three Jars Site, a group code-named Task Force Restoration was set up to recover treasure at Fort Bonifacio and Fort Santiago. On 2 May 1973 a letter was sent to Marcos. It mentioned that Oplan Dry Run would be used to test techniques and procedures of excavation after which Oplan Ligaya could be initiated at Fort Santiago. It also stated that "Upon receipt of the signal from Your Excellency as announced by the Chief of Staff, AFP, on 1 March 1973, conferences and preliminary reconnaissances were undertaken," and that 26 March was D Day (Start-of-digging Day) at Fort Bonifacio for the Task Force.

The Fort Bonifacio site was in a tunnel system under General MacArthur's old headquarters then called Camp McKinley. In the middle of the fort, next to the officer's club and across from MacArthur's living quarters was a circular driveway. In the center was the entrance to MacArthur's bomb shelter. When the Japanese occupied the fort they expanded the bomb shelter into an elaborate tunnel system. By the time the Americans returned part of it had been blown up, either by the Japanese or during the battle to retake Manila, but most of it remained intact.

The letter went on to state that Lieutenant Colonel Porfirio Gemoto sealed off some of the entrances. He then proceeded with the lighting of the tunnels and "checking the pinpointed areas which were believed to have contained the treasures as indicated on our map. Three sets of detectors and instruments were used and all of them confirmed the locations of at least 16 spots."

The letter ended, "In the meantime the men are acquiring the proficiency and ability needed in working vertical and diagonal excavations. They have been successfully testing their instruments, methods, and equipments (sic) and are now ready for Oplan Ligaya." The letter was signed by General Onofre T. Ramos (Ret.), Colonel Florentino R. Villacrusis (Ret.), and Reverend Simeon F. Lepasana.

According to Villacrusis' information, obtained from the eye-witnesses, the Japanese had dug their own tunnels at Fort Santiago underneath the Bastion de San Lorenzo that were much deeper than the dungeon, and buried the treasure there. Those were the targets, but there was a problem. Now the fort was a tourist attraction in downtown Manila. The site would be difficult to excavate without calling attention to the area. During the preliminary probing it was publicly announced that some restoration work was being done. Throughout the search for the treasure such cover stories would become routine. Church sites might also be "renovated" and private property might be "excavated for soil sampling" or other geological reasons.

Villacrusis had been trying for five years to dig at Fort Santiago. Even though he was a member of the task force he, just like all the others, still had difficulty getting approval for any site he wanted. That was the reason for Reverend Lepasana's signature on the letter. Lepasana wasn't a member of the task force but he was invited to join the group on this project simply because he had a relative working in the palace who might be able to influence Marcos' decision regarding Fort Santiago. It didn't work though. Marcos never did give the go-ahead for Oplan Ligaya. Meanwhile, events halfway around the world were shaping the course of Marcos' next treasure hunting endeavor.

In 1974 Marcos heard that the seventeenth century Spanish galleon *Atocha* had been found by treasure hunter Mel Fisher. The gold, jewels, and artifacts salvaged from the wreck were valued at $140 million. At the same time a friend, Victor Nituda, told him that an American psychic, Olof Jonsson, had helped Fisher locate some of this treasure. That fascinated Marcos. He believed in the supernatural and even admitted that sometimes he "heard voices." Imelda, testifying before the Agrava Commission investigating the assassination of Ninoy Aquino, had said that she warned Ninoy not to come to the Philippines, and had told him, ". . . the president is sort of clairvoyant."

Marcos tried to cure his kidney problems by psychic surgery, in which a faith healer supposedly enters a patient's body with bare hands and removes diseased organs. He publicized the *anting anting* (amulet) he received from Gregorio Aglipay, a legendary Catholic priest who founded his own church in the Philippines. Aglipay was a friend of the Marcos family and, just before young Ferdinand went off to war, reportedly gave him a talisman for protection. It was a sliver of magical wood bequeathed down through the ages and supposedly gave the owner magical powers. Aglipay inserted the amulet in his back with an incision made by his own hands, according to Marcos. He claimed that the amulet protected him in battle.

Marcos believed in mystical powers. The use of a psychic on a treasure hunt was nothing new. Perhaps Jonsson could help him. Now I know what you're thinking. Marcos had Laura, the spiritualist. Why did he need Olof? Like I said, never try to rationalize the acts of an irrational man.

CHAPTER NINE

Leber Group

There had been thirteen victims. The police had a madman on their hands. After murdering his victims he would set fire to their homes so that no clues were left. Olof Jonsson was called in. He was taken to some of the burned houses. At one he was handed the charred remains of a rifle. As soon as he touched it he knew who the killer was. He was standing in front of him. It was Officer Hedin, the man who had been assigned as his escort.

The next day Olof reported this to the police officials but by then Hedin had disappeared. His body was later recovered from a river nearby, and a suicide note was found in his room. He confessed that he killed the people after robbing them to support the extravagant habits of a girl friend. He feared that Olof would soon find out the truth. This was in Sweden in 1952. Olof was well known as a psychic even then.

Olof has many talents but he is reluctant to use them unless there is a real need. In 1966 he helped police in Indiana locate three missing girls. At first it was believed they were kidnapped. After three frustrating weeks the police admitted they had no further leads and asked Olof to help. Olof had moved to the states and was living in Chicago at the time. He heard about the case and volunteered his services. After visiting the site where they disappeared he said he was sure the girls were unharmed and still in the Saugatuck area (the place where they disappeared). He also said they had all bleached their hair and changed their hair styles. Olof was correct. The girls soon came out of hiding with their new hair color and hair styles, and admitted they had planned their own disappearance to get away from what they considered to be very boring lives.

In February 1971 *Life* magazine reported on some experiments involving ESP carried out between astronaut Edgar Mitchell and Olof during the Apollo moon mission. That same year *The Psychic Feats of Olof Jonsson* was published documenting his remarkable psychic powers. Since 1982 he has been under contract with the University of Illinois. Scientists there are trying to determine just what it is he's got that nobody else has. Of all the psychics he has the highest success rate in the world — 80 percent — with Zener cards, a form of testing to determine ESP ability.

I met Olof in 1987. After a dozen interviews over a two year period, including a week in the Philippines together, I witnessed his psychic powers many times. While in the Philippines a small dinner party was held in his honor. As usual he had asked that someone bring a pack of playing cards. "For amusement," he always said.

Olof is one of the few psychics talented in all the psychic disciplines. He has levitated objects. He has read the page of a book without the book being opened. He has taken an object involved in a crime and relived that crime. He has done this in front of witnesses and under scientific observation. His experiment with Mitchell on the moon was just a small sample of his extraordinary talents, as was locating part of the *Atocha* treasure. He could do it all, but there was a catch. A lot of energy was required. So usually when there was an audience who wanted to see him perform he would rely on a few card demonstrations. Olof wasn't David Copperfield. The things he did were not tricks. And he didn't like to stand on a stage and wow people with his amazing abilities. He was a very private person but when asked he would try to oblige with a demonstration or two using playing cards.

After dinner Olof asked the person that brought the cards to pass them to the end of the table. The table was quite long. There were twelve of us seated. He asked the person at the end to shuffle them and pass the deck to someone else. Then he asked that person to pick a card out of the deck but do not look at it. "Now I know what the card is but I want Ronnie to tell you." Go ahead, Ronnie. I just communicated to you what the card is."

Ronnie was seated at the other end of the table. He had not touched the cards or seen the one picked. "The ten of diamonds," he said. The card was turned over. It was the ten of diamonds. Olof did several more variations of this same demonstration. He never touched the cards.

But Olof wasn't in the Philippines to do card demonstrations. He was there because of his ability to detect the presence of gold on a treasure site "by seeing its aura," he claimed. This wasn't his first trip to the Philippines for that purpose. Marcos invited him in 1975. Because of his talent he was the genesis of a treasure hunting group.

•

In 1974 Victor Nituda was in the U.S. on business when he read the newspaper article about Olof helping Mel Fisher locate part of the Atocha treasure thirty-five miles off the Florida coast. Nituda was a friend of Marcos. He had written a syrupy account of the president's childhood, entitled *The Young Marcos*, and he was about to go that extra mile one more time.

He flew to Chicago and contacted a friend to help him locate Olof. When they finally met, he told Olof he was a friend of the Philippine president and asked if he would like to go there as a special guest of Marcos. Olof was flattered. He accepted the invitation but said he was already going to the Philippines on another matter. He agreed to call Nituda after he arrived.

The other matter was also a treasure hunt. Just before the Nituda invitation, Olof had received a letter from an air force officer stationed at Clark Air Base in the Philippines. He couldn't recall the name but remembered that his rank was lieutenant colonel. The officer had also read about Olof's success with Fisher and had invited him to come to the base to help locate a treasure believed to be buried by Yamashita. He showed the letter to another new acquaintance, Norman Kirst, who had just approached Olof for help with a treasure site located off the eastern coast of the U.S.

Olof found all this attention from treasure hunters amusing and exciting. He personally had no use for wealth, but if riches were used to alleviate poverty and to help others then he was all for it. With that understanding he agreed to try and help these people.

After reading the note, Kirst offered to sponsor the trip and accompany Olof and his friend, Cary Calloway, to the Philippines. They flew there in September 1974. As soon as they arrived they were informed that treasure hunting on the base was not allowed. So they spent a few weeks searching for some off-base sites but didn't find anything. A Filipino attorney headed the search team. He introduced Olof to one of his friends, another Filipino who had a treasure hunting group called The Professionals. His name was Florentino Villacrusis.

Olof, Kirst, and Calloway decided to drive down to Manila, sixty-five kilometers (forty miles) south of the base, for a respite. Nituda was contacted and Olof was invited to the palace to meet Marcos. After the meeting Olof was invited to stay a few weeks as Marcos' personal guest. He moved into the palace guest house and was provided with a car and driver. While there he managed to get an invitation for Kirst to meet Marcos.

At the meeting Kirst presented himself as an international financier who had brought Olof to the Philippines for the treasure hunt. Marcos appeared to be curious about the treasure and asked a lot of questions. When Olof mentioned Villacrusis' name in the course of the conversation Marcos said he knew him. He spoke highly of Villacrusis and suggested they work together on some treasure sites that Villacrusis knew about. Kirst, not wanting to be left out, convinced Marcos that with his international contacts he could sell the gold without anyone knowing its origin. That was how it began.

Gradually others with talents unique to this undertaking were added to the team. In December 1974 Kirst called Bob Curtis in Reno, Nevada, and invited him to join the group. Kirst had heard that Curtis possessed a new technology for extracting more gold per ton of material. Such a process would be a convenient cover for any abrupt increase in the quantity of gold going out of the Philippines. Any gold bars recovered would have to be laundered — melted down and reprocessed — in order to eliminate identifying marks and to refine its purity. A fair-traded bar on the London Bullion Market required a fineness of 99.5* or better in 1940, just

---

* Some commercial traders required a fineness of 99.99, which is 24-karat, but this would be for highly specialized uses.

like today. But some gold bars refined back then may have been less than 99.5 because they were privately minted and not intended to be fair-traded.

Kirst had called Curtis from Malacañan Palace and introduced him to Marcos over the phone. Curtis had never heard of Kirst before but he listened as Kirst and Marcos spoke of a golden treasure that was theirs for the taking, and Curtis was added to the team. While he was getting ready to depart for Manila a letter arrived from Kirst. It was dated 22 February 1975 and marked "Personal, Confidential, Proprietary Information." It described in some detail the location and value of some of the treasure sites. The amounts were mind boggling. According to Kirst there were thirty-four locations of major importance and 138 lesser locations, for a total of 172 sites. Of the dozen or so sites specifically mentioned, eight of the sites were worth over $5 billion each.

Calloway, an architect, had to return to his job in Chicago. Olof returned with him to resolve some business matters, and then flew to Reno to meet Curtis a few weeks later. On 27 February, Curtis and Olof flew to San Francisco where they were met by Kirst, and they returned to Manila together on 1 March.

At the airport they were greeted by several members of the new group. Villacrusis was there along with his old friend, Cesar Leyran, and a former Philippine ambassador to the United States, Amelito Mutuc. Mutuc was also a friend of Villacrusis and had been asked to assist in legal matters involving the treasure hunt.

They drove to the Hyatt Hotel overlooking Manila Bay on Roxas Boulevard. As soon as they were checked in a briefing was held. Villacrusis started by introducing his two eye-witnesses, Ben and Pol. He presented maps of the sites that Kirst had written about in his confidential report, and went over some recently prepared engineering drawings of a few of the sites. He also explained that Marcos' major concern was secrecy. The whole operation must remain secret. To insure this secrecy, and to protect the Americans, a car and driver was assigned to them, along with security guards in civilian clothes. Also, it was announced, for the sake of security in communication Ver would use the code name Jimmy and Marcos the code name Charlie.

By then a sort of pecking order had been established in the group. While Marcos was the leader with Ver directly under him,

Mutuc had been appointed the coordinator of the working group which consisted of everyone at the briefing plus another colonel who had been around treasure hunting circles for awhile — Mario Lachica. This eleven-man team called itself Leber Group. (Curtis would later bring in more Americans from Las Vegas but they weren't considered official members of the team.) The origin of the Leber name is as confusing as its meaning. Curtis thought it was Rebel spelled backwards. Others in the group thought it stood for "Legitimate Ethical Business Enterprises Related."

Over the next few days they inspected the locations of more than two dozen sites in the Manila area. Only a few appeared to be under excavation. Others showed no sign of attempted recovery. Marcos explained that he had known for several years where the sites were but if all the gold were retrieved at the same time then it would have to be stored and secured while undergoing the laundering process. He had delayed work at some sites because such plans were not yet complete.

That was the purpose of the Leber Group. They were going to resolve all these problems and in the process make themselves extremely wealthy. The timing of the venture was especially propitious. Effective 1 January 1975 Americans could legally buy and possess gold. Gold markets all over the world were already buzzing with increased activity and each day brought a higher price and more incentive for the Leber Group to apply themselves more vigorously to the task.

On 11 March, Marcos invited Olof, Kirst, and Curtis for an overnight cruise on the presidential yacht to his summer palace at Mariveles located at the southern tip of the Bataan peninsula, the scene of so much suffering at the start of World War II. On the way Olof entertained Marcos and the group with a few demonstrations of his psychic powers.

As the boat approached the dock at Mariveles the guests could see a huge Spanish hacienda built on the side of a hill that overlooked a picture-perfect inlet of white sandy beaches and crystal clear, azure blue water. A few miles out, directly in front of them, stood the small, tadpole shaped island of Corregidor, from which General MacArthur departed the Philippines with a promise to return.

The group spent the rest of the day like any other tourists on vacation being hosted by a friend, except their host was the president, and this was the Philippines, and Filipino hospitality was like no other in the world. Some were taken to Corregidor by helicopter for sightseeing while others chose to go swimming, snorkeling, or waterskiing. All the while their every need was attended to by an army of servants.

That evening they were wined and dined like royalty. After dinner Marcos invited the three to his office to discuss the upcoming treasure hunt. One topic of discussion was the metals refining plant required for laundering the gold. Curtis offered to dismantle his plant in Reno and ship it here. This would be the quickest way to get into operation. Marcos agreed.

While they were talking everyone tried to keep looking at Marcos who was seated at his desk. But there was a stunning golden statuette of Buddha about one meter in height sitting on the floor just inside the entrance to his study and everyone kept glancing back at it.

Marcos was obviously aware of this and, far from expressing displeasure at the inattentiveness of his audience, he told them that the Buddha was solid gold, weighed about a ton, and was part of the treasure found at one of the sites but he didn't say which one. (Olof would later say that it had a remarkable resemblance to pictures he had seen of Roxas' Golden Buddha.)

Marcos added that part of the gold found at that site was stored right below his office in a basement vault. After the meeting Ver took them downstairs. In a room about nine meters square gold bars were stacked from floor to ceiling. They noticed that each bar had what appeared to be Chinese markings. Ver said that this wasn't all of it, that there was more stored at the palace, and that this was just the treasure recovered at one site. The group returned to Manila eager to go to work.

A few days later Marcos arranged a meeting between Curtis and Jose Y. Campos. Campos was well known as a close friend of Marcos and the godfather of his son. He had parlayed this relationship and his own business acumen into building the largest pharmaceutical firm in the country, United Laboratories. The company had exclusive contracts to furnish drugs to the military and the health ministry. Campos was also known to be a front for several of Marcos' business ventures. This meeting was for that purpose. They agreed to set up a precious metals refinery which would be a joint venture between United States Platinum, Inc., Curtis' company, and United Laboratories.

The next few weeks were spent studying the various treasure sites. The locations were all over the place. There were sites at Clark Air Base, Subic Naval Base, Camp John Hay, the mountains around Baguio, and in regions further north. Fifty of the land sites were in Metro Manila and the nearby province of Rizal. Several of these were in military camps. The gold stored at the summer palace was reportedly found at Camp Aguinaldo in Quezon City. Another site, the one mentioned in the 2 May 1973 letter to Marcos, was in a tunnel system under General MacArthur's old headquarters. This had also been General Yamashita's headquarters briefly, and was now named Fort Bonifacio. Other sites were in Intramuros, the Walled City, and Fort Santiago, and in places of worship such as the San Agustin, Christ the King, and San Sebastian Churches. The little barrio of Teresa, thirty miles outside Manila, held several major sites. In addition there were water sites in Lingayan Gulf and Manila Bay, and off the coasts of Mindanao, Corregidor, and eastern Luzon.

A water site could mean that chests containing the treasure were dropped off the fantail of a ship at a predetermined site. Or it could be the location of a ship containing treasure that was purposely scuttled or sunk in battle. Pol related a story about one Japanese ship, the heavy cruiser *Nachi*, which he claimed was scuttled in Manila Bay in 1943. It was towing a barge loaded with a million silver peso coins. Without warning a torpedo hit the barge amidships. It split in two and its cargo spilled to the ocean bottom. At the same time two torpedoes blew the *Nachi* wide open and it sank almost immediately. Most of its crew of 1,110 went to the bottom with her. The Japanese submarine then surfaced and machine-gunned the survivors in the water. Pol said that the *Nachi* was torpedoed because it carried a cargo of gold bullion. He watched the sinking with binoculars from the roof of a hotel on Roxas Boulevard.

It was a fascinating story, but it wasn't true. The *Nachi* could not have been sunk in 1943. The official history of U.S. naval operations stated that it survived the Battle of the Java Sea in February 1942 and the Battle of Leyte Gulf in October 1944. It was finally sunk in Manila Bay on 5 November 1944 by Hell Diver and Avenger aircraft from the USS *Lexington*. In 1945 the submarine rescue ship USS *Chanticleer* sent divers down to inspect the *Nachi*. Their search yielded valuable documents about other battles but there was no mention of any precious cargo such as gold.

These mistaken recollections may have been fueled by the visit in March 1975 of some survivors and relatives of the *Nachi* crew who came to Manila to try and recover the remains of the crew. The widow of the ship's commander, Captain Empei Kanooka, accompanied them. The event was widely reported in the media, and may have sparked Pol's emotional recollection. He might have seen a ship sunk that was loaded with silver pesos and gold, but it wasn't the *Nachi*. Even so, when Pol related this story Leber Group was eager to begin excavating the *Nachi*.

Ver was against doing a water site first. He claimed it was too complicated, and suggested that it would be easier to excavate a land site. Someone recommended Fort Santiago. Ver replied that all arrangements had not yet been made with the park commissioner. Teresa I was then suggested. Ver claimed that the owner of this property had not yet agreed to any terms, but that wasn't the real reason.

Raymondo Francisco, the owner, had demanded that his expenses be reimbursed for previous digs. Francisco allowed Villacrusis and Lepasana to dig there in 1972 for about a year but they ran out of funds. And in 1974 Villacrusis and Pol dug at the same site. By the time Leber Group was formed they had dug down to about fifty meters. Villacrusis had recommended that they continue at the same site but Francisco first demanded he be paid for expenses he had already incurred. That was yet another thing intriguing about the projects of the task force. They always seemed to be thinly capitalized. Marcos refused to finance any of the digs. That was always left up to those in charge of a particular excavation.

Ver finally relented and allowed the group to begin searching for the barge and the *Nachi*. By then the crew's relatives and survivors had departed. At the same time preparations were made for excavating the site at Teresa II, the property next to Teresa I. The owner, Mrs. Helena Frankenburger, had given Villacrusis permission to dig.

The search for the *Nachi* was begun first. The Philippine Navy provided a boat. Ben and Pol accompanied Olof, Kirst, and Curtis. Using the map they were guided to the approximate location. Then Olof took over. This wasn't the place, he insisted. Following his directions they anchored several hundred yards away and sent the divers down. They surfaced twenty minutes later and announced that the *Nachi* was directly underneath. Markers were dropped and they returned to shore to make preparations for the recovery.

When they went back out the next day with their equipment the markers were gone. After looking for several hours it was decided to just come back out the following day and locate the *Nachi* again. The search was delayed for two days, however, while the boat assigned to them was used to escort Marcos' yacht to the summer palace. Finally they went back out and Olof again located the cruiser. Blaming it on the currents and waves before, this time wire was used instead of rope when the markers were dropped. In addition Ver agreed to have a boat patrol the area to guard against intruders. When they went back out to begin recovery the markers were missing again and there was no patrol boat in the area. When asked about the patrol boat Ver said it had been called to escort the presidential yacht. Olof tried to find the location again but darkness came and they had to go in. They agreed to try later but by then their efforts were directed elsewhere.

While this work was going on the group set about devising detailed plans for recovering, sorting, boxing, storing, and transporting the treasure. That was when Olof heard that Marcos intended to melt down all the gold, including the Buddhas and other artifacts, in order to hide the origin. He voiced his objections to Ver and to anyone else that would listen, saying that these were a priceless and irreplaceable part of history, but nobody seemed to care.

Curtis made plans to return to Reno. A few days before his departure Marcos called the group together. At the meeting they finalized and signed a formal agreement. It was now official. The value of the treasure would be divided equally into twelve shares.* Olof noticed that there was no percentage allowed for the government. Marcos had decided this wasn't necessary.

Curtis left for Reno on 28 March and Olof departed the day after. Kirst had already left a few days before for his home town in Wisconsin. Curtis was kept busy dismantling and crating his refining plant for shipment back to Manila. He was also busy with another chore.

In December 1974, when he was first contacted about joining the group, his company was having serious financial problems. After he talked to Kirst he contacted Samuel J. Agnew of the John Birch Society in January 1975 and told him about the treasure hunt. He also told Agnew that his company would be used to launder the gold, and asked if he could borrow a quarter of a million dollars to finance the project. Through a complicated loan agreement Curtis agreed to give Agnew's group 22 percent of his share in the treasure in return for a $240,000 loan repayable in three months at ten percent interest.

Now it was April and the loan was due. He contacted Agnew, told him he couldn't pay yet, and managed to convince him that an additional $125,000 in financing was needed. This loan was also granted in return for a percentage of the gold laundering scheme and a promise that the John Birch Society could handle the sale of the laundered gold. Curtis knew that Marcos had assigned the responsibility for selling the gold to Kirst, but he made that promise to Agnew anyway.

Curtis paid his shipping bill, which amounted to $36,000, and departed the states on 18 April. Olof had thought about not returning. Marcos' attitude toward the treasure offended him. Eventually he decided he could do more good by being there. He accompanied Curtis and his engineer, Wes Chapman, back to Manila. Kirst was not informed of their departure. By then there was no love lost between the two.

* The agreement contained twelve names — Mutuc, Villacrusis, Lachica, Leyran, Ben, Pol, Olof, Kirst, Curtis, Jimmy De Veyra, Aristeo T. Ferraren, and Eduardo S. Escobar. De Veyra was Marcos. Ferraren, a retired general, signed for Ver. Escobar, although not a part of Leber, received a share for giving Marcos the use of his construction company for the labor.

Curtis had never heard of Kirst until the day he was called in December 1974. There was no denying that Kirst had granted him this opportunity. That is why he agreed to pay for the air fare of Kirst to fly to San Francisco and then return to Manila with him. Kirst had also asked for a monthly salary of $2,000, plus twenty-five dollars a day for expenses and Curtis agreed.

That is how their relationship began. Now that Curtis was a part of the group he no longer felt an obligation to pay Kirst anything. While in the states Kirst called several times to ask for more money but he was turned down. After Curtis went back to Manila his office telexed him from Reno and said that Kirst was still calling. He wanted to return, and was asking for $5,000 the first month and $2,000 a month thereafter. Curtis told his office to advise Kirst that he wasn't needed in Manila yet.

On the way back to Manila, Curtis read in the newspaper that Johnson Matthey Chemical Limited, a London corporation that refined the Philippine's gold, would assist the Central Bank in establishing its own gold and silver refinery in a new complex in Quezon City. Upon its completion in 1976 all the country's gold and silver bullion could be refined there. This news came as a surprise and ran counter to everything Curtis had discussed with Marcos and Campos.

When they arrived back in Manila it was discovered that Marcos had announced Presidential Decree 263. Now only the coast guard could issue salvage permits, and only with presidential approval. Marcos found out that a Japanese ship had arrived and, with assistance from a Filipino group, began a salvage operation on the Japanese cruiser *Mogami*. It also carried gold, according to Pol. That was enough reason to outlaw the competition. The salvage permit was revoked and the decree announced.

In addition, Luzon Stevedoring Corporation, which provided equipment and services for the operation, was taken over by the government because it was "considered strategic or vital to the national welfare," according to the official announcement. Nobody knew quite what that meant. A few objections to the takeover were raised but they soon died down. All this was easy enough for Marcos. This was the mid-seventies. He had complete control of the country by now and was just beginning to fully exercise his dictatorial powers. But this time he was a little late. Perhaps he forgot that the Japanese already had a twenty-year head start since they signed a salvage agreement in 1955.*

On 24 April, Curtis and Chapman met with Ver to discuss details of the retrieval process. Ver mentioned that Marcos had complained about rumors being circulated that an American group was in the Philippines to assist him in recovering the Yamashita treasure. Until the rumors die down it would be best that they not be seen in public with Marcos, and added that he would be the link between Leber Group and Marcos. This was a veiled warning to both of them. It was no secret that both liked their whiskey, and when they drank they talked. They got the message. From now on they would stop bragging in public about the treasure hunt.

Ver then explained that Mutuc had angered Marcos by volunteering his legal services to one of Marcos' political opponents, Senator Sergio Osmeña, Jr. In addition it was discovered that Mutuc was secretly involved with the Filipino group trying to salvage the *Mogami* behind Marcos' back. Therefore, Ver announced, effective immediately Mutuc was no longer part of Leber Group.

Curtis asked Ver about the newspaper report that Johnson Matthey would soon set up a refinery in Manila. Ver assured them the article was inaccurate, that Marcos had no plans for allowing them to build a plant in the Philippines. Curtis didn't know that Ver was lying, and that already plans were being drawn up for that refinery. Johnson Matthey was one of the London Five, the five-member gold pool which sets the daily price of gold.**

John McAllaster, an associate of Curtis, and his wife Maureen arrived in late April. Curtis' plant arrived shortly afterward on

* The Japanese Foreign Ministry, when asked about the status of the 1955 agreement, stated that one project which called for recovering fifty-seven ships off Manila and Cebu, was completed. The status of a second project, involving another 175 ships, could not be confirmed.

** In February 1986 Dr. David Owen, leader of the Social Democrats, and Brian Sedgmore of the Labour Party charged in the British House of Commons that gold worth approximately 7.25 million pounds had been smuggled into England by Johnson Matthey without payment of taxes from April 1985 until February 1986, and that these activities ended only days before Marcos fled the Philippines. The prime minister, however, refused to set up a tribunal of inquiry.

2 May. It was placed in the warehouse of Doctor Eduardo Escobar, who owned the Age Construction Company. Escobar was a friend of Marcos. He agreed to handle the excavation of the Teresa site. Work finally began in mid-May. The map of the site was first used to determine the area in which to start. Then with Ben and Pol's recollections and Olof's assistance they found the main air vent that led to the tunnel below. Security arrangements were finalized and work was begun.

While the work was going on Pol told the members of Leber Group a story about what had happened there thirty-two years before. In 1943 Teresa was chosen as a treasure burial site. This time no local laborers or Matagumi Kaisha were used on the work crew. Instead several hundred American, Australian, and Filipino prisoners of war were brought in. Over the next few months a huge hole about the size of two football fields and fifty meters deep was gouged out of the earth. A series of concrete tunnels was constructed. The main tunnel was about 300 meters long, fifteen meters wide, and twelve meters high. At both ends were side tunnels about 100 meters long which, on the map, looked like two huge carabao horns. No one was informed of the purpose of the construction.

One day a convoy of trucks arrived with its cargo of treasure. Several hundred small crates, supposedly loaded with gold bullion, were offloaded and placed in the main tunnel, boxes of diamonds and jewels were offloaded and placed in a side tunnel, and then a few trucks containing more crates of gold were driven down into the shelter.

A Shinto priest arrived at the site to bless the treasure. After the blessing the prisoners were ordered into the shelter to offload the trucks. Then several tractors started bulldozing the entrance and covering it with dirt. When the prisoners realized they were about to be buried alive everyone started screaming and running for the entrance. Machine guns mowed them down. After the first rank was slaughtered the others, already half dead from starvation, disease, and overwork, just didn't have the energy or strength to get past the dead bodies blocking their way. They kept screaming and clawing at the grisly barricade as they were entombed. Then the site was booby-trapped with two thousand-pound bombs to insure that if anyone accidentally stumbled on the treasure he would never live to tell the tale. The terrified screams of hundreds of souls could still be heard as the site was covered over and camouflaged to hide its location.

I was unable to confirm Pol's story. But what gave the whole thing credibility, according to some members of Leber Group, was that Pol kept predicting accurately what they would find next in the excavation as they dug down. He said that there would be a layer of charcoal three meters down. There was. Three meters further down they would find a layer of bamboo. They did. Pol then said it wouldn't be long now, that there were only two more levels, one of criss-crossed wooden boards and one of human bones. That was his only mistake. He thought the treasure was ten meters, or about thirty feet, down but it wasn't. It turned out to be thirty meters instead. One explanation for Pol's being able to predict what would be encountered next is that he was able to read at least a portion of the Teresa map. His dramatic story about how the treasure was buried and the prisoners killed could not be disproved, and one incident that occurred later made it believable.

The digging continued. They uncovered the other two layers. At twenty-five meters a large round stone one meter in diameter was discovered. It had a hole about eight centimeters in diameter in the middle. (This is what reminded Pol of the execution he had performed here at Teresa. When the head came off it rolled up against this stone.) Pol said that this rock was about five meters directly above the tunnel. It was difficult for the group to hide their excitement from the work crew, who were not supposed to know what was going on.

An attempt was made to speed up the pace but the work still progressed at a painfully slow rate. The monsoon season, which usually arrived in July, started in June. Now the work crews spent as much time bailing out water as they did digging out dirt. Sometimes their excavation got flooded and slowed things somewhat, but they still proceeded down.

On 8 June they broke through the top of the tunnel complex. Almost immediately everyone smelled a stench and became sick. Some broke out in sores and rashes and had to be hospitalized. Those at the site believed that the gases escaping from the tunnel came from the putrefaction of the hundreds of bodies that had

decayed long ago and been sealed up until now. The doctors thought
that such gasses should have dissipated by now. Still there was a
stench, and something did cause sickness and rashes, which added
credibility to Pol's story.

One morning one of the security guards left the site and
reappeared a few hours later with a military contingent headed by
a colonel known to be loyal to Imelda. He announced that from
now on he would provide security. The confusion disrupted work
for awhile. Although the laborers didn't know the purpose of the
excavation they now knew that two military factions were contesting
each other for whatever was there.

This turn of events was not altogether unexpected. Marcos
knew that Imelda and her brother, Kokoy, were snooping around
the palace trying to find out what was going on with his treasure
hunting. He had issued strict orders that this project was to be kept
secret, even from Imelda. Why he was waging such a campaign
against his wife about this particular matter provided some insight
into what was going on in the palace at the time.

Marcos and Imelda were still close and their marriage was
intact. However, it was about this time that Imelda began to lust
for power of her own. She began to gather her own group of
supporters. Soon it was common knowledge that you had to pay
homage to one or the other. Loyalty to both was out of the question.
Now, like their bedrooms, there were separate power bases. Palace
intrigue was at its peak.

Imelda began her own political career that same year, being
appointed governor of Metro Manila. Later she would be appointed
minister of something called Human Settlements, to help the poor.
And after that she would be elected to the Senate in a Marcos-
controlled election. But now in 1975 she and her brother were the
formidable team. They used Marcos' powers to their own advantage.
Cosmopolitan would call her one of the richest women in the world.
Marcos probably decided that she was rich enough. The treasure
would be his and his alone. Imelda obviously disagreed with him.

It was almost a game, albeit a dangerous one, keeping Imelda
and Kokoy at bay while the search was on. For the most part he
had been able to contain her but she too had her loyal followers
which included a few in the military that didn't belong to Ver's

task force and who would obey her. Marcos suspected that she was the one behind the attempted recovery at Christ the King Church. That's why it was stopped. They had also dug in Fort Santiago and may have recovered two of the shallow sites in the walls. Then the park commissioner, a friend of Marcos, stepped in and refused to allow any further digging. That was why the task force wasn't allowed to dig there.

When the dig at the Three Jars site was stopped the nephews of Don Paquito Ortigas tried repeatedly to contact Marcos and get the site reactivated. When they couldn't, they told Villacrusis that since Marcos wouldn't respond they would contact Imelda. Villacrusis reported this to Marcos, and he ordered that site closed. Undaunted, Imelda still looked around for other sites and finally managed to plant a spy at Teresa II. Here were the results.

Marcos had neglected to inform Leber Group about this situation with his wife. Now things were brought to a critical head. Fortunately the crisis was defused that same day. One of the group was able to get a message to Lachica who acted quickly. That evening he sent Colonel Renato Gemora, the military district commander, to the site with reinforcements. They surrounded the site and demanded the surrender of the Imelda contingent. They finally gave up without firing a shot.

About two weeks after the incident, on 26 June, Olof was in Makati, the financial district of Metro Manila, and ran into Kirst. When Olof said hello, Kirst responded coolly that he had returned at his own expense the previous day to see Marcos about a new business deal. Back at the hotel Olof told Curtis about the chance meeting. They tried to contact Kirst but were unsuccessful. The next morning Kirst appeared at Teresa II with Villacrusis and Cesar. All were decidedly cool to Curtis and McAllaster. The two groups remained divided from then on.

On the morning of 6 July, when everyone arrived at the site they were informed that the workers had hit some metal and cables during the night so work had been suspended. On investigation the metal object looked like a truck fender and the cables, they suspected, might be hooked to the thousand-pound bombs Pol had warned them about. Work was halted and the area secured. Then Curtis, McAllaster, and the lieutenant in charge of security went

to Gemora's office and informed him. Gemora told them to proceed
to Quezon City to the residence of General Ramon Cannu,
Gemora's boss (and legal council for Marcos' PSC).

There they were welcomed warmly by an excited Cannu, who
phoned Ver immediately to relay the information. Ver called them
to the phone and congratulated them but in the same conversation
asked if any of the workers suspected they were digging for treasure.
They said no, that they knew that everyone was still sworn to secrecy
about the project. Ver then told them to go back to the hotel and
wait for further instructions.

What they did not know was that some time in the last twenty-
four hours Marcos had decided that Curtis and his associates were
no longer needed. This sudden change of plan may have been
engineered by Kirst, but the defection of one of Marcos' media aides,
Primitivo Mijares, also happened about this time. Mijares had
defected in February while on a trip to the U.S. and had testified
before a congressional subcommittee on 17 June about corruption
and human rights abuses in the Marcos government.

In San Francisco, Philippine Consul General Trinidad
Algoncel had attempted to reach Mijares and bribe him with $50,000
before he testified. Mijares turned down the bribe and instead went
to nationally syndicated columnist Jack Anderson with the
information. It was in the newspapers in June.

If Marcos was embarrassed by that bit of news he must have
been enraged when he read Anderson's columns of 2 and 3 July.
In those Mijares mentioned that Marcos was looking for "buried
World War II Japanese treasure in the Sierra Madre." Teresa was
in the foothills of those mountains. Thus the mood at the palace
around this time was somber. Mijares had sealed his fate by that
episode. The following February he disappeared, and six months
later his son was found brutally murdered in Manila.

Ver called the next morning and said that a car would pick
them up shortly and take them to a meeting with Lachica. Some
very important matters needed to be discussed. Ver sounded upset.
The car arrived but instead of Lieutenant Sapro Santos, their usual
driver and escort, Ver's personal driver was there along with an
unsavory looking bodyguard. By now they had moved down the
road to the Philippine Village, another five-star hotel on Roxas

Boulevard which overlooked Manila Bay. As they left the hotel, instead of turning left to go to the palace, they turned right and headed for Makati.

Fifteen minutes later they entered Fort Bonifacio, the sprawling military base located next to Forbes Park, the most exclusive subdivision in Metro Manila. In a few minutes they turned into the War Memorial Cemetery, drove up to the memorial and stopped. The national cemetery was an imposing place. Thousands of names of Americans who gave their lives in the defense of freedom were carved on the walls of a huge stone memorial which overlooked row upon row of hundreds of white crosses on the immaculately kept gently sloping green.

They had to wait about an hour before Lachica drove up. He apologized for the delay and explained that he chose the national cemetery as the place to meet because it was quiet. He told them that Marcos was upset about Mijares testimony. He thought that the Americans might have leaked some information to Mijares. The operation would be suspended until it could be determined if there was such a leak.

They headed back to the hotel together. On the way Lachica said it would take about a week for the Philippine Embassy in Washington to finish a detailed report about the matter. Curtis asked if they could return to Reno for that week because they had been neglecting their business. "I know Charlie is upset right now but I assure you we haven't breached our secrecy agreement and we'll only be gone a week," Curtis implored. "Besides, we're leaving our equipment and most of our clothes here."

Lachica said it was okay for Olof to leave since he wasn't needed at that time but he would have to talk with Charlie about them. Olof packed up and left that afternoon.

Ver called the next morning and said it was okay to leave but they should be back within seven days. Curtis and the McAllasters checked out of the hotel on 10 July. They asked the hotel to hold their rooms since they were returning in a week, and departed that afternoon. Wes Chapman had left a few weeks earlier because his wife was about to give birth.

Mutuc returned to Manila about the same time they departed. After being informed of his dismissal from Leber Group he had written to Marcos asking for forgiveness and pleading that he was innocent of disloyalty. He then publicly announced his withdrawal as legal counsel for Senator Osmeña.

Shortly afterward Mutuc flew to the U.S. to see Osmeña, who was there seeking medical treatment. Mutuc asked him to write a letter in support of continuing U.S. aid to the Philippines to the congressional subcommittee which had heard Mijares' testimony. At first Osmeña was reluctant but he agreed after Mutuc reminded him that Marcos still had his nephew in jail in the Philippines. Mutuc then testified on behalf of Marcos before the same subcommittee. When the former ambassador returned to Manila after doing Marcos' dirty work he was once again welcomed back to the fold.

On arrival back in Reno, Curtis and McAllaster discussed the situation. They still hoped to prove to Marcos they were innocent of any wrongdoing. If they could then perhaps Leber Group could continue in operation and they could still receive their share. They obtained a copy of Jack Anderson's column and read it to determine what damage was done. There was only a brief mention of the treasure.

On 12 July they called Mutuc. He assured them that all was well and that Marcos now realized that the testimony of Mijares wasn't as damaging as he had first thought. They asked about the Teresa II site, and Mutuc told them that work was still stopped but the site was under tight security. Mutuc asked when they were coming back. They said that they were ready to return but to find out first if work was ready to resume. They agreed to call back in a few days.

Over the next two weeks they tried to call dozens of times but Mutuc was unavailable. On 1 August he finally took the call. His greeting and manner were the opposite of what it had been before. Tersely he told them that Teresa II was back in operation and that they would still get their share when the treasure was recovered. But he advised them not to return, and added that Curtis' laundering plant, still stored in Escobar's warehouse, was no longer needed and would be shipped back to Reno.

Curtis tried to phone Marcos and Ver but they were unavailable. He then sent a telex which made it quite clear that if the agreement was not honored then the secret of the treasure was in jeopardy. The telex was never answered.

There was one other exchange of letters. Villacrusis wrote Curtis on 28 January and informed him that if he didn't return to Manila he would no longer be considered a part of Leber. He also informed Curtis that the check for $2,410.79, which he paid to the Philippine Village Hotel, had bounced and that he should make it good or a criminal action would be filed.

Curtis didn't bother to reply. Instead he wrote Mutuc on 10 February and warned him that if he did not explain what was going on, then they would take other steps to protect their interest which included going to the press. Mutuc never responded. There was no further communication.

For some reason Curtis waited two years before going public in 1978. He first contacted the former governor of Nevada, Senator Paul Laxalt, explained his story, and turned over a large array of material to back it up. He had taped all of his phone conversations and also had hundreds of documents and dozens of pictures. Laxalt turned this material over to the State Department and asked them to check it out. Eventually they said no crime had been committed so they could not pursue the matter.

Jack Anderson heard about the story and carried it in his column. As a result a spokesman for the Philippine Embassy in Washington finally issued a brief statement from Marcos:

> General Ver has wired me that President Marcos directs that I inform [the reporter] that whatever she has is her own concoction because there is no such plan by the president, General Ver, or Ambassador Mutuc to pick up any Japanese World War II treasures. The allegation about the threat uttered by the president is also denied categorically as a vile and total falsehood.

The threat mentioned by Ver came from Curtis' claim that Marcos had threatened his life if he ever said anything about the treasure hunt.

The story attracted the attention of Steve Psinakis who was always interested in matters involving Marcos. He was aware that Marcos was capable of such things. He was a member of the Movement for a Free Philippines, the largest anti-Marcos organization in the U.S., with a chapter in every major city. At the same time Curtis' story was making the rounds, another story was also going around that Ver had sent someone to the states to assassinate the head of the movement, Raul Manglapus.

Fortunately the movement had its own intelligence network. They obtained the assassin's name and monitored his movements when he arrived in the states. Manglapus and another prominent exile, Eduardo Quintero, who had been a delegate to the 1970 Philippine Constitutional Convention, were able to set up a meeting with the man. He admitted he was under investigation for murder in the Philippines and that he had little choice but to cooperate with Ver or else face the consequences. In the Philippines in 1978 such a scenario was very possible and the consequences dismal. The plan failed when it was made public.

Psinakis was familiar with Marcos and his way of dealing with people. The year before, in October 1977, he masterminded the dramatic escape of Eugenio Lopez, Jr. and Sergio Osmeña III. They broke out of a prison in Manila and flew to Hong Kong on a private aircraft. From there they were flown to the U.S. and granted political asylum. Lopez was the brother of Psinakis' wife and the nephew of Marcos' vice-president; Osmeña's father was Marcos' political rival. Both were arrested when martial law was declared in 1972 and accused of attempting to assassinate Marcos. They were never officially charged but held without bail until their escape.

Marcos had agents in the U.S. threatening, harassing, and spying on anti-Marcos dissidents. Now he seemed to be stepping up these activities. Psinakis decided to conduct his own investigation into the treasure hunt. He interviewed Curtis and other witnesses, listened to the taped phone conversations, and pored over all the documents and pictures. Wes Chapman was contacted. At first he denied everything. But when he was confronted with proof he admitted his association but denied that Marcos had anything to do with it. Chapman was aware of what happened to Mijares and his son the year before and was probably afraid to say too much. Kirst was also contacted. His reaction was the same. At first he denied any involvement but after being confronted with proof he admitted he was part of Leber Group.

The results of Psinakis' investigation were printed in a 24-part story in the *Philippine News* beginning in June 1978. The *Las Vegas*

Sun also did a series of articles. A few weeks later the *Sun* reported that Ver and three unidentified Philippine colonels had secretly entered the U.S. to meet with the Mafia for the purpose of planning to kill Curtis and Psinakis. This caused quite a stir in the newspapers but nothing ever came of it.

Marcos didn't allow the treasure hunt story to be carried in the Philippine press. The only mention was a brief denial by columnist Teodoro Valencia, who was a known Marcos apologist and, incidentally, also the park commissioner whose territory included Fort Santiago. He was the one that had stopped Imelda's excavations at the fort.

In 1978 and 1979 several letters were sent to Olof requesting him to return and help pinpoint the treasure locations. The letters — usually signed by Villacrusis, Cesar, Pol, and Mutuc — all carried basically the same message: Your help would be greatly appreciated. If you'll return we guarantee your safety and a very large reward.

Olof never responded to their pleas. Curtis was never contacted again. Gradually their treasure hunt receded into memory but others were waiting in the wings to take up where they left off.

Fort Santiago, 1930

Fort Santiago Today
The Bastion de San Lorenzo is at far end.

(Photos furnished by National Historic Institute, Manila)

Central Bank, Quezon City
The mint is located here.

Central Bank, Manila
This is the main branch.

(Photos furnished by Joey Reyes, Central Bank of the Philippines)

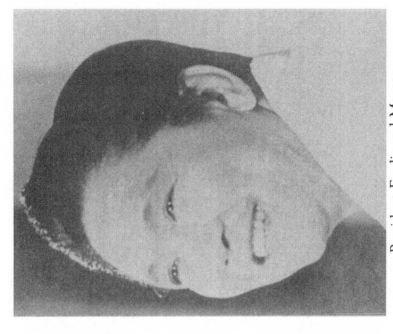

President Ferdinand Marcos

(Photo furnished by University of the Philippines, Alumni Center, Manila)

General Yamashita, 1943

(Photo Furnished by National Historic Institute, Manila)

The gallows where General Yamashita was hung

General Yamashita On Trial
His three lawyers are seated at the table. He is seated behind and
to the right of the lawyer on the right.

(Photos furnished by Philippine National Library, Manila)

Minoru Fukumitsu and Commander Loughlin

The ship *Awa Maru*

Father Bulatao in his office

Left to Right: Pol, Ben, the author, Pedro

訣別 昭和19.7.17 満洲牡丹江

樺沢副官 山下奉文大将 吉田亀

The picture of Yamashita carried around by the author

Roger Roxas and the Golden Buddha
(Photo courtesy of by Roger Roxas)

Roger Roxas and the author

Olof Jonsson with President Marcos on the presidential yacht

Left to Right: General Ver, Bob Curtis, Olof Jonsson,
Norman Kirst, and President Marcos

(Photos courtesy of Olof Jonsson)

Major General John Singlaub
(U.S. Army file photo)

Doctor Noel Soriano

Left to Right: George Wortinger, Doctor Soriano, the author, John Lemmon
Cine Corregidor in background

Coregidor, 1923

(Photo furnished by National Archives, Washington, D.C.)

Cine Corregidor Before the War

(Photo furnished by National Archives, Washington, D.C.)

Cine Corregidor After the War
The work crew prepares to excavate the site

Bastion de San Lorenzo Today
Entrance to Dungeon is in Front

On Top of Bastion de San Lorenzo
Looking Toward Front of Fort

Ted Drinnon and Bob Curtis in Torture Chamber

Jappon on Corregidor
Wearing author's hat and glasses

Attorney Mario Ongkiko

Left to Right: Pedro, the author, Olof, and Ben at the fort

IHS on wall of Bastion

Helmet on display in National Library

Reiner Jacobi

(Photo courtesy of South China Morning Post, Hong Kong)

Enrique Zobel with President Ferdinand Marcos in 1969

(Photo courtesy of Enrique Zobel)

Imelda Marcos

(Photo courtesy of San Francisco Examiner)

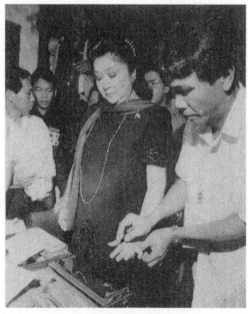

Imelda Marcos Being Fingerprinted In Manila

(Photo courtesy of Daily Globe, Manila)

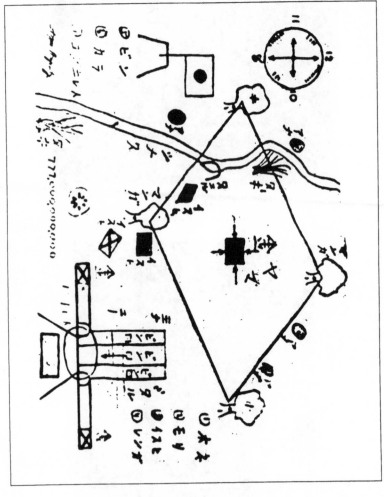

Treasure Map

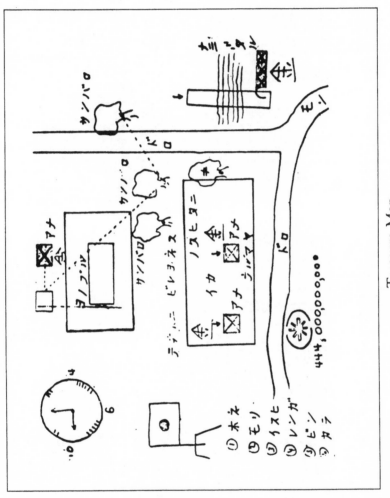

Treasure Map

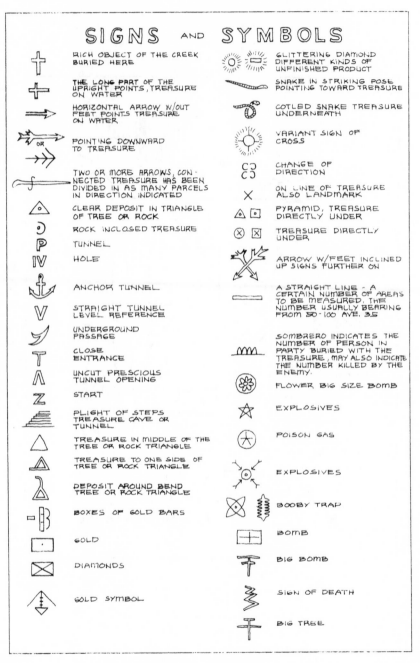

SIGNS and SYMBOLS

RICH OBJECT OF THE CREEK BURIED HERE

THE LONG PART OF THE UPRIGHT POINTS, TREASURE ON WATER

HORIZONTAL ARROW W/OUT FEET POINTS TREASURE ON WATER

POINTING DOWNWARD TO TREASURE

TWO OR MORE ARROWS, CONNECTED TREASURE HAS BEEN DIVIDED IN AS MANY PARCELS IN DIRECTION INDICATED

CLEAR DEPOSIT IN TRIANGLE OF TREE OR ROCK

ROCK INCLOSED TREASURE

TUNNEL

HOLE

ANCHOR TUNNEL

STRAIGHT TUNNEL LEVEL REFERENCE

UNDERGROUND PASSAGE

CLOSE ENTRANCE

UNCUT PRECIOUS TUNNEL OPENING

START

PLIGHT OF STEPS TREASURE CAVE OR TUNNEL

TREASURE IN MIDDLE OF THE TREE OR ROCK TRIANGLE

TREASURE TO ONE SIDE OF TREE OR ROCK TRIANGLE

DEPOSIT AROUND BEND TREE OR ROCK TRIANGLE

BOXES OF GOLD BARS

GOLD

DIAMONDS

GOLD SYMBOL

GLITTERING DIAMOND DIFFERENT KINDS OF UNFINISHED PRODUCT

SNAKE IN STRIKING POSE POINTING TOWARD TREASURE

COTLED SNAKE TREASURE UNDERNEATH

VARIANT SIGN OF CROSS

CHANGE OF DIRECTION

ON LINE OF TREASURE ALSO LANDMARK

PYRAMID, TREASURE DIRECTLY UNDER

TREASURE DIRECTLY UNDER

ARROW W/FEET INCLINED UP SIGNS FURTHER ON

A STRAIGHT LINE - A CERTAIN NUMBER OF AREAS TO BE MEASURED, THE NUMBER USUALLY BEARING FROM 50-100 AVE. 35

SOMBRERO INDICATES THE NUMBER OF PERSON IN PARTY BURIED WITH THE TREASURE, MAY ALSO INDICATE THE NUMBER KILLED BY THE ENEMY.

FLOWER BIG SIZE BOMB

EXPLOSIVES

POISON GAS

EXPLOSIVES

BOOBY TRAP

BOMB

BIG BOMB

SIGN OF DEATH

BIG TREE

Signs and Symbols

JAPANESE CODE

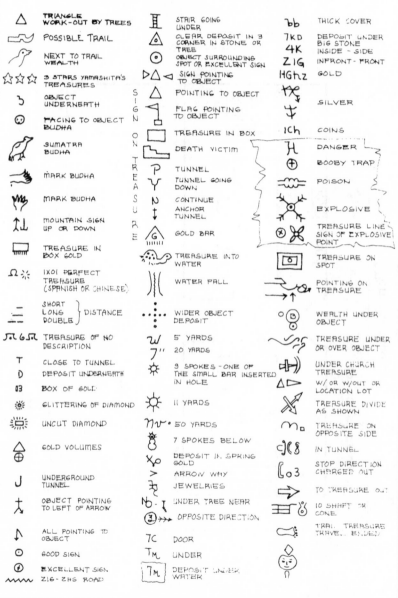

△	TRIANGLE WORK-OUT BY TREES	工	STAIR GOING UNDER	bb	THICK COVER	
⌐◡	POSSIBLE TRAIL	△	CLEAR DEPOSIT IN 3 CORNER IN STONE OR TREE	7kD	DEPOSIT UNDER BIG STONE	
◠	NEXT TO TRAIL WEALTH	◉	OBJECT SURROUNDING SPOT OR EXCELLENT SIGN	4K	INSIDE - SIDE	
☆☆☆	3 STARS YAMASHITA'S TREASURES	▷△◁	SIGN POINTING TO OBJECT	ZIG	INFRONT - FRONT	
ろ	OBJECT UNDERNEATH	◁	POINTING TO OBJECT	HGhz	GOLD	
☺	FACING TO OBJECT BUDHA	⊥	FLAG POINTING TO OBJECT		SILVER	
	SUMATRA BUDHA	□	TREASURE IN BOX	ICh	COINS	
	MARK BUDHA	⌐└	DEATH VICTIM	H	DANGER	
	MARK BUDHA	P	TUNNEL	⊕	BOOBY TRAP	
	MOUNTAIN SIGN UP OR DOWN	Y	TUNNEL GOING DOWN	~~~	POISON	
	TREASURE IN BOX GOLD	N	CONTINUE ANCHOR TUNNEL		EXPLOSIVE	
Ω	IXOI PERFECT TREASURE (SPANISH OR CHINESE)	G	GOLD BAR	⊗	TREASURE LINE SIGN OF EXPLOSIVE POINT	
	SHORT LONG DOUBLE } DISTANCE		TREASURE INTO WATER	□	TREASURE ON SPOT	
	TREASURE OF NO DESCRIPTION	)(	WATER FALL		POINTING ON TREASURE	
T	CLOSE TO TUNNEL	∴∴	WIDER OBJECT DEPOSIT	○B	WEALTH UNDER OBJECT	
D	DEPOSIT UNDERNEATH	u	5 YARDS		TREASURE UNDER OR OVER OBJECT	
03	BOX OF GOLD	7"	20 YARDS			
	GLITTERING OF DIAMOND	☼	9 SPOKES - ONE OF THE SMALL BAR INSERTED IN HOLE		UNDER CHURCH TREASURE	
	UNCUT DIAMOND	☼	11 YARDS	△▷	W/ OR W/OUT OR LOCATION LOT	
	GOLD VOLUMES	nv	50 YARDS		TREASURE DIVIDE AS SHOWN	
	UNDERGROUND TUNNEL		7 SPOKES BELOW	m□	TREASURE ON OPPOSITE SIDE	
J		Xo	DEPOSIT IN SPRING GOLD	)(8	IN TUNNEL	
人	OBJECT POINTING TO LEFT OF ARROW	>	ARROW WHY	603	STOP DIRECTION CHARGED OUT	
↑	ALL POINTING TO OBJECT	玑	JEWELRIES	⇒	TO TREASURE OUT	
⊙	GOOD SIGN	No.I	UNDER TREE NEAR OPPOSITE DIRECTION		10 SHAFT OR CONE	
⊕	EXCELLENT SIGN	7C	DOOR		TRAIL TREASURE TRAVEL ENDED	
~~	ZIG - ZAG ROAD	TM	UNDER			
		7M	DEPOSIT UNDER WATER			

SIGN ON TREASURE

Codes

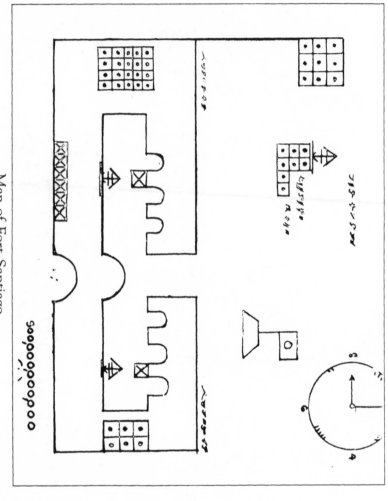

Map of Fort Santiago

(Courtesy of Aida Alejandrino)

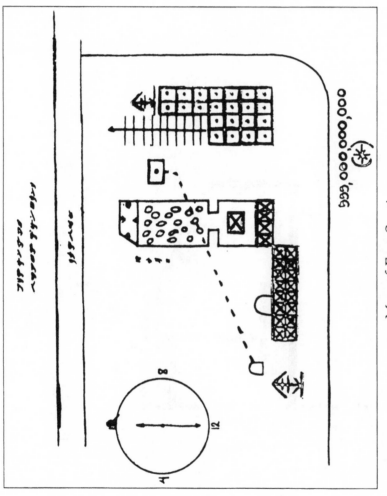

Map of Fort Santiago

(Courtesy of Aida Alejandrino)

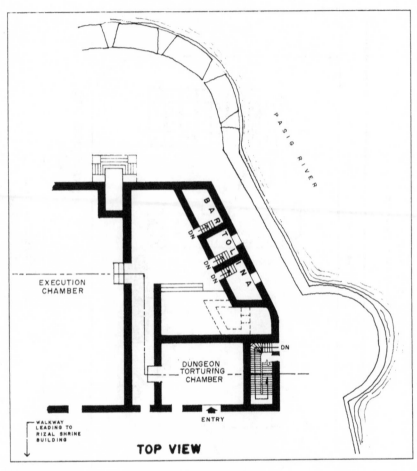

Top View

Bastion de San Lorenzo

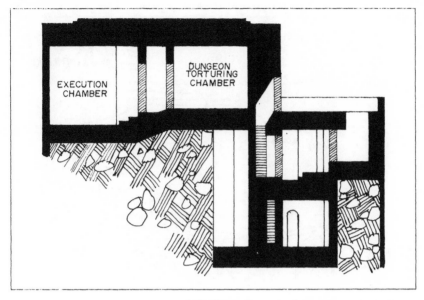

Side View

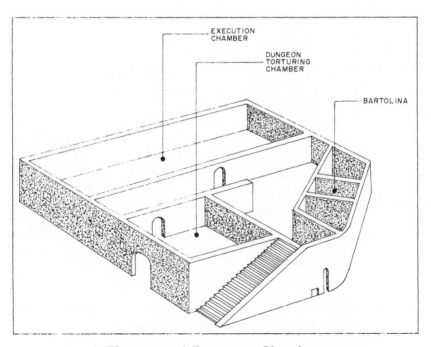

Torture and Execution Chambers
Bastion de San Lorenzo

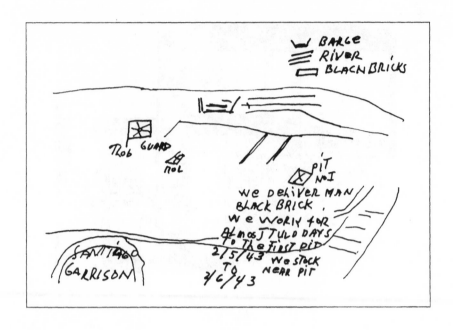

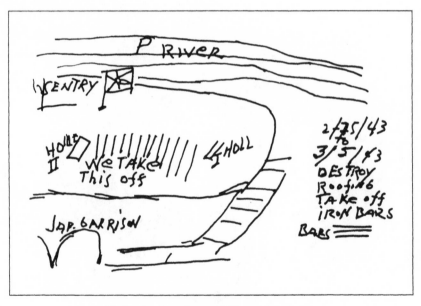

Pedro's sketches of Fort Santiago

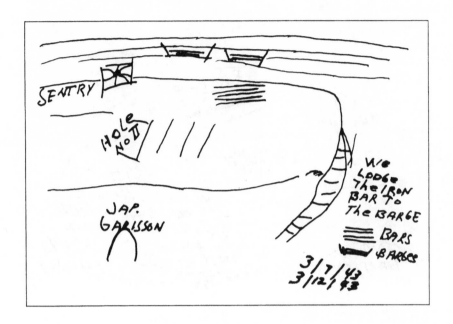

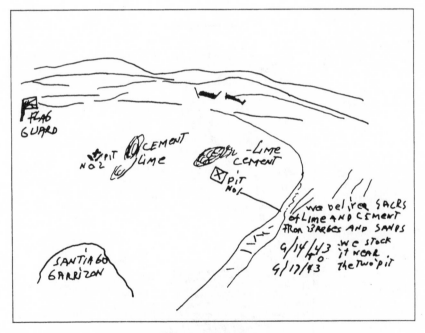

Pedro's sketches of Fort Santiago

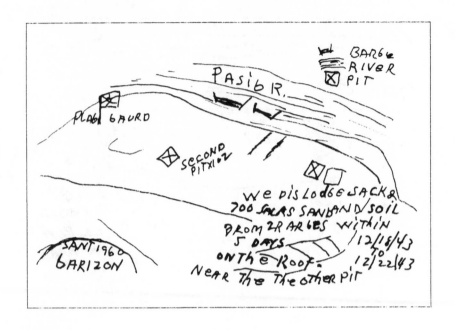

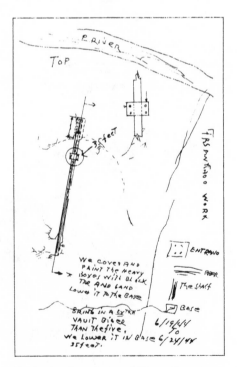

Pedro's sketches of Fort Santiago

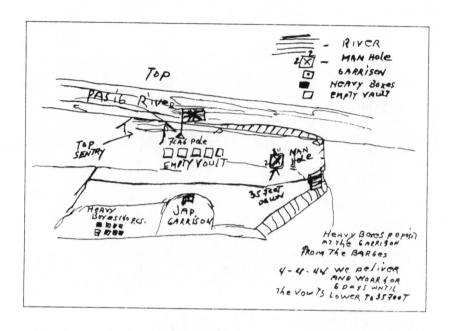

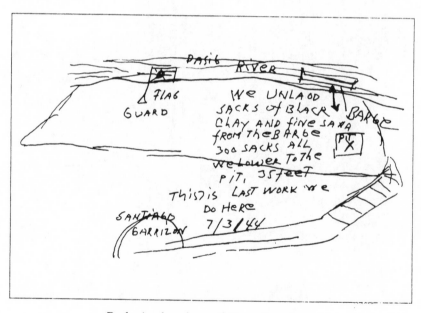

Pedro's sketches of Fort Santiago

Gold Certificate

(Courtesy of Nandeng Pedrosa)

Nippon Star

Retired Major General John K. Singlaub is an honest-to-god hero. His military career is the stuff of legend. As a young army officer in World War II he was recruited into the fledgling OSS, the precursor of the CIA. He parachuted into occupied France to organize the resistance in support of impending allied landings. His case officer for this operation was William Casey, who would become director of the CIA under President Reagan.

Next he volunteered to train Chinese guerrillas in fighting the Japanese in occupied China and Indochina. In one memorable episode just before the surrender of Japan he and a handful of men parachuted onto the island of Hainan to persuade an entire garrison of fanatical Japanese troops to turn over the 400 allied prisoners of war they were guarding. At the end of the war Singlaub was appointed chief of the U.S. military mission in Mukden, Manchuria.

When the CIA was later formed he became the China desk officer at its headquarters in Washington. When the Korean War broke out in 1950 he was called back into the organization and posted to Korea as deputy chief of station. During the Vietnam War he commanded a joint unconventional warfare task force called SOG (Studies and Observation Group) that ran covert operations into North Vietnam, Laos, and Cambodia. He served as a deputy assistant secretary of defense from 1971 to 1973, and in 1976 became Chief of Staff of all U.S. forces in South Korea. In 1977 President Carter announced that all U.S. ground forces would be removed from South Korea. Singlaub publicly denounced the proposal. As a result he was transferred out of South Korea to another assignment. The following year there was a second confrontation with the president regarding his policies. He decided it was time to retire.

Singlaub is also an American, a word that seems to mean more to a veteran. He does not like those who are opposed to the American way of life. To be more specific he hates communists and everything they stand for. As a civilian he became active in conservative causes and anti-communist movements. He served as chairman of the World Anti-Communist League and headed its American chapter, the U.S. Council for World Freedom. His friend, retired Lieutenant General Daniel O. Graham, the former director of the Defense Intelligence Agency, became its vice-chairman.

With the election of President Reagan and the appointment of William Casey as head of the CIA, Singlaub was once again back in favor and those in the know were aware of this. But he maintained a respectable, and judicious, distance between his causes and the government. This was made clear in 1986 when Lieutenant Colonel Oliver North's operation, code-named Enterprise, was exposed.

In 1982 Congress passed the Boland Amendment. The White House and the CIA were ordered to cease funding the Contras, who were trying to overthrow Nicaragua's Sandinista government. This was a matter of grave concern to devout anti-communists. To get around the amendment North, working for the National Security Council, secretly struck a deal with Richard Secord, Thomas Clines, and others to run an operation called Enterprise. In 1986 when it was exposed a list of the conspirators read like a who's who in covert operations. Singlaub was never indicted for this operation, however, because he was not a part of it. He had chosen instead to work with some of his friends from the private sector to legally garner sanctioned but unofficial worldwide support and assistance for the Nicaraguan resistance.

In hindsight, the Enterprise operation was foolhardy, something Singlaub was not. Friends described him as a bit too forthright when it comes to speaking his mind, which was probably why he always seems to be surrounded by controversy. But that possible flaw is offset by other qualities. He was known as a clear and concise thinker given to introspection. He would have to be to survive in his present occupation. A lot of people don't like his anti-communist stance. They would like to bring him down, to destroy him literally or otherwise. Many have tried. None succeeded.

Singlaub was not one given to flights of fancy or chasing rainbows. So why did he decide to join a group of Americans halfway around the world on a treasure hunt? Such a venture might be misunderstood if the wrong people found out. They would grind him up and spit him out if he were wrong. Singlaub knew it was a gamble. But he also knew, after examining the evidence, that he was right, so it was worth trying. He had the courage of his convictions, so he went for it.

·

In 1983 Cesar Leyran came to Houston, Texas, to look for someone to back him financially in his treasure hunting projects. After Leber Group had dissolved in 1975 he had immigrated to the U.S. later that year, but he returned to the Philippines soon after to resume his search for gold. A short, wiry, chain-smoking dentist who never practiced dentistry, he was a loner by nature. As long as people could remember he only cared for two things, searching for gold and chasing women. Some people thought he had the fever.

It was difficult to explain the fever since it wasn't a medical condition. It was a state of mind, an attitude associated with treasure hunting. It affected a lot of newcomers. They arrived on the scene excited but quite normal, wishing to become an instant expert in this arcane art. Usually they had invested money which entitled them to visit the site and find out what was going on. Then the process began, not the process of treasure hunting but the process of acquiring the fever. The tales were told, old maps or sketches were brought out, and an eye-witness flavored the scene with an anecdote or two: "I was there in 1943 when they buried the treasure..."

The greenhorn listened reverently. His brain received and processed the information like any other data. But it wasn't like any other data. This was a riddle and the solution could be worth millions. And sometimes thinking about the end result could cause left lobe lockdown. The brain ceased to function normally. An incredible transformation took place. First there was a grin, a big shit-eating grin. Then the eyes started to glaze over and the breathing quickened. He might start pacing back and forth and flailing his arms about, all the while muttering things like, "Only thirty meters down...a hundred million dollars."

Gradually he was consumed by this one thought. Conversation about anything other than treasure was adroitly brought back around to the only subject on his mind — treasure. Contact with reality was lost and, along with it, all hope of ever succeeding. He was just too impatient to formulate and implement a precise plan of operation. He couldn't be reasoned with. He knew it was there and that was that. Soon his impatience would lead to a mistake that caused an accident or a misunderstanding. Gradually his friends and crew abandoned him. He was left alone with his dreams which turned into nightmares. Soon he was a broken man. The fever had claimed another victim.

Fortunately most of the time the person snapped out of it before the condition ran its course and the business at hand continued. Some didn't, however, and they were the dangerous ones in the business.

Cesar wasn't dangerous and he didn't have the fever. He was just relentless in his quest like a California panhandler of old. If he could scrape a little money together he would be on the site digging. If he couldn't pay the rent he would sleep on the site. Everybody that worked with him swore that he knew more about treasure sites than anyone besides his friend Villacrusis, but he had never found the end of that proverbial rainbow. Perhaps the reason was his personality. He was known as somewhat of a tyrant on the job. He was the boss and he wanted everyone to know it. He drove his men mercilessly, some say aimlessly. Or maybe it was his choice of partners. In twenty years of searching he had teamed up with this bunch or that group and, in the end, an internal squabble over leadership or money or some other matter would cause a breakup, and Cesar would be on his own again.

In Houston a treasure-hunting associate, Norman Haines, introduced him to a doctor by the name of Roger Cotrefell. Cotrefell, somewhat of a grand promoter himself, was impressed with what Cesar said, and enthralled at the prospect of a treasure hunt. He called a friend, Ron Healy, and both listened to Cesar describe treasure burial sites containing billions of dollars in gold and jewels. That did it. They were hooked. The three headed for the Philippines. There they linked up with two former Leber Group associates, Amelito Mutuc and eye-witness Pol Giga.

Their first undertaking was a water site in Calatagan Bay, located in Batangas province a few hours drive south of Manila. According to Pol, in 1944 the Japanese had blasted a hole in a reef offshore in about five meters of water. They then used a donkey engine set on a platform on stilts on top of the reef, along with an endless cable and a big drop bucket, to gouge out a slot from the reef about twenty-two meters deep. Into this slot they deposited a cache of gold bullion and jewels, refilled the hole, and cemented the top of the reef.

Now, forty years later, they were going to attempt to recover this long-buried treasure. It was an unfortunate choice. This was Cesar's first water site. Underwater excavation was hazardous and costly, and trying to locate gold underwater was chancy at best. But they were not to be dismayed. Pol said it was a big one.

With high hopes and a flurry of activity the group descended on the site. Divers eventually located what appeared to be a cut in the reef approximately eighteen by thirty meters, and Pol pointed out a marker that could have been man-made — a large coral head stuck or cemented on top of a granite boulder. The excavation began. For the umpteenth time Cesar was going to try and realize his lifelong ambition.

During this period the grand old man of Philippine treasure hunting passed away. Colonel Villacrusis was a Christian Scientist and believed that all the body's ills could be cured with prayer. Unfortunately the spiritual healing that he waited for never came. He became sick. His condition worsened, and he sank into a coma. His family finally decided that perhaps a hospital could better cope with the situation. They rushed him there, but it was too late. Doctors diagnosed his condition as an acute inflammation of the urethra. He died the next day, on 27 May 1984.

At the death of his friend Cesar became unofficially the dean of treasure hunters in the Philippines. Not many people knew about his new title. It wasn't the kind of thing announced in the newspapers, nor did it come with a hat or insignia that he could 'wear. There was no need. Those in the business knew that he was now the man with the most knowledge and experience. Because of this he began to attract more people from different walks of life, and possibly the best organization for treasure hunting ever seen in the Philippines began to form up around him.

After arriving in the Philippines, Cotrefell only stayed a few months and then went back to the states. Healy remained and in early 1985 a friend, Allan Forringer, came over from Pittsburgh to have a look. Forringer liked what he saw and decided to stay. Others joined the group that year. John Harrigan came in from Memphis, and John Granbush from Denver. Tom Polk and John Voss followed them. These people were connected in some way to an organization called the National Commodity and Barter Association. Its headquarters was in Denver. Its members were primarily Mormon. One of its purposes was to correct the alleged injustice of the U.S. tax system. Granbush was the president of the organization. He took a keen interest in the treasure hunting activities and helped finance the operation for awhile.

As the number of foreigners grew it was decided that a more formal organization should be set up. A company was formed in Hong Kong called Nippon Star. Harrigan was its first president with Forringer its chief of operations. With their organization the Americans convinced Cesar, for awhile, that they could run a better show. Granbush returned to the states. Healy and Polk stayed awhile longer and then returned also. Voss continued to travel back and forth.

Nippon Star continued its excavation at Calatagan Bay throughout 1985 but they were having a lot of difficulty. The concrete or whatever it was on top of the reef was very hard. Progress was slow and costly. Work would stop occasionally until more funds were raised. This haphazard stop-and-go operation went on until finally they decided that another site might be easier.

There was also another reason for such a decision. Cesar had entered into this agreement during the Marcos era, when one had to be constantly aware of the latest intrigues in political and military circles. The only law that prevailed in treasure hunting was the law of the jungle, and Ver ruled that jungle. Cesar had been well steeped in these nuances, and had allied himself with Villacrusis for this reason. But Villacrusis died, the revolution came, and Marcos and Ver were gone. A new treasure hunting strategy was now required. They vacated the site but one member of the team decided to stay there and continue with another group.

An American, Al Meyer, had been hired as a diver. In true treasure-hunting fashion, as soon as he thought he knew enough he decided he didn't need Cesar and Nippon Star anymore. He broke away and was somehow able to interest Francisco Sumulong, the president's uncle, in the project at Calatagan Bay. Cesar knew Sumulong. He also knew he was well-connected so no fuss was raised. The political winds were blowing in a different direction in the palace now. Besides there were plenty of other locations, and he had learned his lesson about water sites.

With his new contact, Sumulong, Meyer wangled an invitation to meet with Aquino on 9 March. Meyer claimed to have a piece of equipment, which the group referred to as an Atomic Box. It could detect gold underwater, supposedly. He wasn't the first to claim to have a special machine. Another Nippon Star associate, Norman Haines, also laid claim to a special technology. And there were others who preached the merits of their own inventions. Someone claimed he could fly over any area, take pictures with a special camera and film, and pinpoint the location of any treasure buried below the earth or underneath the water. It was called satellite something-or-other, and the charge was a flat $100,000 per site. That, too, was wishful thinking. Such a technology did not exist.

There were other devices, metal boxes of various colors, shapes, and sizes with antennas sticking out and wires running here and there. One looked like a battery-operated chrome divining rod. Another resembled a space-age pistol. The pistol device had a compartment where a small piece of material — gold, silver, or whatever — could be placed. Then the pistol was held out away from the body. It was supposed to start twirling — the barrel was on ball-bearings — when it located the material. It seemed like every treasure hunter had his own particular device that could do wondrous things, but the proof was in the pudding and there was no proof of anyone ever having a successful recovery using any of these gadgets.

Jack Anderson heard about Meyer and his device and mentioned him favorably in his column a couple of times. This caught the attention of newspaper columnist Tom Valentine in Chicago, who invited Meyer to put his device to a test. Meyer accepted and gave a demonstration, but failed the test. About the same time Meyer recruited another diver to assist him at Calatagan Bay. Soon enough this diver also started making claims about his own super device which he called a Proton 4.

Whatever devices were used, only one thing was certain. Sumulong's group poured a lot of money into the Calatagan Bay site but no gold was ever found. After that venture, Meyer, still unsuccessful, tried to drum up some publicity. He called Dale Van Atta, Anderson's associate, and announced that he and Roger Roxas, of Golden Buddha fame, were going back to the mountains to retrieve the rest of the treasure at the Golden Buddha site. Roger denied this but it didn't matter. By then Anderson was no longer interested in atomic boxes and treasure hunts, and there was no more mention of such things in his column. This did not dissuade Meyer. He continued on his quest, as did Haines. Both are still out there digging somewhere.

After the revolution Nippon Star quietly went back into operation. They worked several sites during 1986. One was in Cavite, about an hour's drive south of Manila, at a private residence that had been the headquarters of a Japanese commander during the war. It was believed that one of the tunnels dug to hide this treasure was started in the kitchen of the house in order to conceal it from the garrison stationed outside. So that's where they started digging, in the same kitchen.

Two more sites were located on the property of University of the Philippines at Los Baños, and very near where General Yamashita was executed. Formerly the underground headquarters of the Japanese army stationed in the area, it consisted of a vast tunnel network housing ammunition and supplies, medical aid station, kitchen, and other facilities. The treasure was believed to have been placed in two separate tunnels and then both areas booby-trapped and back-filled. (According to Roger the treasure still at the Golden Buddha site was buried in a similar fashion although the tunnel complex was smaller.) The fourth site was located on Mount Banahaw, also in the province of Laguna. It wasn't long before an eye-witness appeared on the scene. This time it was Pedro.

Since Villacrusis died Ben had gone back to Bambang, and Pol had kept to himself mostly, not offering his services to anyone after the Calatagan Bay project fizzled. During the time when part of Marcos' military were out searching for gold, each eye-witness seemed to have his own informal sponsor, either military or someone closely associated with the military such as Cesar. Villacrusis would invite Pol, Ben, or both to help at a site, and sometimes Cesar would invite them, no doubt with the permission of Villacrusis. Pedro's sponsor was usually Lachica. Those days were over and Pedro was the first eye-witness to adapt to the new ways. He became a sort of free agent, hiring himself out to the highest bidder.

Now things were different. There were no more threats of prison or death and no more working just for rice. There was also one more important, almost imperceptible, difference. After forty years, the stigma of being a *makapili* was gone. Few people seemed to know or care what that meant four decades ago. Now Pedro was a free man in more ways than one. So when a member of Nippon Star approached him one day he graciously agreed to help, for a large fee. As an added bonus his sons were also hired.

Pedro had been busy the last ten years. After digging at Cabuyao in 1974 he had gone with Lachica to Teresa and excavated a site on the property of Mrs. Helena Frankenburger. They dug there off and on for about a year and then stopped. Work was resumed in 1975 when Leber Group picked this as their first site but for some reason Lachica didn't include Pedro in the group. That year he worked with another group in Palanan, Isabella, and claimed they were successful but he couldn't prove it. In 1978 he worked at a nursery site in Los Baños with General Jose Marcos Lizardo, a cousin of Marcos, but they found nothing. He was inactive for a few months until someone finally came calling again in 1979 with another treasure hunting invitation. This time it was Cesar Leyran, and he had Pol with him.

Pedro and Pol had not seen much of each other since the war. Their paths had crossed a few times — once in 1949 and again in 1956 — but these were brief encounters with other people around and they never discussed their adventure. Now Cesar asked them to work together at a site in Bauang, La Union, with him and a friend, Doctor Ernesto Palanca, a surgeon at Cardinal Santos

Hospital in Manila. Pedro and Pol caught up on each other's activities. They were amused to find out that while Pedro was digging with Lachica on the property of Mrs. Frankenburger at Teresa, Pol was just over the hill digging with Villacrusis on the property of Francisco Romero. They dug at Bauang for two years but stopped in 1981 for lack of funds. They helped Palanca again in 1984 at a site in Santa Rosa, Laguna. They dug there for a few months but ran out of funds again.

In 1985 Pedro worked at another Laguna site in nearby Canlubang. He had been contacted by four Japanese, one of whom had been a Japanese engineer employed by the Matagumi Kaisha civilian construction corp, and knew Pedro during the war. They had already secured permission from the military. It was a typical Ver-controlled task force operation. The site lay on the property of a widow. No one bothered to ask her permission. Instead the Japanese had approached an influential congressman and made him a generous offer. Afterwards they were then allowed to go in with a Ver-sanctioned military team, headed by Major Dumlao and Major Barangan, the brother of General Barangan, and attempt a recovery. They worked there until the February revolution and then made a hasty departure, leaving three deep, gaping, and dangerous holes. Pedro doesn't know if they were successful because they wouldn't allow him on the site the last few days they were there.

Afterwards Pedro went home as usual. It wasn't long before he was contacted again, this time by Nippon Star. He was ready, for a fee, and they went to work on the site located on Mount Banahaw, about halfway up the mountain at a little place called Majayjay. This was one of the sites where the smelly, brownish-green, tarlike substance was encountered. They dug a hole about two meters square down to twenty-nine meters, doglegged five meters to where they were directly under one of the markers, then dug down another fifteen meters to where the substance was found. After they cleaned it out of the hole water began to seep in and fill up their excavation. They were able to escape but the water rose eleven meters. A pump was brought in to get the water out but every time it stopped the water rose again to the same spot. That problem bothered them the whole time they were on the site. They eventually ran out of funds and abandoned the site.

Allan Forringer ran the day to day operations of Nippon Star. There were rumors that he might be CIA but that's all they were. Just about any American who came to the Philippines and acted the least bit out of the ordinary would start the secret-agent rumor mills churning. "Out of the ordinary" could mean that he didn't appear to have a job. Or, if he did, it wasn't with a typical American company. Or it could mean he had foreign or mysterious friends of questionable background. His secret agent stock went up when Singlaub came to the Philippines to view the Nippon Star operation. But it wasn't Forringer who invited Singlaub. He didn't even know Singlaub, nor did anyone else in the Nippon Star group. One day in May 1986 John Harrigan got an idea. He heard about Singlaub and his activities through a newspaper or magazine article, and thought that maybe he could interest him in what they were doing.

After a few inquiries he was able to contact Singlaub through his U.S. Council for World Freedom office in Phoenix, Arizona. At the time he was retired from the military and best known for his chairmanship of the World Anti-Communist League which raised money for anti-communist groups. After a brief discussion Harrigan was able to get an invitation to meet with Singlaub in Washington, D.C. He flew there, explained the Nippon Star venture, and asked if he would be interested in joining their group. Later Singlaub flew at Harrigan's expense to Memphis, Tennessee, where he met Forringer and Polk. After the meetings he agreed to go to the Philippines and take a look.

Singlaub came over in June and observed the operation. While there he met with General Fidel Ramos, armed forces Chief of Staff (who became the defense minister and then was elected president). During their military careers their paths had crossed occasionally so the two already knew of each other. Singlaub advised Ramos as to why he was in the Philippines and the group he was associated with. He also called on Secretary of Defense Juan Ponce Enrile, U.S. Ambassador Stephen Bosworth, his political counselor, and the head of the U.S. Military Assistance and Advisory Group (MAAG). All these calls were social. Singlaub was too well known to visit the Philippines without at least saying hello and explaining what he was doing there. A week later he returned to the states.

In July he was in Taipei on business so he flew over to Manila for a one-day visit. He reappeared in September. By then he believed that the treasure was real. He convinced Nippon Star to enter into a joint venture with a new company called Phoenix Exploration Services, Ltd. Phoenix was registered in the U.K. but there was nothing British about the new setup. Phoenix was owned by Helmut Trading, a company registered in Liberia under bearer stock so its true ownership could not be traced. Singlaub was elected chairman and a friend, Lieutenant General Robert L. Schweitzer, was elected chief executive officer of the new venture. Schweitzer had been deputy director of the National Security Council at the beginning of the Reagan administration. Then he was assigned to the Pentagon and spent several years on the army general staff. In 1984 he was assigned to the Inter American Defense Board as its president. In 1986 just before Enterprise was exposed he retired from the army and joined a Washington consulting firm called Geomilitech Consultants. Singlaub was also associated with Geomilitech.

Singlaub wanted to recover the treasure in as professional a manner as possible. He and his group convinced Nippon Star that this operation should be run in a military fashion and that they were the ones to run it. Three retired U.S. military officers, provided by Geomilitech, and three retired Philippine military officers were brought in to help reorganize the project. A new table of organization was drawn up, and the treasure hunt resumed. At this time Singlaub aligned himself with Teodoro "Teddy Boy" Locsin, Jr., then special counsel to the president and also her speech writer. With this direct line to the palace the group believed they would have no problems in securing permission to search for gold.

With the kind of contacts that Singlaub had established it was difficult to understand why Nippon Star could not obtain better advice in their reorganization. They committed several strategic mistakes. First they chose as their attorney someone who was a legal adviser to Raymond Moreno, a known associate of Ver. Moreno would later plead guilty in U.S. federal court to three counts of conspiracy involving embezzlement and tax fraud. The evidence proved that Moreno and an associate were acting as agents for Ver in purchasing communications equipment for the Philippine military. They required the subcontractors to double the amount of their invoices and kickback the money to them. Moreno was fined and placed on probation.

The same attorney suggested that Nippon Star set up their office in the Technology Center, which was the location of a communications company owned by Moreno. About the same time an advertising executive was hired to handle Nippon Star's publicity. It just so happened that this executive also handled publicity for Marcos' political party. These seemingly innocent associations would soon come back to haunt them.

Financing continued to be a problem. As a result the group would dig awhile and then wait for more money. Then dig some more and stop until more funds arrived. During this period Cesar left the group under a cloud. It had something to do with money as usual. He had been responsible for the birth of Nippon Star, and now he was the first victim of the new group's organization.

In October another old friend from OSS and CIA days, Ray Cline, came to Manila to attend an international conference on security. Singlaub did not attend the conference but he and Cline managed to meet. It was because of Singlaub's association with friends like Cline and Schweitzer in the U.S. and his association with Locsin in the palace that a rumor was passed around that the operation was jointly sanctioned by President Reagan and President Aquino. Nothing could have been further from the truth. Neither Reagan nor Aquino knew about or sanctioned the endeavor, nor did they ever discuss it. Another rumor was that the treasure hunt was a secret CIA operation. When asked about CIA involvement, Singlaub said that the CIA probably was aware of the efforts being made to recover the treasure but they were never a part of any of these efforts.

In December 1986 Harrigan and Forringer came to the U.S. to see Bob Curtis. The story of the 1975 treasure hunt was still being passed around. Curtis had put the word out that now that Marcos was gone he would be willing to return to the Philippines to search for treasure if he were approached by the right group. There was one other thing he said that convinced the financial supporters of Nippon Star that he was needed. He claimed to have all the maps.

Harrigan and Forringer flew to the states and called him. After a brief explanation Curtis agreed to meet Forringer in Las Vegas. The result of that meeting was that all parties agreed to meet in Hong Kong as soon as possible to discuss a possible working

arrangement. The meeting was finally set for 11 February at the
Mandarin Hotel. There Forringer introduced Curtis to Singlaub
and other members of the group. After four days of discussion an
agreement was signed.

While this meeting was going on in Hong Kong the
Philadelphia Inquirer printed a story that Singlaub was recruiting
American Vietnam veterans supposedly for the purpose of training
some members of the Philippine military in counterinsurgency.
Singlaub being who he is, the story was given a lot of press. The
San Francisco Examiner followed through with its own story. It
reported that Singlaub was setting up an arms-trading operation
in the Philippines and was developing contacts with allies of Marcos.
The story cited the association with Moreno's lawyer and the
Technology Center, and also noted that the advertising executive
they hired had worked for Marcos' political party.

All this came as a shock to Singlaub. He had no intention
of befriending anyone associated with Marcos and he definitely
wasn't dealing in arms or training soldiers in the Philippines.
Somebody was obviously being fed erroneous information in an
effort to discredit either him or what he was really doing in the
Philippines. Of course all those loose connections to Marcos didn't
help matters.

The local press swarmed after Ramos and asked if the stories
were true. He emphatically denied it. Singlaub then flew back to
Manila and called his own press conference. He said he was not
training anyone in the Philippines and announced that he was there
on a treasure hunt. He proceeded to explain what his group was
doing and that the government would receive 75 percent of whatever
treasure they found. The truth, he hoped, would help defuse the
tense situation, but it didn't. The rumors only got wilder and the
numbers bigger. Now it was reported that Singlaub had secretly
brought in thirty-seven Special Forces veterans to train selected units
of the Philippine armed forces.

The Singlaub publicity did not sit well with the palace. It
effectively sounded the death knell for Nippon Star. Quietly the
word went out from Malacañang* that the palace did not want

---

* Malacañang is spelled with a g when referring to the seat of government
without the word palace affixed.

itself associated with a treasure hunt. After his press conference in Manila, Singlaub returned to the states to be available as a witness in the Iran-Contra congressional hearings which were just starting. It is rather ironic that a few weeks after his return President Reagan announced he was providing an additional $10 million for two years of increased CIA involvement in the Philippine government's counterinsurgency campaign. Singlaub, however, did not return to the Philippines.

While Singlaub was busy fending off reporters in Manila, Nippon Star and Curtis decided to go ahead with their first project which was to recover a site on Corregidor. Nippon Star supposedly obtained a permit to dig on the island, and Curtis supposedly knew where the treasure was. Their working relationship got off to a rocky start. One supposition turned out to be false, and the other was never proven to be true. In July 1987 government authorities ordered them off the island, saying they had no right to be there. A subsequent examination of their permit showed that it was fake. Before being ordered off they had tried one of Curtis' sites and found nothing. They were working on a second site which had thus far produced no evidence of a treasure.

The retired military officers returned to the states, and Generals Schweitzer and Singlaub resigned from Nippon Star. No gold was ever found. Ultimately they failed, not because they didn't have the talent and organization, but because of the negative publicity which led to the lack of cooperation from the government. Whether or not the Marcos connections had anything to do with guaranteeing their failure may never be known. Marcos may have wanted Nippon Star to fail so it would still be there when he returned, and in 1987 he had serious intentions of returning.

Cesar, in the meantime, had returned to treasure hunting on his own. He decided he didn't need the U.S. military or anybody else to help him. And Curtis decided he needed to form another group and raise some more money.

CHAPTER ELEVEN

Corregidor

In 1987, following a cabinet meeting, Doctor Emanuel V. "Noel" Soriano, national security director, met with President Aquino in the Cabinet Room at Malacañan Palace.

"I have to leave in a few days to see a man in the states who may have some very important information about the Marcos gold."

"Do you really have to leave?" she asked. The 28 August coup, the most serious attempt to date to bring down her presidency had occurred twelve days before.

"Yes, ma'am. It's an important national security matter." If the information he had was correct, he explained, then the Philippines just might be one step closer to recovering gold worth billions of dollars, money that the country desperately needed.

Noel returned to his office and called me. "It's a go," he announced. The knot in my stomach tightened. I had provided most of that information. Five days later we departed for the U.S.

I met Noel in 1978 when he was president of the University of the Philippines. He taught a course in the doctorate program at the college of business. Our relationship was typically student-professor at first, but later we became friends when we discovered a mutual interest, the overthrow of Marcos.

In September 1983, a month after Ninoy Aquino's assassination, Noel wrote an open letter to Marcos urging him to step down. It was a brave gesture which required a lot of soul searching but it just wasn't healthy to come out in the open against a man who had total control of the country and who was known to be vindictive toward his enemies.

"Why?" I asked, pointing out that it was almost suicidal to fight Marcos.

"That's not the point," he said, "I have to do this, for my children."

Now he was a marked man, followed everywhere by gun-toting henchmen, and called at all hours of the day and night and told that he and his family were going to die. That didn't dissuade him. He was still at the barricades during the demonstrations, feeling the sting of the high-pressure water hoses, gagging at the stench of the tear gas, and staring down the barrels of the riot guns.

When Corazon Aquino agreed to run for president he was a member of the steering committee that managed her campaign. By now everyone knows of the Miracle at EDSA which threw Marcos out of the country and thrust her to the helm of the ship of state. Later Noel joined the cabinet as national security director and chairman of the cabinet crisis committee. While in this position there were five attempts to overthrow her, and five times he chaired the committee that brought the nation back from the brink of anarchy and chaos. He had earned his spurs.

Short, bespectacled, and balding, he looked like the mild-mannered bookish professor he once was. He first earned an engineering degree from University of the Philippines and then went to the states for further study. After earning a doctorate from Harvard he returned to the Philippines and found his niche in education. Academia was his life until Marcos came along and changed all that. He still couldn't believe it. It seemed like only yesterday that Ver's men were following him. Now he was the national security director and they were hiding from him. He decided that his first task would be to dismantle Ver's spy network and install an apparatus whose concern was national security, not intimidation.

I flew to Manila one day in early September 1987 and called him. "I've got to see you now."

"Okay, but only for a few minutes. I'm very busy," he said. I went over and was ushered into his office immediately. It was 6:00 in the evening.

"I just want you to listen to what I have to say and decide for yourself what it means." Before I left at 10:00 that evening it was agreed. If the president would allow it, we had to leave for the states as soon as possible.

That's how it all began. It would cost Noel his job, and four men their lives. But that evening in September we didn't know this. All we wanted was to find out if there really were billions of dollars in treasure buried in the Philippines. If there were it would help the Philippines enormously.

·

When the typhoon hit Corregidor that night it sounded like a freight train coming through the room where I slept. The rain pounded the tin roof and the wind howled as I wondered how much more the little concrete building could take. It was times like this when I would recall the words of my mother — "Why don't you get a regular job, Charles?" — and wonder why I never listened to her infinite wisdom.

After almost twenty years in Asia I knew this was a big one. Later the final tally would be announced. More than 700 died. It was the worst typhoon in twenty years. Fortunately I didn't know this at the time. I just knew that tomorrow was Thanksgiving and this was a crummy way to spend it.

Almost three months had passed since that first meeting with Noel about the treasure but it only seemed like yesterday. Now I was on my first treasure hunt which was about to end in failure because of the big blow and because of the U.S. Navy Seabees camped about 100 meters from the door. As I lay there I wondered for the hundredth time if we were doing this right.

On 16 September, Noel and I departed Manila on separate flights in order to avoid attracting any attention. We linked up in San Francisco and flew on to Las Vegas to meet with Bob Curtis, the center of all this attention. Earlier in the year I had been working on a book about Marcos' hidden wealth and was looking for people who had participated in the Leber Group treasure hunt. I finally located Curtis in Las Vegas. He agreed to see me in early August. This led to a series of interviews.

He began by giving me a copy of the 24-part series which Steve Psinakis had written for the *Philippine News* in 1978. In addition he had pictures, engineering drawings, and tape recordings to back up the story. He said there were some things he couldn't include in his story in 1978 but now he could talk about them. One thing was that he had the maps.

Curtis explained that during the Leber Group operation all the maps had been brought to the hotel by Ben and Pol. After doing this several times they decided to keep them there. They had rented a conference room for project meetings. The maps were hidden behind a panel concealed by the refrigerator behind the bar. When there was no one around he had gone there and secretly photographed 171 of the maps. He didn't photograph the map of the site that Ver claimed had already been recovered. Afterwards he sent the photographs to the states.*

The other thing he couldn't talk about before was that he had almost been executed before he left the Philippines. He proceeded to relate the incident when he was taken to the national cemetery to meet with Colonel Lachica, but with a new twist. He said that when they arrived there both he and his partner, McAllaster, were taken to open graves and forced to kneel down. A pistol was held at his head and cocked. They were about to shoot when he told them that he had sent all the maps of the treasure sites to the states and that if they shot him then the locations of all the sites would die with him. Because of this they backed off. They even allowed them to leave for the states by promising to return in two weeks.

He said that what he told Lachica was not exactly the whole truth. He had photographed the maps and sent the pictures, not the originals, to the states. That evening, after the incident at the cemetery, he went back to the hotel, took all the originals from the hiding place, and burned them. So now he was the only one with copies of all the maps.

There was no reason not to believe him. After all, his story had been checked out by Steve Psinakis, Jack Anderson, and the members of Nippon Star among others. Before I could ask he volunteered the information that the maps were stored in a safe deposit box at a secret location in Las Vegas. He rarely showed them because Marcos and many others knew their enormous value. He knew that there were people constantly watching and following

---

* Curtis thought that there were 172 maps. This jibes with statements made by other members of Leber Group although Ben claimed there were more.

him. As proof that he had them, however, he showed me one picture of a map. It was the Teresa site which Leber Group had been excavating when he left the country.

During this period I also met some of his associates, people that had joined him in his crusade to return to the Philippines and take his rightful share of the treasure which Marcos had cheated him out of. That was the line they espoused and it was believable. These people were on the whole nice, unassuming, successful businessperson types. They contributed toward Curtis' low-key image. They also contributed money, or at least they helped raise the money for the coming crusade. Several of them were actively going around showing some of Curtis' newspaper articles and pictures and selling shares. A 1 percent investment in the project cost $400,000. Or an investor could buy a smaller share, say one-tenth of 1 percent, for $40,000.

I had gone to Las Vegas twice for two two-day interviews, and was back home in San Francisco slaving away at the computer one day when Curtis called me. In a weak raspy voice he said "I'm in the hospital in Burlingame. I had an operation."

He went on to say that he had flown to San Francisco for a meeting and was at the airport waiting for a plane to Las Vegas when he had some kind of attack. They rushed him to the nearest hospital, which was in Burlingame. Part of his intestine was removed. He almost died. He had already been there three days but only now was he strong enough to make a phone call.

I went to see him and asked if he needed anything. He sent me on a few errands, and my wife and I took Yolanda, his wife, out to dinner. He was there two or three weeks so a routine was established. I wrote in the morning. In the afternoon I took the twenty-minute train ride to Burlingame to visit with him for a few hours. He had nothing to do but rest and talk, and he loved to talk. Everyday he provided more interesting details about Leber Group, the maps, the eye-witnesses, and his close encounter with death at the War Memorial Cemetery.

It was the end of August and I was scheduled to leave for Manila on business in a few days. I went to the hospital to say goodbye. One of his group, John Lemmon, had just returned from the Philippines and was there to see him. We met and talked briefly.

When he heard I was leaving he asked if I could help get them a legal permit for Corregidor. He then told me what happened to Nippon Star. He was with them on Corregidor when the government helicopters arrived and they were ordered off the island at gunpoint. That had happened on 23 July, a week before I met Curtis the first time. John was upset about this and implied that Nippon Star didn't have all the government clout they claimed to have.

I was surprised at the outburst because I didn't know him and here he was telling me about things that were clearly none of my business. I also remember Curtis' reaction at the time. He seemed a little upset. I don't think he wanted me to know about the incident because he hadn't mentioned it in our interviews. He had told me that the reason for his decision to stop dealing with Nippon Star was that he found out they were being financed by the John Birch Society. He didn't like the Birchers because Agnew had sued him for nonpayment of the money he had borrowed in 1975. I felt rather awkward and murmured something to John like, "I'll see," and left.

John and Curtis must have discussed this after I left because Curtis called me the next day. He said he would appreciate anything I could do but confided that one other group had already contacted him. They were powerful politically in the Philippines, and they wanted to join him. He went on to say that he hadn't made up his mind yet but he wanted an official invitation from President Aquino before he returned to the Philippines. He also wanted the government to provide his security because Marcos might still be after him. He asked if that could be arranged. I said I would try.

When I met with Noel in Manila I told him everything. My only suggestion was that he talk to Curtis and examine all the evidence firsthand to judge for himself whether or not he should get involved in such an undertaking. If Curtis were for real, and he seemed to be, then it would be in the best interest of the Philippine government to deal directly with him instead of allowing a politically powerful individual access to the treasure.

In the Philippines, like most Third World countries, money was power. It could buy a lot of votes, enough to easily put a man in Malacañan Palace. That was the situation and the reason for haste. Noel could not afford not to talk to Curtis. Too much was at stake. Since Curtis was too sick to travel Noel had to go there as soon as possible. In addition there was the hope that if a government minister visited Curtis then he would be impressed enough to show the rest of the maps.

We flew into Las Vegas the morning of 17 September and immediately started to work. That more than anything was a testament to our sincerity. They don't call the town "Disneyland for Adults" for nothing. It is glitzy, fun-loving, and fascinating. At least that was what we heard. The only time we got to see the action for ourselves was when we walked through the lobby of the hotel early in the morning going to work and late in the evening coming home from work. In case I didn't mention it, Noel was a workaholic. A twenty-hour workday was his norm. Mine was ten, maybe twelve. We had a lot of fun together.

The meetings took place at Curtis' home. He went through the same spiel with Noel as he had with me, showing the same photographs and the same documents, and playing the occasional tape. By the end of the second day Noel was convinced, but Curtis still had not volunteered to show any maps other than that one photo of the Teresa site. We discussed the matter and decided not to press the issue. If Noel could get him a permit then he would surely show us that map and that would open the door to the other maps, we hoped.

There was one awkward moment during the meetings. During our interviews Curtis had told me that Pol Giga was a former Japanese general and Ben was a Japanese admiral, and they were the ones that had been in charge of the treasure burials during the war. This was also mentioned in the 24-part series that Psinakis had written. While in Manila I had met with Boni again and told him about the Leber Group treasure hunt. He said that he didn't know Ben, but he had known Pol a long time, and he definitely wasn't Japanese. Noel was told about this and he decided that Curtis should know the truth. At the meeting he was told that his information about Pol being a Japanese wasn't correct, that he was a Filipino.

Curtis appeared to be upset. "But that can't be true. Pol is Japanese. He and Ben were in charge of the whole thing. They told me so..."

He went on like this for a few minutes but eventually composed himself. This matter was only brought up one more time, several months later, when both Ben and Pol denied in front of Curtis that they ever said anything like that. They were both definitely Filipino. Curtis didn't say anything then.

That evening back in the hotel room we discussed the last two days' meetings. After going over every detail one last time Noel finally said, "Okay, I'm convinced that there is something here. I'll try to get Curtis a permit, but only if you work with me on this."

I told him that whatever he wanted was okay by me. Now I was committed. Before we left Las Vegas the next morning he called Curtis and told him he would try to get him a permit for Corregidor. Curtis asked that this be done in the name of International Precious Metals, Inc., a company which he and his wife had formed earlier in the year.

There was also another reason for Noel's trip. When we left Las Vegas I asked him to stop in San Francisco and relax for a few days with my wife and I. We could digest the treasure information together and discuss possible strategies. Noel said he would stay overnight but then he had to leave the next morning on some government business. He didn't say what that business was at the time but later he told me.

He flew to London and met with a group to discuss the security of President Aquino. After five coup attempts he just wanted to be certain everything that could be done to protect her was being done, and this group was the best in the world at that. He studiously avoided mentioning this part of the trip to the president. No sense in alarming her, he reasoned. As a result the British Special Air Service agreed to assist the Presidential Security Group in improving the capability of its primary mission — protecting the president. Although the trip to Las Vegas was important, it served as a cover for the other mission.

On returning to the Philippines, Noel inquired into the official procedure for applying for a treasure hunting permit and initiated the process. At the same time he asked Curtis to write a letter to the president and explain who he was and what he wanted to do. Curtis wrote the president on 23 October 1987 and sent the letter to Noel for delivery to the palace. Noel was provided a copy. As soon as he read it he called Curtis. He was concerned about one paragraph which read:

> You may or may not remember me, for we met in Las Vegas briefly in late 1978 or early 1979 when Steve and Presy Psinakis, your late husband, and Raul Manglapus discussed the advantages of the release of the Treasure story for the MFP [Movement for Free Philippines] and the embarrassment it would cause Marcos.

The problem, Noel pointed out, was that the president's late husband was still in jail and could not have attended that meeting. After a lengthy discussion it was decided to go ahead and use the letter anyway. Noel explained to the president that it was an honest mistake.

While all this was going on some members of Nippon Star were still trying to get Curtis to remain with their group. They set up a meeting in Las Vegas for 29 October. Curtis had asked me to be there so I flew in also. There were six members of his group, four from Nippon Star, Curtis, and myself. I was surprised when he introduced me as the "Philippine government representative." I wasn't Filipino and I wasn't representing the Philippine government. He knew this. That kind of stunt, I would find out, was typical Curtis. After three days the Nippon Star group left without any concessions but during those meetings I learned more about Curtis.

He loved an audience. He played to it as well as any actor. What was discussed and what was decided in those meetings could have been accomplished in a few hours. But these people wanted him for something and he wanted his friends to see it. He milked it for all it was worth and then some. At one point he brought out all his documents, pictures, newspaper clippings, and that one map of Teresa, and for several hours told the gathering what an important person he was.

On 3 November, Noel called from Manila and told Curtis the permit was approved. Preparations were begun for the trip. Curtis was still too sick to travel. He asked me to go over for a few weeks to help set up the operation since I was familiar with the Philippines. I asked Noel if it was okay. He said yes, so I agreed.

Curtis chose two other people from his group to go with me. John Lemmon, who had made one trip already, and George Wortinger, who was currently popular with Curtis because he had recently found an investor who put in $150,000 for the project. George was a Vietnam vet so Asia wouldn't be much of a shock to him.

George and John were not paid any salary for their efforts. Their airfares, hotel, and food were paid for but that was all. The same was true for me. Curtis had inferred that everyone would be given a share of whatever was recovered but there was nothing in writing. He also offered Noel a share. Noel politely turned him down, stating that wasn't allowed since he was a minister, but whatever accrued to the Philippine government and the Filipino people would be reward enough for him.

Another surprise was in store when Curtis got us all together for a briefing. He explained that we were going to excavate the site on Corregidor which Nippon Star had been working on when they were ordered off the island. As he talked he drew a sketch of the site on a piece of paper. We all looked at each other. George knew what we were all thinking so he politely interrupted and asked where were the maps and engineering drawings.

"Oh, this isn't a map site," he said. "The map sites will take too long. This is a quicky site which I know about." He went on to explain that there were four major sites on Corregidor, buried underneath the big gun batteries, but these sites called for much greater financial and logistical requirements so they would have to wait until he was there to direct the operation.

This was disconcerting but only for a moment. At the time everyone was excited about getting underway. Any site was okay and the quicker the better. Before leaving we asked if Pol and Ben could be contacted to assist us. Curtis replied that they were in hiding and wouldn't talk to anybody but him, so it would be a waste of time. As we departed the general feeling around the IPM group was that they were going to succeed where Leber Group and Nippon Star had failed. Once again an assault on the legendary treasure was about to begin.

When we flew into Manila on 7 November there was already a serious time constraint. Months before, plans had been made for the U.S. Navy Seabees to refurbish the Pacific War Memorial on Corregidor. Work was to begin on 9 November. Noel asked the president for a two week delay. The president informed the American Embassy, and the Seabees mission was put off for two weeks. Now we had until 23 November to recover. This was enough time, according to Curtis, so we went ahead with preparations. The permit wasn't actually signed until 11 November but we had already been given the go-ahead. We had a lot to do and a short time to do it in.

Communication to the island would be by radio. I set that up while John and George went about purchasing all the supplies and equipment that would be needed. We hired the work crew from a local construction firm who had recently worked at Clark Air Base, so they already had security clearances.

Government responsibility for Corregidor lay with Tony Gonzalez, the minister of tourism. We met with him and arranged for our stay on the island. In addition he provided us with an engineer, John Andres, to oversee the excavation since we were on government property. A reliable but old and creaky tugboat was found and leased for a month. On Sunday, 15 November, we cast off for Corregidor.

Corregidor was established as a regular army post in 1908 and named Fort Mills. Before the war it was considered good duty by the soldiers stationed there. There were excellent facilities to enjoy during their free time — a golf course, officers club, non-commissioned officers club, a swimming pool, first-class theater,* a stable for horseback riding, and beautiful white sandy beaches. San Jose was the largest of five barrios on the island. Nestled in a cove, it was home for many of the families of the Philippine Scouts, the elite U.S. Army fighting unit comprised mostly of Filipinos.

As war clouds loomed on the horizon the little island became a beehive of activity. The Washington Naval Treaty of 1922 prevented any new armaments from being added. Still the Coast Artillery had thirty-three guns of various calibers and twelve 12-inch mortars to make ready. As 1941 drew to a close the soldiers were

---

*Trivia question: What was the last movie shown in the theater? Hint: "Frankly, my dear, I don't give a damn." Answer: *Gone With The Wind.*

in an upbeat mood, excited and anxious in anticipation of an impending Japanese attack. Mercifully they could not know that Corregidor would be bombed into oblivion at the start of the war. Nor could they know that the name of this little place would become a legendary symbol of courage for fighting men the world over.

The war came, and passed. The island took a heavy toll. Its glorious dead were buried. Corregidor became a national shrine. As we stepped off the boat I said a prayer to the ghosts of the valiant men who had been here before me, and promised not to disturb them.

The day after we arrived on the island a squad of Scout-Rangers, the Filipino equivalent of the Green Berets, arrived supposedly to conduct maneuvers, but their main purpose was our security. Led by Captain Jess Delosa and First Lieutenant Roger Saritiano, they occupied the ruins of the old headquarters building, about 100 meters from the theater which was our main site. Half the squad was actually on maneuvers all the time — the island was an ideal place for that — while the other half hovered nearby just in case.

All expenses of the operation were borne by IPM, the permit holder, as spelled out in the permit. While it could be said that security for the operation was paid for by the government there were other ways to view the situation. They were on legitimate maneuvers, receiving valuable training in the field. They were also there to protect the government's interest if we made a recovery.

Since this was public land, the law regarding treasure stipulated that the government would receive 75 percent of the recovery* and the permit holder 25 percent. The soldiers were fed by us. In this regard we were as generous as we could be. A cook had been hired and the tugboat constantly made supply runs back and forth bringing the best food that money could buy for the crew and the soldiers.

John stayed on the island with Andres and supervised the work crew. George handled resupply. I coordinated the overall effort with Noel and the committee. A government permit required that a

---

* If the treasure were on private property then the landowner and treasure hunter could negotiate a fair split. The gold would first have to be turned over to the Central Bank, however, and the government would receive its share through taxes.

committee be set up to.monitor the treasure hunt. It was composed
of one member chosen by the permit holder, IPM; one member
chosen by the Presidential Security Group (PSG), the president's
representative on the committee; and a chairman chosen by the
two members. Curtis appointed me his temporary representative
until he was well enough to come to the Philippines. Colonel
Voltaire Gazmin, commanding officer of the PSG, was the
representative chosen by the president. Noel was chosen by Curtis
and Gazmin to be the chairman.

A procedure had to be set up for getting the treasure from
the site to the Central Bank safely and quickly after it had been
found. That wouldn't be easy in a country where being poor is the
norm and where some people would cut off your finger to steal
a ring.

While struggling with this problem the radio base station was
set up in Noel's office and code names were assigned for security.
Captain Delosa's code name was Leader. Andres' name was Chief.
John's was Jimmy, because that had been Ver's code name during
the Leber Group treasure hunt. Mine was Charlie, which had
nothing to do with my real name. It had been Marcos' code name.
George's was Lucky, Gazmin's was Cavalry, and Noel's was Neil.

There was a reason behind Noel's almost-transparent code
name. While we were holding the talks at Curtis' home in Las Vegas,
one of his associates arrived unexpectedly and walked in on the
meeting. We wanted to keep these meetings confidential and no
one was to know that a government minister from the Philippines
was involved. In his best covert manner, as soon as Noel saw the
man enter the room, he got up, walked over and said, "Hi, my name
is Neil." The name stuck.

Our first site was in front of the ruins of the theater at Topside,
the topmost portion of the island, where most of the army post's
facilities — the headquarters building, the parade ground, the
theater, the officer's club, swimming pool, golf course, and the
famous mile-long barracks — had been situated. Now all that
remained was the gray skeletal remains of the concrete structures
standing among well manicured lawns and beautiful old trees that
towered over everything. The island had had forty-two years to
heal its wounds and it did so magnificently with the help of the

Department of Tourism. The Pacific War Memorial, dedicated to
the valiant men who died here, had been erected on Topside years
ago. It was showing a little wear and tear but the Seabees were going
to remedy that starting 23 November.

The first site was called Ticket One, because of its location
in front of the theater. Another site, Ticket Two, was inside the
ruins. Before leaving the states Curtis had given John a metal
detector and trained him in its operation. While testing the area
the detector picked up a large reading underneath the concrete
driveway to the memorial.

There had been stories that Marcos had already recovered some
sites and then had the treasure reburied until he could find a way
to get it out of the country. This could be one of those reburial
sites, we thought, so the crew was split up. At Ticket One excavation
was begun on a hole about two and a half meters in diameter. While
this was going on part of the crew began digging at the suspected
reburial site. One evening, to speed things up, some C-4 explosive
was brought in and part of the driveway blown to smithereens. The
only thing found was huge chunks of concrete reinforced with steel
rods. It was suspected that the steel rods were responsible for the
strong signals picked up in the area. The roadway was repaved
during the night. There was no more talk of reburial sites.

Excavation at Ticket One continued. The crew dug straight
down for six meters and then tunnelled in toward the building.
Progress was slow. It was the rainy season in the Philippines. That
meant it rained every day, and every night, almost all the time.
This didn't stop the digging though. A large tarpaulin made an
excellent tent that covered the work area. The digging went on,
rain or shine, but nothing was found. So the direction of the tunnel
was altered and digging continued, and nothing was found. And
it kept raining.

Every three or four days John crossed over to Mariveles or
Cabcaben, the nearest towns on the mainland (the big island,
Luzon, where Manila was located) with phones. He would call Curtis
and report on the progress of the excavation. The frustration could
be seen in John's face when he returned from these trips. We weren't
getting anywhere and 23 November was fast approaching. It was
decided that when the Seabees arrived we would just keep digging

as long as we could and give them some cover story if they happened onto the site.

On Monday, 23 November, the Seabees arrived. They came in style, by helicopter and ship. They were going to be here a few months so they brought everything, including the kitchen sink. There was a laundromat, a small theater (films could be viewed on a video cassette recorder), a mess hall that could have fed an army, a canteen, portable showers and toilets, and the tons of equipment they were going to use to redress the wrongs committed on the memorial.

In addition to the refurbishing job they fanned out over the island and did all kinds of civic-action deeds. There were basketballs for the kids and a free medical clinic for the locals to name a few. It was impressive. Finally the officer in charge wandered over to the Ticket One site one day to say hello. He was nice and polite but wondered what was going on. We told him we were digging for World War II artifacts. "Yeah, right," he replied with a large smirk on his face.

We went about our business and they went about theirs but it was a small island. They knew what we were doing and they knew we couldn't talk about it. In spite of the awkward situation we all got to be friends during the few days we were together.

I took the tug back to Manila on Tuesday. As soon as we landed I was handed a weather report. A typhoon was headed our way and it was a biggie. Corregidor was notified by radio and on Wednesday I headed back over to make sure the site was secured and our people protected.

As expected the Scout-Rangers were ready for any eventuality. They were tied down and ready to ride it out. "Part of the routine," Delosa told me with a smile.

The work crew had made themselves a comfortable home in the ruins of the theater. There were a few standing walls and a roof over part of it. The men had situated their bunks in this area so as to avoid the wind and rain that had already become a regular part of their own routine. All that was left to do was to lash down anything that was loose.

John and Andres were staying in the caretaker's house located directly across the street in front of the ruins of the headquarters

building. It was a six meter square concrete block structure with
a cement floor and a tin roof. I had stayed there overnight a few
times before. It looked stable. Later I would have serious doubts.
By mid-afternoon rain had begun to fall. The wind was picking
up and the seas were too choppy to risk a boat trip. I radioed the
base that I was staying, found an extra bunk next to John's, and
settled in for the night.

Normally I liked the rain. The pitter-patter of the drops as
they hit the tin roof could put me to sleep in seconds. And it did.
As night fell I drifted off to dreamland. Some time later I woke up
wondering what all that noise was. The pitter-patter wasn't there
anymore. Now there was a crescendo of... what? My first thought
was, "It's Chinese New Year. Everybody's beating on pots and pans."
But the noise was louder than that. And I was wet. For a few
moments I wondered why it was raining sideways. Then I
remembered. "You awake?" I whispered in the darkness.

"What do you think?" shot back the reply. We checked our
gear and passed the word to the caretaker and his family in the
next room that if the building collapsed they should head for the
Scout-Ranger's command post across the street. Then I lay there
listening to the roar of the wind and rain and the noise it made
on the roof, wondering at the same time what regular job I could
get when this thing was over.

There was another faint noise coming from somewhere. After
awhile I realized it was the Seabees breaking camp and heading for
Malinta Tunnel at Bottomside near the docks. The big trucks could
barely be heard above the din of the typhoon as they lumbered
up and down that narrow road most of the night. At some point
fatigue overcame the noise and I slept.

When I woke it was light and the roar of the typhoon was
gone. Now the only sound was a light rain. We hurried to the theater
to see if the men were okay. They were all sitting around a campfire
smoking and drinking coffee. Other than the tarpaulin collapsing
the site was intact. The Scout-Rangers were already up policing their
area and getting ready to go on maneuvers as if nothing
had happened.

But the island had been hit hard. Trees were down everywhere.
Limbs, leaves, vines, rocks, and pieces of anything and everything

were scattered all over. The place was a mess. A heartening sight was to see the Seabees clearing the roads, putting up power lines that had blown down, and helping the islanders put their homes back in order.

John and I discussed the situation and decided to call it quits. We had done our best and the treasure wasn't down there where it was supposed to be. The whole day was spent closing down and preparing for departure. A temporary plug was constructed out of plywood, placed over the hole, and covered with dirt. The area was roped off and a danger sign placed in front. The caretaker promised to watch the site and keep everybody away until we could report to the committee and decide what to do. (Later, when we realized that an extension to the Corregidor permit wasn't forthcoming, the hole was filled in.)

The Scout-Rangers said they would pull out after we left. John and I crossed over to Mariveles in the tugboat. George was waiting there with a car to drive us to Manila. The tugboat went back to Corregidor, picked up Andres and the work crew at nightfall, and departed for Manila.

When we got back to the hotel we realized it was Thanksgiving. We went out to dinner but nobody was in a mood to celebrate. The project was a failure. This was supposed to be a sure thing and we were going home empty-handed. We could always blame the typhoon but that was a cop-out. There was little time to think about it, however. Everybody wanted to go home but first there was work to do. The equipment was cleaned and stored, the radios were turned in, and the crew was paid and released. In two days the operation was closed down, and we departed for the states.

After Curtis had received permission to search for gold at Corregidor he asked Noel to also get him a permit for Fort Santiago. This was already being worked on when we left the Philippines. Noel called Curtis in the states on 2 December and said that the fort permit was approved. When they called and told me about Fort Santiago I recalled my last visit there, and wished them well. But soon enough I was back on the team on the way to Manila again.

CHAPTER TWELVE

Return to the Fort

Bob Curtis was tall, over six feet, handsome, and aristocratic in appearance. With his grayish-white hair and pencil mustache there was a vague resemblance to Prince Ranier of Monaco, with one small exception. His clothes were all cut in the western style and, casual or formal, set off with cowboy boots, cowboy hat, and a big belt buckle. His manner and dress were similar to another man from Las Vegas, Bob Kerkez, who was investigated by the PCGG for allegedly attempting to sell gold. At one time I thought the two were the same man using two different names, but they weren't.

Curtis also was egotistical, in a maddening sort of way. He loved to grandstand and did so at every opportunity. But the man was charming and he did possess a certain gift of gab. He always smiled as he talked. He would look straight at me with his ice-blue eyes while he confidently and calmly recalled his role in Leber Group, or rather his version. His ego always played a large role in these interviews, so this had to be factored in. For example, he claimed that he was appointed as head of Leber Group after Mutuc was dismissed. Others involved with the group said this wasn't so.

There was more. In explaining his role in Leber Group, he claimed that the president of Costa Rica had met Marcos in a meeting in Cancun, Mexico in 1973 and told him about the "secret process" which he possessed that could extract more precious metals from a ton of dirt than any other process known in the world at that time. That is why, Curtis claimed, Marcos had ordered Kirst to contact him to join the group. The president of Costa Rica did attend the Cancun economic summit, and Marcos was there also, but it took place in 1981, six years after Leber Group's project. When I pointed this out to Curtis he said that they also met there in 1973. A check of Marcos' travels showed this wasn't true but Curtis wouldn't change his story.

During one interview, while showing me all his newspaper clippings and pictures, there was one picture of a group of Filipinos standing in a road carrying signs printed in Tagalog. He used it to expound on the dangers of treasure hunting in the Philippines. He said that those people were communists blocking the road to one of the treasure sites near Teresa. I replied that communists usually didn't carry signs, and that these signs were not that difficult to read. I had seen groups carrying similar signs many times in the Philippines. This group worked for a company named Foremost and they were on strike for higher wages.

Once while displaying the Teresa map he pointed out that 2,000 year old Japanese script had been used on the map, and very few people could decipher it. This didn't sound right, so I called the Japanese Embassy in Washington. A staff member confirmed that there was no such thing. The oldest written Japanese language was dated 712 A.D. and emanated from Chinese characters. All writing today stems from the Meiji period of 100 years ago when the Japanese were taught for the first time how to write and speak the same way. Besides, the script on the maps was easily readable by anyone fluent in Japanese. That never was the problem. It was the codes and symbols that were indecipherable.

The misinformation he kept putting out was demoralizing. I considered dropping him as a primary source but then decided that there was a larger truth here somewhere, and that's what I was after. Curtis was a member of the Leber Group with Marcos. He did go on a treasure hunt. And he had the maps.

In trying to be fair, I dismissed his mistakes and exaggerations as the work of an overactive ego. Besides, he wasn't the first person to get carried away and exaggerate his own importance in an interview. The way members of his new group viewed him was that he had shortcomings, but he was charming and determined to find that treasure.

When John, George, and I returned from Corregidor empty handed our degree of skepticism had been raised a notch. Then we got the word that IPM had a new permit to search for gold at Fort Santiago. Curtis announced that this was a sure thing and he would lead the group this time. The euphoria of the moment swept away the doubt.

.

The fort operation could have been started immediately but Curtis wanted to be in on this one. He needed more time to recuperate from his surgery, so everyone celebrated Christmas before gearing up. Again Curtis asked me to help out and again Noel concurred, so I stayed on. John, George, and I received what Curtis called Christmas presents — letters stating that we now each had a .0125 percent share in IPM which was worth $5,000 according to him.

I flew to Las Vegas in January for a briefing. The fort operation was a map site but it would be a quicky. "All I need is a sledge-hammer and a few hours, and it will be all over," Curtis said.

John, George, and I looked at each other. Now where had we heard that before? And hadn't he said something about map sites taking longer? Curtis still hadn't shown us the Fort Santiago map, so as usual George asked if we could see it.

Curtis replied that it wasn't necessary, that this time the job was a simple one. George started to say something but Curtis cut him off and announced that after this site he would be prepared to do ten other recoveries while in the Philippines. That seemed to placate everyone. "But I'm still not bringing any maps," he said, and went on to explain that it would just be too dangerous, that the maps were too valuable to take over there. "I'll memorize each map before I go to Manila. That is all we'll need," he said.

His promise of ten sites was greeted with enthusiasm, so nothing more was said about maps. Anyway even if the map of the Teresa site didn't contain 2,000 year old Japanese script it still appeared to be just a jumble of Japanese words, codes, and symbols. If he wanted to memorize ten of those instead of bringing the maps that seemed to be okay with everybody. Curtis asked me to leave for Manila first and make the advance arrangements. Then he, John, and George would join me two weeks later. I departed on 27 January.

Like Corregidor, the fort had also taken a tremendous pounding in the war. In February 1945, during the liberation of Manila, it was the scene of incredible carnage. The Americans were outside the fort blasting away with their artillery but the Japanese would not surrender. Company L of the 129th Infantry entered the fort supported by tanks, and a wholesale slaughter ensued. With their bazookas, machine guns, cannon, and flame-throwers, they made a bloody mess of over 400 Japanese soldiers.

After the battle the GI's went through the fort to make sure there were no more Japanese surprises, and came upon a sealed door. It was the entrance to the dungeon. They kicked it in and found 600 prisoners, all dead from suffocation, torture, starvation, and disease. It was the final act of horror of a place that stood as mute witness to so many horrors. Over the last three hundred years thousands had languished in those subterranean cell blocks. Most, like the 600, never saw the light of day again.

Afterward U.S. Army engineers cleared the area of all ordnance and left. The fort lay neglected for the next twenty years. Squatters took over the area and all others avoided it if they could. Trash and excrement littered the grounds. Then in the mid-sixties Imelda Marcos developed some interest in restoring it while serving as first lady to first-term President Marcos. There were probably ulterior motives. Imelda reportedly excavated several sites in the front wall of the fort near Bastion de San Francisco and recovered several dozen drums containing silver coins.

Gradually the fort was restored. The squatters were removed and the grounds cleaned. During the seventies it was transformed into a national park with flowers, manicured lawns, and shade trees. Jose Rizal, the national hero, had been imprisoned here before he was executed by a Spanish firing squad in 1896. The building where he was incarcerated was declared a national shrine. Now the fort was a beautiful and quiet place where strollers could get away from the hustle and bustle of city life and lovers found a quiet corner to be together.

The Bastion de San Lorenzo was the location of our site. Located at the far end of the fort if one approached it from the city, it jutted into the Pasig River and overlooked Manila Bay. The entrance to the infamous dungeon was located just a few paces from its front door.

The front portion of the Bastion was dominated by a large room approximately thirty meters long and nine meters wide. It was once a storeroom for the powder of Spanish cannons. The Japanese decided it could be put to better use. They converted it into a torture chamber. For convenience the execution chamber was located just down the hall to the left. To find it you entered the front door of the Bastion, walked into the torture chamber, turned left, walked about thirty paces, went through a doorway into a hall, turned right, walked another thirty paces, and entered a doorway on the left. It was a larger room than the torture chamber and somewhat messier, the favored method of execution being decapitation, or beheading. Some of the former prisoners who survived still recall the smell coming from the room down the hall. The day the Americans retook the fort, fifty bodies were found there stacked like cord wood in a corner.

As part of the restoration the dungeon was cleaned out and restored. Inside the Bastion a new cement floor was installed in the torture chamber. The doorway that led to the hallway and execution chamber was cemented over, making the rest of the Bastion inaccessible. The roof was patched so that visitors could take the stairs to the top and look out over the bay. There was one ugly gaping hole in the roof measuring about three meters by five meters and covered with an iron grill, proof that Marcos' men had been there.

In 1981 Villacrusis finally got his wish to dig at the fort. He had been trying since he returned from Japan in 1968. He contacted everybody he knew that had power and influence with Marcos, but he had gotten nowhere. This didn't dissuade him though because no one else had been able to secure permission either, including veteran treasure hunter Tony Pratts, Cesar Leyran's friend. He had successfully negotiated an agreement at Christ the King in 1970. He formed a company in 1971, General Mineral Resources, and applied for a permit to excavate at the fort. His efforts went on for several years but to no avail. And in 1977 a group of World War II veterans using the name of Marcos' old outfit, the Cagayan Fourteenth Infantry, headed by Luis D. Villon, tried to get permission to dig there but they too were turned down despite pleadings from various influential sources.

The closest Villacrusis had come was in 1973. The task force had implemented Oplan Dry Run at Fort Bonifacio. They then asked to implement Oplan Ligaya, the code name for Fort Santiago, but that was never approved. After that he was kept busy with the Leber Group and the Teresa sites for awhile.

One day in 1981 Villacrusis took his wife, who had breast cancer, to a spiritual healer by the name of Aida Alejandrino. Villacrusis was aware that she had also treated Imelda, so he asked if she knew Marcos well enough to approach him without telling Imelda. When she said yes he told her about the fort and the treasure hidden beneath it. He showed her the maps and engineering drawings and said that thus far he had been unable to get a permit. Aida said that she would see what she could do. To his surprise a few weeks later she called and said she had permission.

They immediately began excavating the top of the Bastion. Aida's brother, Doctor Gil Gadi, was placed in charge of the operation along with General Barangan and Villacrusis. They decided to work only at night. A hole was opened up in the roof. They dug there for about three months removing tons of backfill. They were ordered to stop while Marcos was away on a state visit to Saudi Arabia, but resumed work after he returned.

In late 1981 work was halted abruptly and never resumed. There were rumors that some boxes containing six tons of gold had been removed but these couldn't be substantiated. When they abandoned the excavation they left a large hole, a sort of backhanded tribute to the Marcos style. A 300 year old fort, which was a glorious part of Philippine history and its antiquities, had been mutilated and then abandoned. Later a protective iron grill was placed over the hole but no effort was made to repair the damage or restore the Bastion.

According to Curtis there was another treasure left in the Bastion in addition to the one Marcos may have found. Our target was the cemented doorway in the torture chamber that once led to the hallway and execution chamber. As explained in Las Vegas, all he had to do was knock a hole in that doorway. On the other side was a room which held the gold.

On arrival I checked into the hotel, dropped my luggage, and took a taxi to the fort, anxious to make sure that the target was intact. I casually strolled around the fort acting like a tourist and finally wandered over to the Bastion. A locked wrought iron gate barred the entrance. After a few enquiries I was led to the manager's office and met Mr. "Bando" Bandoja. I asked if it would be possible to go inside the Bastion and look around. He not only agreed, he insisted on taking me there himself and acting as my tour guide.

The iron gate creaked open and we walked in. It was dark inside and the place was half-filled with musty-smelling furniture, damp rope, broken glass, and old shelving. Bando apologized for the disarray. He said that the chamber was being used as a temporary store room. I tried to act attentive as he talked, all the while groping my way toward the end of the room where the cemented doorway was supposed to be. Finally I was there, and my heart sank.

There was already a hole almost one-meter in diameter knocked in it. Bando found a flashlight and I peered inside. There was a hallway half-filled with dirt, rocks, and debris. The hole wasn't big enough for me to squeeze in but a smaller Filipino could manage it. One of the roving photographers was enticed into climbing in, taking some pictures, and describing the area for me. That hallway should have gone to the right for at least thirty paces but it didn't. There was a cement wall after four or five paces. I reported this to Curtis who said not to worry, that it was the opposite wall parallel to the cemented door that was our target.

There were a lot of preparations to make before Curtis' arrival and the start of the operation. The radios were checked and the base station was set up again in Noel's office. I checked with the construction company and eight of our twelve-man Corregidor crew were available so they were rehired. Andres wasn't available for this project so a civil engineer, Arnel Pan, was hired to supervise the crew. Curtis wanted protection around the clock. Noel arranged for two close-ins to provide security on twelve-hour shifts. When Curtis, John, and George flew in on the evening of 8 February we were ready. We hoped Curtis was. The success of this venture depended on whether or not he really knew where the treasure was.

Noel and I met them at the airport like visiting dignitaries. They were whisked though immigration and customs, out to curbside where the vehicles were waiting, and over to the hotel within minutes. We were staying at the Mandarin, the same hotel we had used for our base of operations in November.

Curtis was taken straight up to his suite and checked in there. John and George took care of themselves. They checked in and renewed old friendships with the hotel staff. Curtis wanted to check in under a code name but Noel said he should give his real name. Anyway, he was assured, the hotel had agreed to offer code one security which meant that if anybody called there for him or asked for him at the desk the standard reply would be, "Sorry, sir. There's no one here by that name."

The name Curtis had wanted to use was the same code name he used in the U.S. when we communicated with him — George Armstrong. He believed that in a past life he was General Custer, George Armstrong Custer to be specific, the youngest general in U.S. history and the dashing cavalryman of Little Big Horn fame who never met an Indian he liked. Noel explained to Curtis that his old code name didn't mean anything in the Philippines, that the Filipinos had never heard of George Armstrong. Besides we all had code names that were a single word, and he had an even better one this time — Quarterback. He liked it. A quarterback was a leader.

Once again time was a critical factor. The permit was for ninety days and it had been issued two months ago. We had less than a month to do whatever we were going to do. Work began the next morning. The committee was set up. Noel was the chairman, Gazmin was the PSG representative, and Curtis was the IPM representative. A twelve-man detail was seconded to us from the PSG to provide security at the fort.

The fort was under the jurisdiction of the Department of Tourism so once again we met with Minister Gonzalez. At first we discussed the possibility of using as our cover story that we were making a movie. After a lengthy discussion we decided that it would be better if we didn't disturb the normal routine of the fort. It was a favored attraction both for tourists and locals. We would work at night, starting an hour after the fort closed in the evening and stopping at sunrise.

On 12 February the operation began. At 8:00 in the evening a motorcade of three cars silently drove up to the entrance of Fort Santiago. Bando was at the gate to let us in and turn over the keys to the Bastion. He never even asked why we were there. His instructions had come from the top and, as far as he was concerned, that's all he needed to know.

At the same time a contingent of soldiers arrived to take up their positions around the Bastion. There were four in uniform during our night shift, and four in plain clothes during the day while we were away. In addition to Curtis, John, George, and I, a fifth American had been added to the group. Ted Drinnon had flown in from Las Vegas a few days before. He was a big guy, almost two meters tall and about 118 kilograms. Naturally his code name was Tiny.

Work began. A larger hole about one meter square was knocked in the cemented doorway. The crew removed enough dirt, rocks, and debris from the hallway to get to the opposite wall, They jackhammered a hole there and found it was filled with dirt. Several small holes were jackhammered and the results were the same. The chamber that supposedly contained the treasure was backfilled from floor to ceiling.

The hole in the opposite wall was enlarged to more than one meter square and the crew began removing the backfill. It was hard to believe but we were tunnelling inside the Bastion as if we were tunnelling inside a mountain. Subsequent testing would reveal that the entire inside of the Bastion, with the exception of the torture chamber, was backfilled from floor to ceiling.*

Over the next few days a routine was established. We would arrive at the fort as the sun went down and start work. Arnel Pan, the engineer, supervised the work done inside the tunnel. Two of the crew used small Makita jackhammers to break up the dirt, two more shovelled it into the buckets, and the other four would relay the buckets to the mouth of the tunnel and dump them.

The crew took turns at the various jobs, drilling for thirty minutes; then bucket relay for thirty minutes; then working the shovels. At 9:00 in the evening there was a fifteen minute break, and at 11:00 there was a break for dinner which was a big meal.

---

* Soldiers stationed here before the war stated said the Bastion was used for offices and living quarters for the headquarters general staff. Later, when the backfill was removed, some World War II artifacts were uncovered, indicating it was done during or right after the war.

After that there was a fifteen minute break at 2:00 and 4:00 in the
morning. Around 6:00 we would stop work, clean our equipment,
sanitize the area to make sure nobody would know we had been
here, lock the iron grill door, and quietly depart.

Taking our instructions from Curtis, we tunnelled in three
meters, then dog-legged right, and tunnelled another two meters,
shoring as we went along. The tunnel was a little over one meter
across and almost two meters high. It was shored up with two-by-
four and two-by-six timbers and three-quarter inch plywood. Curtis
never went inside the tunnel. He was still too sore from surgery
to do anything strenuous. Instead he sat in a lounge chair and passed
the time by watching television on a tiny portable set he had
brought. If a problem arose or if instructions were needed we would
relay the situation to Curtis and he would tell us what to do.

At the end of the two meter dog-leg a wall was encountered.
Curtis was informed, and he said to start down. A larger area was
dug out, almost two meters across, two meters deep, and two meters
high. This small chamber would serve as our base. To the right
of that we started digging a hole. We were down almost two and
a half meters when the cave-in occurred. We had been excavating
for ten days.

It happened at 10:55 on Monday evening, 22 February, just
five minutes before the dinner break. I had been in the tunnel for
over an hour and had just come out. Ted was about to go in, and
we were discussing the progress of the digging when a noise was
heard behind us. It sounded like a muffled Filipino shout, "*Oy!*"
We turned toward the tunnel entrance.

There were more shouts and two of the crew literally dove
out of the opening in the wall, yelling, "Sir, cave-in. Cave-in!"

We ran toward the entrance and were almost bowled over by
two more of the crew scrambling out. One of them was Effren
Maguindanao, the head of the work crew. "Sir, the end of the
tunnel. It caved in. Three of my boys are trapped. We have to hurry.
We have to get them out," he shouted.

The chamber and the hole beside it had not yet been shored.
We kept delaying it because of the viscosity of the dirt. It was thick,
red, moist, sticky clay. It had to be pealed off the shovel. Arnel
had been standing at the end of the shored up part of the tunnel

monitoring the digging when I walked out a few minutes before. Neither of us observed any signs at all of an impending cave-in. There were no stress fractures or anything to indicate in the slightest the approaching tragedy.

I could hear shouting inside, "Bernie, *hilaan, hilaan* (let go, let go)." Bernie Castillo, one of the crew, had been at the start of the receiving line which was at the end of the shored up part of the tunnel facing the chamber. His job was to receive the bucket of dirt from Raul, who was in the chamber, and pass it back down the line to the tunnel entrance. Bernie was standing there when the ceiling caved in directly in front of him and the walls began to collapse. When he saw what was happening he did an incredibly brave thing. He dove into the chamber headfirst and tried to grab Raul. Everything happened so fast and so quietly that the rest of the crew stood there for a few seconds too stunned to believe what they saw.

When they realized what Bernie had done and that the tunnel was collapsing on him and Raul they grabbed Bernie's legs and began to pull. They got him halfway out. Now only his head and shoulders were covered but they couldn't pull any further because he wouldn't let go of Raul. Only when he began to choke on the dirt and couldn't breathe anymore did he give in and let go, and they pulled him out.

He still wouldn't give up. He ran out of the tunnel, found a steel bar, and ran back inside, hoping to punch a breathing hole in to Raul. As he punched he kept yelling, "*Sandali lang, kukunin kita, sandali lang* (Hold on, I'll get you, hold on)."

We heard the sound of Raul's muffled voice. "*Bilis. Bilis. Hindi ako makahinga* (Hurry. Hurry. I can't breathe)."

Bernie kept yelling but now his sobbing drowned out his words. After a few minutes there were no more sounds from Raul.

Now the shored up part began to creak and dirt began to cascade out from under the plywood sides. Everyone was ordered out. Outside a head count was made. Arnel, Effren, Edwin, Bernie, Frank, Mariano, and Romulo were accounted for, but two were missing. Raul Copino and one more, Sonny Garcia. Effren said Sonny had been down in the hole filling the buckets and passing them to Raul. He never had a chance.

As soon as Effren told me about the cave-in I radioed Noel that we had an emergency. After explaining what happened he said he was coming immediately with help. While Bernie was trying to punch a breathing hole to Raul, Effren and the crew had grabbed the jackhammers and ran around to the side of the fort to try and knock a hole in the wall. It was hopeless. The walls were more than a meter thick. There was no way to reach the caved in area except through the tunnel, and now strange creaking noises were echoing through it as if the whole thing were going to collapse at any time.

Noel called a friend, Del Lazaro, head of Benguet Corporation, the largest mining company in the Philippines. Within forty-five minutes Noel, Del, a mining engineer and a geologist were at the fort. They inspected the site and said it was too dangerous to go inside. The fact was that we were tunnelling inside a very large room whose ceiling was six meters above us, and this entire room had been filled with dirt, sand, and clay for at least forty years. That cave-in caused hundreds of tons of dirt to displace. Until Del could get more mining engineers to inspect the tunnel we could not go back in.

John and George drove up to the Bastion at 11:00. They had gone to get the food for dinner and arrived just in time to see the last desperate moments of the crew as they tried in vain to rescue their friends. The reality of the situation began to sink in. There was no hope.

We did our best to comfort the crew. With the exception of Arnel, they had all been with us on Corregidor. Raul had been going to school in between jobs studying to become an engineer. Sonny's nickname was Jappon because he looked Japanese. He had found a half-wild kitten in the Bastion, fed it, and took care of it the whole time we were there. Now it was running around looking for his friend and his dinner. Jappon always fed him at 11:00 but it was almost midnight and the boxes of food lay on the table untouched. When the cat meowed it sounded like a baby's cry echoing in the chamber.

What happened to Raul and Jappon could have happened to any of the crew. Each took his turn inside the chamber and in the hole. That didn't make it any easier to accept though. Everybody was upset and scared, including me. I had been in that chamber for over an hour. It collapsed a few minutes after I came out. That's the way life was, I guess. When you're least expecting it — Whammo! You're face to face with your own mortality. But like we used to say in Vietnam, coming close doesn't count except in horseshoes and grenades. Even so, I could still hear that little voice inside for a long time afterward saying, "YOU could be next."

Still reeling from the shock of Raul and Jappon's death, we had two major problems to contend with: how to handle the operation which was supposed to be secret; and how to handle Congressman Peping Cojuangco's party. The cave-in had occurred on Monday night. Even before this we had already been advised that we couldn't dig on Thursday night. Cojuangco was hosting a victory celebration for the winning candidates in his PDP-Laban political party. It would be held in front of the Bastion. It was decided to keep the accident secret until after the party.

The mining engineers showed up early Tuesday morning. The Bastion was closed to the public, supposedly for repairs. The area was roped off, a sign was posted, and the guards politely turned away the curious. Extra work crews were hired and quietly brought in. Our original crew was told to go home, that they were still on salary, but they didn't have to work. Some went home. Others wanted to stay and help. We let them decide.

Bernie wanted to stay. He didn't want to go back in the tunnel so at first he helped take the dirt by wheelbarrow from the fort to the river. Then he became listless and just hung around watching the others work. The next day he showed up drunk but he still just sat in the corner watching. The day after that he showed up drunk again. There were some complaints from the workers, but he was left alone. He wasn't bothering anyone. Bernie was waiting for us to find Raul and the wait was putting him through his own private version of hell. He didn't need any more problems.

A round-the-clock recovery operation was begun. Now there was no thought of stopping work during the day. The shoring in the tunnel was reenforced but the engineers decided that the safest way to recover the bodies was to go in from the top. A hole was cut in the roof directly over the cave-in and this area was shored up from the inside.

Ted and I were standing together in the Bastion when one of the engineers came out of the tunnel and told us that is was okay to start work again. We looked at each other. That voice was still there, only fainter. "YOU could be next," it reminded me. Ted started toward the tunnel but I hung back.

"Let's go," he bellowed. I followed. He led the way as we entered the tunnel. It was smaller now, a little over one meter high, so we had to either crouch or crawl. Ted crawled; I crouched. It was five meters long. I had measured it before. But today it seemed more like fifty meters. As we crawled, crouched, and groped our way along, I could smell the damp earth and the odor that death had left behind. It would be a long time before that stench went away. We finally made it to the end. Now where the base had been was just loose dirt and some scaffolding which reenforced the roof. We looked up so that our faces could catch the breeze coming through the hole above. Beautiful blue sky and white clouds could be seen. We scaled the scaffolding and climbed onto the roof. Ted got out first and held out his hand to help me up. I was hoping he wouldn't notice my shaking. If he did he didn't say anything. Over the next few days the tunnel shrank back down to normal size, the little voice went away, and my shakes subsided.

The tons of earth were slowly removed, bucket by bucket, through both the tunnel and the roof. While this was going on the investigation into the cause of the cave-in was completed. It may have been a booby-trap. The tunnel was dug through thick viscous layers of clay. On two or three previous occasions we had encountered a layer of fine, coffee-colored sand about twenty-five centimeters thick. Once this sand was exposed to the ventilation in the tunnel it dried out and trickled down onto the floor, leaving small cavities in the side of our tunnel. Eventually these would collapse. Sometimes it would be almost unnoticeable. A few rocks or shovelfuls of dirt would fall. But once an area one meter square just slid off the side of the tunnel onto the floor. We cleaned it up, checked the plywood sides, and went on digging.

What no one realized at the time is that when those cavities collapsed they caused the dirt and clay around that area to be displaced, and there were hundreds of tons of earth all around us. It was never determined for certain that this caused the cave-in — no one reported seeing any of these layers of sand in the chamber or the hole before the cave-in — but there was no other explanation.

We labored day and night for three days. Jappon's body was found first, on Thursday afternoon. By then the smell was overwhelming. Everyone wore surgical masks to hide the stench. The heat and humidity of the Philippines helped to speed the process of decomposition. He was only recognizable from the blue pants he wore. A body bag was lowered from the roof, Jappon was placed inside, and hoisted up by rope and pulley. By prior arrangement, the coroner drove up in an unmarked station wagon, put the body in the back, and drove away without incident.

The fort was closed on Thursday to get ready for the party. Trucks had already begun delivering the tables and chairs so no one took notice of the station wagon. Because President Aquino was expected to attend, the security being set up was tight. We were asked to stop work at noon but we continued until Jappon was recovered and then left. The party wouldn't be over until late. Then the area had to be cleaned and the tables and chairs removed, so we were asked not to return until Friday morning.

We had been so busy trying to recover the bodies that a group meeting wasn't held until Thursday evening. There never was any debate on whether or not to go public with our operation. That was a foregone conclusion. Two men had been killed and their families had to be told the truth. The details of what to say were worked out. Noel asked me to be the official spokesman. From now on nobody else was to talk to anyone about the operation or the accident.

Curtis was visibly upset at this announcement but everyone else breathed a sigh of relief. He talked too much and we all knew it. On several occasions we had gone out for a drink together. After a few whiskeys he would turn to the nearest waitress, bartender, or whoever was around, say something like, "Do you know who I am?" as if he were in some credit card commercial, and then launch into one of his hero diatribes while hinting at what we were doing. He did this too many times after constantly warning us that any breach of security would result in our expulsion from the project.

When we arrived for work early Friday morning it was obvious that the press already knew something. There were about a dozen reporters waiting outside the roped off area. I announced that a press conference would be held at 2:00 that afternoon, and we went back to work. As we entered the tunnel the smell jolted us back to reality. Raul was still down there somewhere and we had to find him.

When the time drew near for the press conference I stopped working, cleaned up a little, and tried to mentally prepare for what could only be a very unpleasant situation. There was a twenty minute delay because Noel had called on the radio and asked me to read the prepared statement to him again. He did that about six times, each time changing a word or rephrasing a statement, and reminding me what could and couldn't be said.

When I finally walked outside to face the media I couldn't believe my eyes. There was the largest crowd of journalists, photographers, and television cameramen I had ever seen. And nobody was smiling. "Good afternoon," was all I remember saying. I know I read the statement and answered their questions — it was on the evening television news — but if stage fright were a disease we'd all be dead. I had plenty to go around.

Somehow I got through the press conference. Little did I know that was only the beginning. There would be many more, and they were not enjoyable. Filipinos did not look kindly on foreigners coming over to their country and killing their sons and brothers in a greedy pursuit of riches. I had always wondered what an ogre was. Now I knew. To paraphrase the cartoon character Pogo, "I have found the ogre and it is me."

We recovered Raul's body the next day. Bernie rode with his friend to the funeral home and stayed with him until he was buried.

That ended the sense of urgency that hung over the ordeal like a black cloud but it didn't end the media attacks. Some of it was downright ridiculous. Most countries which have a free press have their own version of the National Enquirer. The Philippines' was no exception.

We were depicted as CIA of course but it didn't stop there. We recovered the treasure and loaded it in a submarine which had docked alongside the fort, one story charged. It went on to explain that the cave-in was planned by us to kill all Filipino witnesses to the recovery. Another story was that we had murdered the two and put them in the tunnel to make it look like an accident because they had stumbled on the treasure first. This story was given some veracity when reporters got hold of a police report which stated that a Sonny Garcia had been stabbed to death that night. This made for a few headlines until the police announced that two people named Sonny Garcia had been killed that night and the stabbing victim was a different man.

Such stories only helped to exacerbate a very trying situation. Reporters waited in ambush outside the Bastion and hounded the crew, trying to get them to criticize the Americans, but to no avail. A lack of facts never prevented some reporters from writing a juicy story, however. Naive and unsuspecting, those of the crew that talked found out the hard way that what they said and what they were quoted as saying were two different things. Some of them became so upset at the media that they started sleeping at the Bastion, afraid to go out. A sort of siege mentality set in. It was us against them so we circled the wagons. We counselled and protected the crew as best we could.

We mourned the deaths of Raul and Jappon more deeply than anyone outside our group could imagine. Everything that could possibly be done was done. The families were visited. All expenses for the wake and the funeral were taken care of. We had insured each worker for ₱100,000 ($5,000) but we found out that in the Philippines it can take a year or longer to receive such benefits, so we paid them immediately.

One day about a week after the funeral I was working at my makeshift desk inside the Bastion and a letter arrived. This wasn't out of the ordinary. Many people sent letters requesting assistance in their treasure hunts. When I opened this one I was surprised to see it was from the sister of Jappon.

"Dearest Charles Dougald," it began in broken English, "I write this letter to express how grateful I am to your concern to my brother." The letter went on to say that she didn't blame me for his death, and that she was very thankful for my kindness. The English wasn't that good but that didn't matter. It was the most eloquent letter I'd ever received. As I read, my mind wandered back to November and Corregidor.

One day I was in the hole checking on the excavation with John. Some of the crew were up top taking a break and I could hear them laughing about something. When I climbed out Effren

was standing there with just a hint of mischief showing in his eyes.
He said, "Sir, I hope you don't mind. We took some pictures with
your camera. Could you develop them and bring them back to us?"
I agreed and left for Manila shortly afterward.

A few days later I was back on the island. Each time I came
over I would bring something for the crew. This time it was Hershey
chocolate bars. I was passing them out when Effren asked about
the pictures.

"Yeah, they're in here somewhere," I said, fumbling through
my kitbag. I had dropped them off to be developed when I arrived
back in Manila and picked them up just before getting on the boat,
so I had not seen them yet.

"Here they are." I tore open the envelope and began looking
at the pictures and passing them around. When I got to the one
they were looking for a cheer went up, like someone had just scored
at a football game. The picture was of Jappon with my hat and
sunglasses on, striking an extremely pompous pose.

"Jappon!" I yelled as I threw down my bag and started chasing
him. It was all in fun of course. The crew laughed themselves silly
over that. I saw Jappon's sister a few days after receiving the letter.
She gave me a copy of that picture. She said it was his favorite.

"What's that?" The question brought me back to the present.
I looked up. George was standing in front of the desk staring down
at me holding the letter. Apparently I didn't look too well.

"Are you okay?" he asked.

"Hurrumph," is all I could manage through the lump in my
throat. "Damned dust," I finally muttered as I stood up and walked
away while wiping my eyes. I carried that letter and picture with
me for a long time until it began to get a little worn. Then I put
them away with my important papers.

George had come to tell me that John was leaving. He had
caught some kind of bug and just kept getting sicker until finally
Curtis ordered him to go home. The funny thing was that he was
the health nut of the group. He took a lot of razzing because of
all the vitamins he took, and because of the little potable water
machine he installed in his hotel room. He was such a straight-
arrow — he didn't smoke or drink — but he was a good man and
a hard worker. He would be missed.

Despite the accident and the bad publicity the president still supported us. In early March we received approval for a thirty-day extension of the permit. This did not sit too well with some who wanted us to fail. It wasn't anything personal. The treasure hunt had become a political issue. Overnight it had become page one news in the foreign press and, since the president had sanctioned the operation, it was an ideal opportunity for those not in favor to embarrass her. They certainly tried hard enough.

CHAPTER THIRTEEN

The Digging Continues

"**G**et out," they were ordered. Mario Ongkiko got out of the van with the others. "You can't ride any further. Walk from here," one of them said. So the men — some of them past middle age — trudged the hundred odd meters in the hot mid-morning sun. Sweating and out of breath they finally arrived at the building, entered the foyer, and were told to sit and wait.

After an hour someone came in and curtly announced, "He will see you now." As they all got up he became agitated. "Not you," he said in a raised voice, gesturing for Mario and the other two attorneys to sit back down. "Just you four."

Mario watched the commissioners disappear up the stairs. Within minutes they were back. Without a word they all silently headed for the door and walked out. It was almost noon. The sun was higher in the sky and hotter, but the walk back was easier. It was over now.

This arrogant display of power took place on 24 November 1984 at Malacañan Palace. The seven were men of impeccable repute, attorneys and businessmen chosen because they were incorruptible. (Actually there were five attorneys, but only three made this trip.) They were members of the Agrava Commission, appointed to investigate the assassination of Ninoy Aquino, and had just delivered their report which was separate from the report of Judge Corazon J. Agrava, the Commission head, because they disagreed with her on several points. Both agreed that Aquino was shot by a military escort. Agrava's report, however, named only seven suspects and specifically stated that General Ver was not implicated. The report of the other four named twenty- six suspects and included General Ver, Marcos' friend.

The four commissioners walked into Marcos' office. He wasn't there so they remained standing. In a few minutes he walked in and sat down at his desk. He did not even look at them. Finally one of them broke the silence and said, "Mr. President, we are here to submit our own report."

Marcos coldly eyed them for a moment, and then curtly replied, "Put it there," motioning toward a corner of his desk. As the report was placed on his desk he said, "I hope your conscience is clear." He signed the receipt for the report, slid it toward the commissioners and said, "You may go," dismissing them with a wave of his hand without looking up.

The day before, when Agrava delivered her report, she was driven up to the palace steps, immediately ushered in, and greeted warmly by Marcos. Agrava and Marcos had been classmates at the University of the Philippines Law School. She had graduated in 1938; he in 1939. They were old friends. She had done the best she could under the circumstances and he appreciated it. He wasn't so appreciative of the others, however. All they got was a stare that said they were marked men.

That's the way it was back then. One didn't come out openly against Marcos. Ninoy's murder was supposed to send a message to that effect. When these men — four commissioners and five legal counsels — were asked to serve on Agrava's panel, it was akin to volunteering for the most perilous military assignment behind enemy lines in war time, only worse. There were no friendly lines to come back to, and the enemy was all around, all the time, threatening. They served their country for a year and in doing so committed the worst crime of all, standing up to Marcos. Paradoxically, they were guilty because they were innocent. Had Marcos not been overthrown their fates were sealed. But he was, and they earned their well-deserved niche in history.

Mario was typical of the group. He was eminently respected in his own profession and possessed a rare quality — an iron-willed determination to stand up for what he believed in and do what he thought was right. Very few people ever got the call to stand up and be counted, and even fewer, when called, had the courage to do so. He did, despite the certainty that he would be about as popular as a leper. He did, despite the death threats that came in the night. He did, because it's what his father would have done.

The youngest of twelve children, Mario followed his father, a judge, into the legal profession when he was admitted to the bar in 1957. Slender with gray hair, the eyes behind his spectacles belied the bloodlines of his Chinese ancestors. A chicken farmer on Saturday and lay minister on Sunday, he still managed a game of golf now and then. During the Agrava Commission hearings the media described him as quiet, self-effacing, and hard working. Filipinos are always wont to compare their local heroes to a U.S. counterpart. The closest thing in the states to Mario's courtly manner and gracious disposition would be Ben Matlock, the lawyer from Atlanta played by Andy Griffith on the television series. If anyone could, and would, protect a bunch of wild, greedy foreigners it would be him.

•

Every morning as I walked through the lobby of the hotel on the way to work I would check the headlines at the newsstand nearby. "TREASURE HUNTERS NOT ALLOWED TO LEAVE P.I." and "TREASURE HUNTERS CHARGED WITH HOMICIDE" were two of the nicer ones on this particular morning. Now the press conferences were being held daily outside the Bastion. I would make a brief announcement about what we were doing and then answer questions for about thirty minutes. A strategy session was held every evening to discuss what information could be given out the following day. We had received word about the homicide charges the previous evening. That would be the topic today. What would tomorrow's topic be, I wondered. Every time we thought it couldn't get worse, it did.

The next day the Senate released a statement warning that we could face criminal prosecution for desecrating a national shrine. Nobody seemed to notice that we were digging at least a hundred meters away from that shrine. The same day we were informed that Noel, Curtis, and I were invited to testify before the Senate committee on education, arts, and culture. ("What happens if I decline the invitation," I asked. "You don't want to know," came the reply. I decided to attend.)

We all knew this wasn't going to be fun. In addition to the announcement about our desecrating a national shrine, they had passed a resolution to suspend all diggings for treasure. The palace rejected the resolution and told us to continue. We decided it was time to get a lawyer. Noel said he had a friend, a member of his Monday night poker club, that had some experience in this kind of thing. He would see if he was available. At our next strategy session Mario Ongkiko was introduced.

We knew who he was. His reputation preceded him. I've always been interested in how people of position and importance handle themselves. They come in all flavors. Some are the nicest people you'll ever meet. But there are others who start believing their own publicity. They walk around with an exaggerated opinion of themselves, their nose stuck high in the air. The Tagalog expression for this is *supplado*. Dealing with such people can be a pain in the rear end. I expected Mario to be one of these. Success in his profession, and he was at the pinnacle of that, demanded that he be tough, aggressive, and sure of himself, in other words egotistical. I couldn't have been more wrong. He seemed to be cut from the same mold as Noel and Gazmin, a quiet professional who always seemed to exude warmth and confidence.

In attendance at a typical strategy session would be Noel, Curtis, George, Ted, and myself. John had already left the country before the hold order was issued. Depending on the situation others might be invited. Another attorney, Ely Alumpay, also from the poker club, would sometimes come over and provide valuable insight into our legal problems.

Now that we were holding daily press conferences, a public relations firm was hired to handle our image, so a representative would sit in on that part of the briefing. Gazmin, who was officially a part of the committee that oversaw the project, did not attend these sessions but Noel kept him advised.

That night there were several topics of discussion: the progress of the digging; the security of the site which had to be tightened because of the reporters and the curious onlookers; the day's headlines and how to handle the next press conference; our criminal charges; and our Senate invitation. Mario sat through the session until the Senate invitation was brought up. Then he took over and briefed us.

"Expect the worst," he warned. "These are politicians and they will be playing to the gallery. It could turn into a circus but don't let that rattle you. When you answer a question try to explain your side but be as brief as possible. I'll be right beside you. If you don't know how to answer a particular question just ask them, 'May I consult with my attorney.' They won't deny you that right. Just remember, don't get upset and be brief. Listen to the question and answer it as briefly as possible."

He emphasized the need for brevity. Talking too much would just give them more ammunition that could be used against us. We listened in rapt attention. Our testimony at this public hearing could ruin the project and us with it.

The hearing did not go well. The senators were polite but firm in their criticism when they questioned us. I kept to Mario's advice and tried to answer all questions with a yes or no. When further elaboration was required my answers weren't much longer.

Unfortunately Curtis forgot all about the importance of brevity. Somewhere along the way he became infected with a serious case of "watch syndrome." We all know people like that. You ask a fellow what time it is and he tells you how to make a watch. A book could have been published from his testimony entitled, "All You Ever Wanted To Know About The Fort Santiago Gold Recovery Project But Were Afraid To Ask." When asked a question he just couldn't stop talking.

During his testimony it was brought out that after the 1975 treasure hunt he was sued in court for swindling. This was common knowledge to his IPM associates and it was also mentioned in Psinakis' articles. When this came up at the hearing he was visibly nervous for some reason.

The senator's criticism of us was mild compared to that reserved for Noel. Such open hostility toward a government minister wasn't expected. Their questioning was relentless and unmerciful. Over and over, one point was hammered home. The director of national security had more important things to do than to help foreigners hunt for treasure. It was a long day.

Later we received another invitation. This time the House of Representatives wanted us to come over for a chat. We dutifully trooped over and gave our testimony again. They were not so hard on us but Curtis continued his loose-lips act. It was ironic that one of his favorite expressions among the group was, "How is he in the trenches?" referring to one's ability to cope under pressure. Naturally behind his back we all started greeting each other, "How's Curtis doing in the trenches?"

It was only half funny. He was slowly falling apart. At the strategy session each evening, he made a ritual out of reading the day's bad publicity in each newspaper and then moaning and complaining, "Did you see that? Oh, this is terrible. What are we going to do?" And on and on.

After Mario joined us he observed Curtis' ritual. Then he stepped in. He knew Curtis was upset so the matter had to be handled delicately but firmly. When Curtis asked for the umpteenth time what we were going to do, Mario suggested that, for starters, Curtis could stop reading the newspapers. He smiled as he told Curtis, "We really don't need anyone to remind us of our problems. We need help with our solutions. Let's concentrate on the positive. Okay?"

Mario devised a strategy. From then on we were to forget about the accident and concentrate on our work. The press would be treated as nicely as possible. They were allowed into the Bastion for photographs. This reaped some dividends. There was still some negative reporting but not as much as before. The tide began to turn. Only once did we falter. It was a stupid mistake.

At one session Curtis told us that we were within two weeks of a recovery. The reason for his pronouncement was that, after going back to work, we continued to excavate the same hole as before. At about the ten-meter level a cement floor was encountered. We had it analyzed. It definitely was not from the Spanish period — they didn't use cement in construction of the fort — and could be of World War II vintage. Curtis got very excited. He was emphatic in his belief that the gold lay just beneath this floor and that we would be there in two weeks. I guess we all wanted to believe this, so it was announced at the next press conference. Looking back I could kick myself for falling into such a trap. We didn't need to set a time limit, but we did. The next day the announcement was made and the following day the headlines proclaimed "FT. SANTIAGO GOLD DUG UP IN 15 DAYS."

When the cement floor was reached we began jackhammering a hole about one meter square. About sixty centimeters down we encountered five centimeters of fine sand and then more cement. We jackhammered through another sixty centimeters of cement and found five more centimeters of the same fine sand. There were four levels of this cement, each sixty centimeters thick and each separated by a few centimeters of sand. At approximately thirteen meters we broke through the floor and encountered wet sand. There was also flowing water indicating we were at or below the water table.

We constructed a boxlike structure approximately one meter square out of marine plywood. The plan was to push this into the sand, use shovels to dig out one meter of sand, place another plywood structure above it, push it into the sand, and shovel further down. But it didn't work. Every time sand was shoveled out more would come in. It was like scooping up a handful of sand in the desert. More sand would just fill in the hole where you scooped. We wondered if the whole fort lay on this sand foundation. If it did then its removal would just cause the foundation to collapse.

We decided to measure its depth. A pipe five centimeters in diameter was used as a probe. It was pushed down to a depth of ten meters. There were three meters of wet sand, followed by seven meters of mud. The probe couldn't go any deeper. No floor could be located. As the two-week time limit approached our anxiety increased. When it expired the newspapers announced our failure and our credibility suffered.

Curtis continued to be a problem. He couldn't sleep and he was constantly nervous and irritable. Finally a doctor was called. Curtis was put on tranquilizers in the daytime and sleeping pills at night. This helped but he obviously was not a well man. He still insisted on being a part of the operation. In order to keep him occupied he was allowed to give a few interviews to the media. But when he came to the fort he wasn't as helpful as he could have been.

At the fort Curtis used the same metal detector we used on Corregidor to test the site. With the exception of John, who barely knew how to operate it, none of us knew a thing about this technology. We assumed that he did. One day George came to the fort. He looked around to make sure Curtis wasn't there and motioned for us to join him in a corner of the Bastion.

"That metal detector may not be giving us accurate readings," he began. "I talked to a geologist today and he said it is effective

only to a depth of fifteen meters." The muffled curses echoed across
the chamber. By now we knew that the treasure was probably a
lot deeper.

"Something has to be done," someone said. "Somebody has
to bring this up with Curtis," said somebody else. I'm sure it wasn't
planned but as if on cue four pairs of eyes turned toward me. I looked
behind me to see what they were looking at. Then I realized I
was elected.

Curtis' reaction was expected. "My detector works and if you
don't like it you can shove it." He would not allow any other tests
conducted at the fort. We decided something had to be done about
that. If we couldn't go through him then we'd go around him.

The permit to search for treasure in the fort originally
had a ninety day time limit. This was extended another thirty
days when we announced that a recovery would occur within two
weeks. This of course didn't happen and the palace began to get
antsy. When another extension was requested the palace granted
it, but on several conditions.

The Intramuros Administration was asked to oversee the
project. They were in charge of restoring the old Walled City, of
which the fort was a part. They appointed a committee consisting
of an archeologist, sedimentologist, conservation expert, civil
engineer, architect, and historian to observe our operation and
provide guidance. In addition, a geologist, mining engineer, and
structural engineer were hired as consultants; a one-million peso
bond ($50,000.00) had to be posted to cover the cost of restoration;
another P840,000 ($42,000.00) had to be put up which would be
forfeited should IPM abandon the project; and each worker had
to be insured for P100,000 ($5,000.00).

When Curtis turned us down on the request for further testing
we went to Doctor Ben Austria, our consultant and head of the
geology department at University of the Philippines, and told him
about the cement floor and the sand below it. He suggested to the
committee that we core drill the area and obtain samples of the
earth's subsurface.

About a dozen holes were drilled to a depth of fifty meters
and core samples were taken to derive a cross-section of the different
kinds of material encountered down to that depth. We wanted to
determine if the material was geologically endemic to that area or

if it was placed there by man. There was also the outside chance that one of the safes or a gold bar might be hit or cored by the drill.

When Curtis first arrived he would not allow us to contact Pol and Ben. We had asked him in the states about contacting them but he said that they would only talk to him. That was understandable then but now we were all in Manila. The excuse he gave now was that they may be working for someone else and they might spy on us. With Noel's permission I located Pol and he agreed to come to the fort. That first meeting with Curtis was strained but friendly. From then on Pol was brought to the fort several times a week.

One day Pol showed up at the fort with two sketches he had made. One was of a cube approximately one by two by two and a half meters. Pol said that the cube represented the vaults. They were Mosler safes taken from the Central Bank and other banks in Intramuros in 1942. Underneath was the following note:

1. Six (6) vaults in three chambers.
2. Each vault contains 450 gold bars.
3. Fifty kilos (50 kgs) per bar.
4. Country of origin:
   A. Sumatra
   B. Burma
5. 30 Meters Deep

The other sketch was a top-view of the Bastion, and indicated how these vaults were laid out in a chamber thirty meters below. The location was not even close to where we had been digging. The nearest vault to our hole was five meters away. Pol explained that marble slabs were taken from the ruins of old Intramuros and laid on the floor of the chamber. Railroad ties were laid across these slabs. The vaults were laid on the railroad ties. Then the chamber was backfilled. So we could not expect to find a tunnel down there.

The core drilling began. Although Pol had indicated a depth of thirty meters, the geologist or someone on the committee requested a fifty meter depth to determine the geological makeup of the sub-strata beneath the Bastion.

One core sample yielded minute quantities of gold flakes at the thirty-meter level. Another sample yielded a piece of marble fused to an old railroad tie at the forty-meter level. The location of the two samples was near our original hole and ten meters from where Pol indicated the nearest vault should be. Nobody, however, was faulting Pol. He was drawing sketches from memories of forty-four years ago. The piece of marble fused to the railroad tie was proof enough for us that he knew what he was talking about.

The hold order barring us from leaving the country was lifted on 21 April. Now we could leave anytime. Quietly plans were made to get Curtis out of the Philippines and back home. Marvin* arrived from Las Vegas about this time. He was a member of IPM and a good friend of Curtis and his wife. He was also the one that had walked in on our meeting in Las Vegas and Noel introduced himself as Neil. Now Marvin met Noel and found out who he really was. At the same time Noel asked for his help.

Marvin was the closest friend of Curtis in Manila so Noel asked him to convince Curtis to go home. Marvin did his best, but Curtis still refused. He was needed in Manila. The operation would fall apart without him, he reasoned. Marvin reported this to Noel, who decided there was no other way but to confront Curtis. With the backing of the group in Las Vegas a meeting was held in Manila. Curtis was told that he was a sick man and that being around the operation only made him worse. He wasn't going to get better until he went home. He still refused so IPM played its trump card. The project was almost out of money, he was told, and no more funds would be forthcoming until he went home. Only then with great reluctance did he give in.

Noel assured Curtis before he left that he was still the head of IPM and that his share in the project was protected. Then he was asked to provide the map of the fort to help with the recovery. He agreed to send a copy to Noel as soon as he got back to Las Vegas.

Noel maintained contact with Curtis by phone and correspondence, and kept him informed of our progress. When the map didn't arrive within a few weeks he called and asked Curtis again, and again he promised to send it. A month passed and still no map. Noel called and asked him again. This time he said he

* Not his real name. He preferred to remain anonymous.

was afraid of the mails, and asked Noel to meet him somewhere to personally receive the map. They agreed to meet in Tokyo, but these plans fell through when Curtis called and said he was sick again. Instead he sent some engineering drawings and explained that these would be more useful than the map. Noel politely pointed out we already had copies of those, and again asked for the map. When Curtis replied to Noel's fourth request in eight weeks he finally ran out of excuses. He said he had a problem with turning over the map. He never explained what his problem was nor did he ever turn over the map. We would soon find out why.

The number of Americans left on the project slowly dwindled. After Curtis departed George had marital problems and had to leave. (An incurable romantic, he soon divorced number five and married number six, a Filipino. A year later he divorced her.) Ted left soon after that for personal reasons. That left Marvin and myself. One day we were discussing the situation at the fort. "I wonder if he really has the maps," Marvin said, referring to Curtis. I thought that was a strange thing for him to say.

"Marvin, when I was in Las Vegas last September, Curtis told Noel and I that you had seen the maps. You're saying you haven't?" I asked.

"No, I haven't seen the maps. I thought you and Noel had," Marvin said. We looked at each other for a moment, then headed for the telephone.

The answers we got from different members of the group in Las Vegas were varied. "I thought you saw them," or "Marvin has the key to the deposit box so he must have seen them." But the message was clear. Everyone in IPM believed someone else had seen the maps. The photograph of the map of the Teresa site was the only map Curtis had ever shown anyone.

Then we started backtracking. One weekend in March the group had taken a trip to Corregidor. Curtis acted as our guide and showed us the locations of what had been four artillery batteries during the war. The rusting hulks of the big guns were still there. The difference between these and the other batteries, he exclaimed, was that a major treasure site lay thirty meters beneath each of them.

At one particular site he bragged that he had sent an Australian group to recover the site in 1981 but he gave them the

wrong coordinates so they failed. He had told us a similar story
in Las Vegas. We didn't get the point then and we didn't get it
now. George or somebody asked him again why he did that. Curtis
replied that he was testing them. We once again traded that look
of perplexity which had become all too familiar in this project when
dealing with Curtis.

Next Curtis gave Nippon Star two sites and they were not
successful. Then he sent us to Corregidor to do a quicky site, which
was actually one of the sites he had provided to Nippon Star, and
we failed. This was followed by another quicky site at Fort Santiago
which turned into a disaster.

Then there was his comment that he was going to memorize
the maps to ten sites. By now we had seen copies of maps belonging
to others seeking our help, so we were becoming familiar with the
different codes and symbols although we didn't know what they
meant. There was no way he could memorize that much detail on
each map. There was a strong possibility that he wasn't using any
maps at Corregidor or the fort. He was going by what others had
told him in 1975, and either that information was incorrect or he
didn't remember that well. That is why the Australians and Nippon
Star had failed, and we weren't doing that great.

These inconsistencies were reported to his group in Las Vegas.
They were not amused when they found out about the maps. A
lot of money had been raised primarily because of this particular
claim. The most serious misrepresentation of course was to President
Aquino. In his letter to her he had also boasted about having the
maps. In the same letter he claimed to have met her husband in
Las Vegas. This wasn't true either since Ninoy was still in prison
in the Philippines. Now we realized that what heretofore had been
considered an honest mistake was really an outright lie.

There were more surprises. When the public relations firm was
hired to combat our negative publicity each of us was asked to fill
out a bio-data form. I kept copies of these for our records. Curtis
stated in his that he had worked for Bank of America and that
he was co-founder and developer of the BankAmericard in 1959.
When I mentioned this to Marvin he gave me that funny look again,
the same look he gave me when I asked him about the maps.
"Charlie, that's bull shit," he said. An inquiry with Bank of America
confirmed Marvin's malodorous but accurate comment.

Curtis' story about being taken to an open grave for execution at the War Memorial Cemetery didn't sound right either. Why he didn't tell Psinakis about such an important incident is beyond reason. And, if the story were true, why Marcos allowed him to leave the Philippines stretched the imagination. Finally, there was no mention of this incident in his letters and telexes to Marcos, Ver, and Mutuc afterwards.

Later I would find out from Ben that the maps were never stored in the hotel conference room. General Onofre Ramos kept them in his possession since the day Ben delivered them in 1968. Ramos died in the late seventies. Nobody saw them after that. In 1989 a source at the palace gave me a file folder containing photocopies of about fifty of these maps. They were found in the palace in Marcos' files after the revolution. By then it was obvious. Curtis didn't have any maps. But he raised money and brought himself considerable prestige by leading people to believe he did.

We finally did get hold of the map of the fort — actually there were two maps — quite by accident. In the process of attempting to interview all persons involved in one way or another with the treasure at the fort Noel put me in touch with Aida Alejandrino. She was responsible for getting Villacrusis a permit to dig at the fort in 1981. One evening she was recounting this story, and pulled out a scrapbook. Inside were the engineering drawings and the two maps. I realized then that I already had a copy of one of those maps. It had been in the file folder found in the palace.

Other treasure hunters had provided us with lists of codes and symbols to help decipher the maps but they weren't much help. One of the major lessons we learned was that modern technology was much more useful than a map in locating buried objects. Only after a map site was recovered would we be able to determine with certainty what these codes and symbols really meant.

We returned to the business at hand — making a recovery at the fort. All of Curtis' surprises were behind us, or so we thought.

CHAPTER FOURTEEN

The Con Man

Epimaco Velasco was angry. Someone in the office had leaked his letter to the press. Now they were out there screaming for more information. He tried to fend them off while thinking about how to explain this to his boss when he returned. He knew he had to be careful. Whatever was said was sure to make the headlines tomorrow.

The National Bureau of Investigation in the Philippines is the equivalent of the FBI in the U.S. Occasionally the NBI requests, through the American Embassy, that the FBI provide any information they might have on certain Americans doing business in the Philippines, particularly with the government.

The NBI made such a request regarding IPM and its members. The FBI agent assigned to the embassy, Mike Pretoro, acted on the request and delivered the report to the NBI. When it arrived it was too good to keep secret, or so some officials thought. Requesting anonymity, they leaked the information to the press, and now Velasco was on the hot seat.

The officials had not provided a copy of the report to the press. Instead they showed them a copy of the transmittal letter from Assistant Director Epimaco Velasco to Director J. Antonio Carpio, which stated in part, "Undoubtedly, IPMI [International Precious Metals, Inc.] has been involved in dubious racketeering activities and Malacañang must be advised about it."

Velasco dealt with the press as best he could. He confirmed that a report had been received but refused to disclose its contents. "All I will say is that a copy has been forwarded to Malacañang, and the NBI is conducting its own investigation."

It hit the newspapers the next day. "DON'T DEAL WITH GOLD HUNTERS, GOV'T TOLD," was one of the headlines. Noel called the palace and asked about the report, but no one there had received it yet. Then he called his friend, Director Carpio, but he was out of town. Now the reporters were calling for a comment. All he could say was that he had not received any report and neither had the palace, so he had no comment. Carpio returned a few days later and provided Noel with a copy. It wasn't good.

The report actually was about Curtis, not IPM, but that was academic. Curtis was head of IPM and the palace had supported its project. It stated that Curtis was indicted on 15 September 1977 and charged with a two count violation of Title 18, Sections 1341 and 2314 of the U.S. Codes. On 3 January 1979 he was sentenced to five years imprisonment (suspended) and placed on probation for five years.

The report stated in part: ". . . investors were defrauded when Curtis claimed he had developed a 'secret process' for extracting precious metals from sand and dirt. . . Curtis admitted once having the idea of setting up a gold manufacturing company in the Philippines. Under the guise of producing gold from ore, he would melt down cached Japanese gold artifacts, and claim the gold had come from his 'secret method' of processing ore. To further add credibility to his story, Curtis claimed President Ferdinand Marcos had knowledge of the Japanese gold caches and agreed to Curtis' efforts to locate the hidden caches. . . Curtis claims he was forced to flee the Philippines in October 1975 because President Marcos learned of the gold retrieval operation. Another version states that he was expelled from the Philippines for writing numerous bad checks."

This was not the Agnew lawsuit we were all familiar with. This was a federal criminal indictment which occurred during the time Curtis went public with his Leber Group story in 1978. He had neglected to tell us about this. As soon as it hit the newspapers the president ordered an investigation. The NBI kept a lid on the report. Other than the "dubious racketeering activities" charge the press knew nothing else. As the results of the investigation rolled in we were shocked. There was a lot more to Curtis than any of us imagined.

•

After Curtis left the Philippines some changes were made in the way we operated. Mario was now the official legal representative of IPM. He, Noel, and I met two or three times a week to review the situation and to plan.

Another change was that all three eye-witnesses were allowed to come to the fort. Pedro had not been allowed while Curtis was there. When Pol had told me about Pedro we went to see him in Calamba, Laguna. He told his story of how he was a prisoner and worked for a colonel named Yugurra. Then he showed a few sketches of the fort which he made in 1943 and 1944. When I told Curtis, he said he didn't trust Pedro since he wasn't a part of Leber Group.

After Curtis left, Pol helped locate Ben in Nueva Vizcaya. Then he contacted Pedro in Laguna and all three came to the fort. They shared their recollections of how the treasure was buried there.

Pedro had seven crude pencil sketches on scraps of note paper. He showed them one at a time and explained his renderings. The first was dated "2/5/43 to 2/6/43" and depicted the top of a building and a barge in a river next to it. There was a half circle in front indicating the entrance to the building, and underneath was written "Santiago Garrison." This building was the Bastion de San Lorenzo. Next to it was the Pasig River. On top of the Bastion a Japanese flag was drawn, and underneath it was written "Flag Guard." Also on top were two squares. One was marked "pit no. I" and the other "no. 2." To the right were a series of horizontal lines indicating a stairway that led from the roof to the ground. In the lower right hand corner there was a notation: "We deliver many black brick. We work for almost two days to the first pit. We stack near pit."

Pedro explained: "My group arrived at the fort for the first time on February 5th, 1943. There were thirty of us and two Japanese soldiers. A barge was already tied up at the river side of the fort. Using a crane we unloaded a cargo of black brick onto the roof next to hole number one which was about three meters square. There was another hole of the same dimensions about thirty meters away but all the brick was stacked next to the first hole and then lowered into it.

"This treasure site was the largest I worked on. There were a lot of people involved, maybe several hundred. I recognized the Matagumi Kaisha (the Japanese civilian construction corp). They helped build many of the tunnels at the various sites that I worked

on. They didn't know about the treasure. They were supervised
by military engineers and just dug the tunnels and left the site before
the treasure arrived. I also noticed a large group of Chinese from
Formosa (Taiwan) helping. They wore some kind of uniform, brown
pants and shirts, but didn't appear to be military. I would guess
there were also a few hundred prisoners of war working on this
site. It took two days to unload the barge and put the brick in the
hole but we only worked in the daytime. At night we were taken
to the Jai Alai Club nearby to sleep. We finished our work and
left on the evening of February 6th."

Pedro showed the next sketch. It was similar to the first,
depicting the top of the Bastion and the Pasig River beside it. The
main difference was that in the space between the two holes there
were some parallel lines drawn with a notation underneath: "We
take this off." The sketch was dated "2/25/43 to 3/5/43" and the
notation in the lower right hand corner stated, "Destroy roofing.
Take off iron bars." The next sketch was also similar. Dated "3/7/43
to 3/12/43" with a notation, "We lod (sic) the iron bar to the barge."

Pedro explained that his group returned to the fort eighteen
days later, on 25 February. They tore up the roof and loaded the
iron reinforcing bars onto a barge. The whole roof, which was
approximately forty-five meters wide by fifty-five meters long, wasn't
affected. Only the area between the two holes, about thirty meters
long by ten meters wide, was torn up. They finished on 12 March
and departed.

Pedro showed the next four sketches and continued with his
explanation. His group returned to the fort six months later, on
14 September. They worked for three days, unloading sacks of lime,
cement, and sand from a barge.* This time they stacked the sacks
next to hole number two and left on 17 September. Pedro said that
in between assignments at the fort they worked at sites in Rizal
province just outside Manila and Laguna province nearby.

Three months later, on 18 December, they were ordered back
to the fort. They spent five days filling sacks with dirt that came

---

* Tabo Ingles, the guerrilla that was taken to the roof of the Bastion in August
1943 before being imprisoned in a cell right outside the fort, does not recall
any of this activity. But he admits he wasn't feeling his best when this occurred.

out of the two pits. Pedro said there was some tunnelling but he was not yet allowed inside. He estimates that his group filled 700 sacks. These sacks were taken away by truck. Pedro's group left the fort on 23 December and returned to the prison compound at U.P. Los Baños where he spent Christmas.

On 4 April 1944 Pedro and his group once again found themselves on a work detail at the fort. Their first job was to unload five vaults from a barge. Each was a little more than one meter in height, width, and depth. The vaults were lifted off the barge by crane and deposited onto the roof of the Bastion. Then they unloaded some wooden boxes, each about the size of a shoe box. It took two men to lift each of these small boxes which were taken into what Pedro called the Japanese garrison but it was also the torture chamber. He didn't recall the exact number of boxes unloaded, only that there were several dozen.

For the first time Pedro was allowed into the pits but, as usual, it was only down to the ten meter level. Another crew was responsible for the next ten meters. Using cables and pulleys the five vaults were lowered down to the base at the first ten meter level where he and a few men were waiting. From there the vaults were lowered down to the base at the next level. Pedro recalled that the dimensions of the shaft that extended down the next ten meters appeared to be larger than the first. They finished their work on 10 April and left.

They returned again on 19 June and spent five days moving boxes from the garrison to the roof and down into the pits. He recalled that, before lowering them, the boxes were placed in larger containers such as metal boxes and sealed. Then each container was coated all over with black tar and rolled in fine powdery sand. The Japanese engineers claimed that the sand had been mixed with a chemical that made it antimagnetic. (There was no such technology. If there were, they would have surely used it on their underground mines, making them impossible to detect.)

An extra vault, of the type seen in banks and bigger in size than the other five, was brought in and also lowered into one of the pits. They left on 24 June but came back nine days later to unload 200 sacks of black clay and fine sand from a barge, which was then lowered into one of the pits. This work took only one day and they departed again.

Pedro's last visit to the fort was in late August 1944. He doesn't have a sketch for this visit, but he recalled that he was there until American planes appeared over Manila Bay and the bombing started. The first American air strike came on 21 September. The targets were Clark Air Base to the north, Nichols Air Field nearby, and the shipping in Manila Bay. Neither the fort nor the city were bombed for fear of harming civilians but now everyone worked around the clock. He left for the last time after this.

Pol's information about the marble slabs and railroad ties had already indicated that he had some knowledge of the fort back then. One of the sketches Pol provided noted that there were six vaults. Pedro's sketch noted there were five and that a sixth, larger vault was added later. The measurements of the vaults also differed but not by much. Pol and Pedro's information was not exactly alike, but Pol claimed he had drawn his sketches from memory and Pedro's were drawn at the time he was there. The two pits Pedro kept referring to appeared to be at each end of the area noted by Pol's second sketch, which showed how the vaults were laid out in three chambers below.

Pol concurred that there were about two hundred people working at the fort site. He said that the pits were dug down to the thirty meter level, a tunnel was excavated at that level, and then three chambers were prepared for the actual placement of the treasure. They were below the water level so they diverted the water by sandbagging the area and using water pumps. According to Pol, all the treasure had been placed in the chambers by 4 November 1944 because that was the date he and the three Japanese lieutenants were ordered to conduct a final inventory. After the inventory was completed the tunnels were backfilled with rocks, clay, and sand. Most of the backfill consisted of dirt from the excavation which had been taken to Honolulu Iron Works in the port area nearby, dried and powdered, and taken back again. The backfilling took almost three months. Pol remembered that the job wasn't finished and the roof repaired until mid-January. The American First Cavalry Division entered Manila on 3 February 1945.

Ben said he didn't come to the fort until about November 1944. He could not recall much detail but he remembered there were a lot of men working at a frantic pace. Everyone seemed to be moving around double-time. He and Kawabata only stayed there a few days. Then they went to the San Agustin Church in Intramuros, and after that to a site in Santa Mesa also in the Manila area. He thought that Kawabata may have been on some kind of last-minute inspection tour. In January they were ordered to head north to Baguio.

Those were the eye-witness' recollections of the fort. I didn't meet Father Bulatao until January 1989. That was when the regressions began. The information given by Pedro and Ben during our interviews turned out to be the same under regression but Pol's comments couldn't be confirmed this way.

While core drilling, a geophysicist from the University of the Philippines, Doctor Ernesto Sonido, was hired to test the Bastion and determine if there was anything buried down there. He ordered the roof cleared for testing so the drill rig was taken off. In the first test a total-field magnetometer was used to determine if there were any anomalies in the earths magnetic field directly beneath the Bastion. There was, so a second test was conducted to determine the resistivity of the anomaly. Gold, silver, and platinum are extremely low in resistivity. The test showed very low resistivity readings at about the thirty-five or forty meter level in a rectangular area about ten meters wide by thirty meters long. This area included our original hole and the area indicated by Pedro and Pol.

This was a crucial point in the project. How were we going to recover treasure over that wide an area that deep? Our geologist, mining engineer, and structural engineer were brought in for several joint meetings with the Intramuros Committee. Jun Orobia, head of the Intramuros Administration, chaired most of these meetings, along with his associate, Felix Imperial.

Felix was the chief architect assigned to oversee the restoration of the Walled City. Two more experts in their respective fields were brought in at this time — Gabe Casal from the National Museum and Doctor Serafin Quiason of the National Historic Institute. I remember sitting in the first meeting and thinking to myself, "Within this group were over a hundred years of education and experience in all phases of the expertise we needed. If they couldn't do the job then it couldn't be done."

I've already mentioned my friendship with Gabe. He became a mainstay and placed many of the museum's resources at our disposal. All artifacts dug up were immediately turned over to him. These normally consisted of broken Japanese pottery but every now and then we had some excitement. One day some old bones were found. Work was halted while they were rushed over to the museum. They turned out to be those of a carabao.

Another who went out of his way to help was Felix. He patiently introduced me to the Intramuros Archives where I spent many afternoons poring over old maps, engineering drawings, and manuscripts about the history of this ancient stone fortress.

The results of Sonido's testing were presented to the group. Then they were asked: "How do we get to whatever is down there?" Several suggestions were considered. One was to dig a shaft outside the fort and straight down forty meters, then tunnel in toward the treasure. This method would not harm the Bastion. Another was to go in from the roof of the Bastion and sink a steel casing approximately two meters in diameter straight down forty meters. The roof had already been inspected and found to be fifty to eighty-five years old. The Americans had replaced part of it around 1900, and the Japanese had also replaced it while they were there.

The most efficient, and costly, method would be to cut a hole in the roof that covered the area that tested positive and go straight down. Everyone favored this method. In addition to finding the treasure, we would be removing all the backfill for the first time since the war and then restoring the Bastion, all at IPM expense. The Intramuros Administration couldn't lose, and they stood to gain a lot more if we were successful.

Several construction companies were asked to submit bids, and the Philippine National Construction Corporation was chosen. They estimated the cost to be ₱18 million ($900,000) and the time frame about four months.

At dawn one day during the first week of August a convoy of trucks, cranes, and bulldozers pulled up to the rear of the Bastion. A small army of construction workers swarmed over the roof as we looked on. The largest and costliest assault ever attempted on this legendary treasure was about to begin.

Two tragedies occurred during this period. On 13 June, one of the men on our security detachment, Sergeant Mark Navales, was shot and killed while off duty. Six weeks later, on 5 August,

Corporal Aurelio Sayson was killed in the same manner. Both appeared to be professional jobs. The *modus operandi* was similar to other killings in Manila by "Sparrow" units — three-man assassination teams trained by the Communist New People's Army — who used selective assassination as a form of terrorism. When Navales was killed the newspapers reported it and attributed the killing to the Sparrows, but none mentioned that he worked with us. Then Sayson was shot and the press again reported another killing by the Sparrows. Still there was no mention of his assignment. Now two soldiers of our twelve-man security force had been killed within six weeks of each other. Gazmin ordered a thorough investigation into the matter and more briefings were held on security, but the killers were never caught.

I remembered them both. They were good men. Navales was a handsome guy with the military bearing of a professional soldier. He was usually asked to stand behind me during the press conferences because of his good looks. Sayson was tall for a Filipino, over 1.8 meters. Always well mannered and usually quiet, he sometimes startled me with a loud, "Sir," and a salute when I would arrive at the Bastion. At the wakes I offered my condolences to the bereaved parents, but I had no answer to the "Why?" written all over their faces.

Two weeks later I was in the states at home one afternoon and the phone rang. When I answered it a voice with a thick Filipino accent said, "Hello, Mr. McDougald. If you return to the Philippines you will get the same thing that Navales and Sayson got." Then he hung up.

On my return to Manila I reported the incident to Noel and told him what I wanted to do. He gave his approval, so I called a friend of mine who had served with me in Special Forces twenty years before and was still in that line of business. After explaining my situation he arranged for two of his associates to fly over and check my communications and security arrangements. They flew in, quietly worked with the operation for a few months, and flew out again. No one ever knew they were there.

By then Marvin had returned to Las Vegas. He was the last of the regulars to leave. Other members of IPM came and went. They would stay a few weeks or a month and then return to their jobs in the states. It was a less than ideal working arrangement. Most wanted to be helpful but it was difficult to place an American in a foreign environment for the first time, ask him to do a job that was equally foreign, and expect him to contribute anything worthwhile. Valuable time was wasted finding a suitable place for them in the operation. By the time they began to make a contribution they would be ready to leave.

The ten by thirty meter section of roof was removed. Four small rooms and a hallway were discovered directly underneath, adjoining the torture chamber. The four rooms were about the same size as the hole left by the Marcos excavation, about three and a half meters wide by six meters long. The hallway was part of the one I had first seen behind the cemented door, which extended about four or five paces and then ran into a wall. This was the other side of the wall.

Beginning with the room beside the Marcos hole we labelled them chambers one through five, with the hallway being number five. The Marcos hole had not tested positive so it was not included in the area of excavation. These chambers were all cleared of backfill down to the five meter level where an adobe and brick floor was found. It wasn't old enough to be of Spanish origin, but it was determined that this was the original floor level of the Bastion.

Some interesting markings were found on the walls of these chambers. There were the letters *IM* which, according to Pol, were the initials of a Japanese engineer named Morita who had worked at the fort. There were also other symbols —a cross, a coiled snake, and some wavy lines. These resembled some of the symbols on a list I had been given by another treasure hunting group. There were several of these lists around. I had been given three or four, most of which contained the same symbols. No one could tell me where they came from, but the symbols were supposed to provide more information about the treasure. For example, a star meant explosives; a hand meant there was a statue of Buddha with the treasure; a coiled snake meant the treasure was directly underneath; and a turtle meant the treasure was underwater. There were wavy lines, dotted lines, horizontal lines, and vertical lines, sometimes with another symbol and sometimes not. All were supposed to mean something but until a site was recovered we wouldn't know for certain.

A unique symbol found on one wall were the letters *IHS* with a cross setting on top of the *H*. No one knew what it meant until one day I was leading a group of Noel's friends on a tour of the excavation. When we got to that wall one of them said, "My god, that's it. It's the same one!"

"The same what?" I asked.

"Come with me," he said.

We drove to the National Library a few minutes away, climbed three floors of stairs, and walked into the reading room. We really weren't like the proverbial bull in the china shop, but we weren't much better. There were six or seven of us and we were not that quiet. A stern look from the librarian lowered all our voices. Another hard look at me and I removed my hat while muttering an apology.

When we saw the display case in the far corner a hush fell over our group. There under the glass was a replica of a beautiful Samurai helmet sitting on a red satin pillow. Red and black in color, the helmet was richly designed with ornate fittings of what appeared to be brass, gold, and silver. Above the visor about thirty centimeters high were the brass letters *IHS*. A brass cross on top of the *H* rose another forty centimeters. It was indeed the same one.

A sign below the helmet explained that this was a replica of a helmet worn by Joan Naito. He was baptized in 1565 in Kyoto, the capital of Japan at the time, and became a fervent Catholic. Because of his faith he put on his helmet the inscription *IHS*, for the Latin words *Jesus Hominum Salvator* (Jesus Savior of Mankind). Persecuted in Japan for his religious beliefs, he was exiled in 1614.* He, his sister, and many of his followers sailed to Manila and established a convent in the district of San Miguel. He died in 1624. We never found out why this cross showed up on a wall in the Bastion.

The rectangular excavation area extended another ten meters past the hallway. This was part of the old execution chamber. We labelled it chamber six. This was also where we had found the

---

* By 1625 Japanese xenophobia had led to persecution of all Christians. Soon afterward, with the exception of a small Dutch trading post, Japan closed itself off to all Western nations for over two hundred years.

gold flecks and the marble-railroad tie core sample. On the other side of this wall was our original tunnel. The backfill was removed from chamber six but there was no floor at the five-meter level. Not until we hit the ten-meter level was a cement floor encountered. The cement appeared to be the same as that encountered in our original hole. There were also four levels, each sixty centimeters thick and each separated by a few centimeters of sand.

At this stage we had cleared chambers one through five down to floor level at five meters, and chamber six down to its floor level at ten meters. A lot of iron pipe and scrap iron had been found in the backfill so another magnetometer and resistivity test was conducted after the iron was removed. The same positive results were obtained,. Chambers one and six and the wall between chambers two and three scored the highest. The Intramuros Committee and Fort Santiago Gold Recovery Committee then met and decided on a change in the excavation plans.

Chambers one through five would be left as is. Even if they were only forty years old, the Japanese had done a good job of restoration. Chamber six would be enlarged to an area about eight meters by thirteen meters and covering about half of the area where the execution chamber had been. We would go down forty meters in this area and then tunnel back under chambers five through one. The four levels of cement were slowly jackhammered and removed. Samples were taken to the National Museum laboratory and examined. They were of the same content as those taken from our original hole in March.

Now water became a problem. The flow was so strong that we suspected the source to be a spring underneath the Bastion. A spring was mentioned in several of the documents in the Intramuros Archives. Water pumps were brought in to control the flow. There was a tinge of excitement. We were now twenty meters down and halfway to our objective. If things went right we would be there in two weeks. But they didn't. They began to go awfully wrong.

The story about the FBI report was leaked to the newspapers on 5 September. Some people demanded that Noel resign. I had not yet seen the report, but I informed IPM in Las Vegas about the negative publicity we were getting, provided them with copies of the newspaper articles, and proceeded with the project. Then Phil Bronstein called me.

Phil and I had met in Manila in 1983 right after the assassination. He had covered the story for the *San Francisco Examiner*. We still kept in touch with each other. When the treasure story made the news he asked for an interview with Curtis. It was granted and he did a story. Now, several months later, Phil was back in Manila and he called again. He commented about the headlines and said, "I have something I think you should see. It's about your friend. I'll send it over."

It was an old newspaper clipping. The title of the article was "Platinum Company Loses Case." It noted that Curtis had been found guilty in a class action suit. The name of the prosecuting attorney was Michael Specchio. I called him in Reno, Nevada. He told me how to write the court clerk in order to obtain a copy of the judgment. When it finally arrived it was worse than I had imagined. This wasn't the Agnew civil suit or the federal criminal action. This was a third law suit.

The suit was brought by "Eureka Trust, Liberty Trust, Mine Properties Investors IV Trust, and the shareholders of defendant corporations," and named over a hundred individuals as plaintiffs. The trial began 5 September 1975, a few months after Curtis returned to the states, and continued on through 1976 when the conviction was obtained on 13 December.

The findings of the case noted that the plaintiffs invested nearly one million dollars and that Curtis "...fraudulently, wrongfully, and intentionally induced Plaintiffs to invest large sums of money... on the assumption that said Robert H. Curtis was possessed of a secret formula for the extraction of precious metals...The court is convinced and the conviction being supported by the evidence that said Robert H. Curtis, whose background largely consisted of automobile and mobile home sales, misrepresented all essential elements relative to the inducement of Plaintiffs."

I had to smile as I read this. In November 1987, before leaving for Corregidor, Curtis had taken me and several members of his IPM group to a warehouse in Las Vegas where we spent the whole day observing him demonstrate this process. He did turn a bowl full of something — he said it was dirt — into a tiny glob of gold. We were sworn to secrecy as he explained that with the money IPM made on this treasure he would build a factory to house all the equipment for his new technology. Everyone in IPM would then become enormously wealthy. That was the line he was putting out. Marvin put out a better line later. "We must have been dummer'n shit to believe that," he said.

The court went on to state that Curtis used the funds "for questionable and unwarranted expenses," and that defendant John W. McAllaster "similarly participated in the fraudulent inducement of Plaintiffs and utilized corporate funds for unwarranted, illegal, and personal gain." The court made specific reference to "flagrant acts of mismanagement" which included "the costly trip to the Philippines to seek sunken treasure" and "the loss and dissipation of corporate assets."

The court also stated: "The fraudulent statements and misrepresentations by Curtis demonstrates to this court an inclination on the part of Curtis to deceive by fraudulent representations if he has to, and he has no qualms about it." The court concluded that the so-called secret process, based on this record, was in reality "a farce, a hoax, and a flagrant misrepresentation."

Curtis, McAllaster, their wives, nine corporations Curtis had formed, and several other individuals were found guilty and ordered to repay investors $750,000. They were also ordered to pay interest on that amount from 1 July 1974. Obviously Curtis began perpetrating this fraud before he left for the Philippines, and even before he obtained the loan from Agnew.

The date of this judgement was 13 December 1976. The Judgment By Consent was dated 16 November 1976. In that case he, McAllaster, and three of the corporations listed in the other suit — Curtis-Nevada Mines, Inc., Marmac Mines, Inc., and United States Platinum, Inc. — were ordered to pay Samuel Agnew $443,198.23, which included the loan, interest, attorney's fees, and court costs. Twenty-seven days later he had to pay back $750,000 plus interest, attorney's fees, and court costs in the other case. Curtis had a bad four weeks at the end of 1976.

I received the information about the class action suit about the same time Noel received the FBI report and showed it to me. I contacted the federal records clerk in the U.S. and obtained more information. At some point during Curtis' two trials the FBI stepped in and ordered an investigation into his activities. An indictment was returned on 15 September 1977 and the third trial began on 14 August 1978.

Curtis and McAllaster were charged with defrauding Samuel J. Agnew by means of false and fraudulent pretenses. Curtis was also charged with offering a fraudulent secret process for the extraction of precious metals. The indictment against McAllaster was subsequently dropped because he was too sick to stand trial. He died soon after. Curtis pleaded *nolo contendere*. He was sentenced on 3 January 1979 to five years imprisonment, suspended, and placed on probation for five years. Specifically he was ordered not to solicit money from anyone for the purpose of enabling him to pursue his secret process. Also he was forbidden to solicit money for any business or enterprise in which he had an interest.

My information was turned over to the legal section at Malacañang. We all knew that we had a major scandal on our hands if this information were leaked. I recalled the day of the Senate hearing. Now I knew why Curtis had acted so nervous. He was afraid his other two court cases would become known, and the palace would know they had backed a con man. I had little doubt that somewhere in the palace plans were being made to get IPM out of town as quietly and as fast as possible.

What Curtis actually did with all the money is a mystery. The first scheme brought in about a million dollars. The second, which was a loan, brought in $365,000. Agnew's loan certainly had not been used to finance any laundering operation as Curtis had told him. The only monies he spent on the Leber Group project was for a $36,000 shipping bill, hotel bills, plane fares, and other minor expenses.

In Curtis' interviews with Steve Psinakis in 1978 he mentioned that Agnew had sued him and that he had pleaded *nolo contendere*. This wasn't correct. Curtis had gotten his cases mixed up. You can only plead *nolo contendere* to a criminal charge. Agnew's was a civil suit and Curtis agreed to a Judgement by Consent. Curtis also admitted to Psinakis that his company was having financial problems before he left for the Philippines but he did not elaborate, and he never mentioned the class action suit in which he was found guilty, or the federal indictment he was under at the time.

Curtis also told Psinakis that after he arrived back in Reno in July 1975 he was told by his employees that Wes Chapman and another employee had run away with all the company financial records because they had been embezzling funds. So his books conveniently disappeared before any litigation was begun. Chapman was not a defendant in any of Curtis' lawsuits.

It is obvious that reporters for the *Philippine News*, the *Las Vegas Sun*, and Jack Anderson's column were all manipulated by Curtis in 1978. He had an ulterior motive of course. He was facing serious criminal charges, something he neglected to tell them about, and wanted some favorable publicity. He provided enough accurate data and detail to prove that the treasure hunt with Marcos did take place, which was great news at the time for those allied against Marcos. But Curtis exaggerated his own importance. Every chance he got he left out the bad parts and embellished the good parts. He then used the 24-part series as a springboard to his next venture. By the time I came along he had added a few new bells and whistles to enhance the image. I didn't mind. Ego gratification wasn't a crime. But fraud was.

Whether or not Curtis ever settled all these obligations with Agnew and the other group isn't known. What is known is that ten years later he had moved from Reno to Las Vegas, formed a new company called International Precious Metals, and was once again soliciting funds for his secret process and another treasure hunt in the Philippines.

Noel, Mario, and I met to discuss this strange turn of events. By now we were no longer dealing with Curtis. He had resigned as president after returning to Las Vegas. IPM was advised of the situation. It was decided that we should continue with the operation since we were so near. A successful recovery would solve a lot of these problems.

On 24 September the newspapers surprised us again. This time it was Noel's turn. "₱1.4-M PAYOFF FROM FORT DIGGERS BARED," was one of the headlines. It was the lead story in every newspaper. Noel was accused of taking a payoff of ₱1.4 million from IPM. This was absurd. He never asked for or received a penny. The president ordered an investigation. He was eventually cleared of any wrongdoing but for a few weeks the media were relentless in their loose reporting of the incident. And once again there were calls for his resignation.

Two weeks later, on 7 October, the president visited the fort. Although some of her advisers and confidants had been there, it was the first time she had made an appearance. It was mostly ceremony. The committee was introduced. She met the eyewitnesses. And she was taken on a brief tour of the excavation. The visit was brief, about thirty minutes, but she wasn't there to gather information. She was there to bolster Noel's confidence and to quiet the storm of negative publicity he was getting.

We all wondered what was going on in the palace, and how the Curtis matter was being handled. Four days after the president's visit we found out. The on-site manager of the construction company walked up to me at the Bastion and said, "Charlie, I just got the word. I've been ordered to stop work at six o'clock. We're shutting down the operation. I'm sorry."

I called the manager's boss. He said his instructions came from the Office of the President. Noel went to the palace that afternoon and returned in the evening. The news wasn't good. The last extension on the permit had expired and the request for another extension had not been granted, so we had been operating without a permit. This was technically illegal. Before in this situation the palace had told us to continue unless advised otherwise. Usually that meant they were processing the request. But this time we suspected a different kind of paperwork was being processed. The next day our suspicions were confirmed.

We received a letter from the Office of the President. It stated: "It is confirmed and/or clarified that you are hereby restrained and/or disauthorized from engaging in any digging... In the meantime, you are hereby ordered to continue restoration works at the Fort as called for in your contract."

The only good news of the month came a few days later. Mario told us that, after a full investigation, there wasn't enough evidence to proceed with the homicide charges again us. The case was dropped.

Early in the evening on Monday, 24 October, I got a call on my radio from Noel. He asked me to meet him downstairs in front of the hotel. This wasn't out of the ordinary. Many times, when the information was considered confidential, I would go down, get in his car and we would drive around the block or just park and talk. This time the information was more sensitive than ever before. "I just came from a meeting with the president. She asked me to resign. There is no rush. She just asked me to make the necessary preparations."

We sat there a long time, not saying anything. Then he said he had a dinner party to attend, so he had to go. He wasn't glum. He didn't even look upset. That was Noel. He wasn't one to get overly emotional in times of crisis. He could keep a stiff upper lip as well as anyone. He would attend the party and be just as entertaining as if he hadn't a care in the world, while his hopes for a treasure recovery went down the tubes. Because of some important matters of government his resignation was delayed until February.

Olof Jonsson came to Manila in December. We had been trying to arrange his visit for almost six months but he couldn't come until then. Even though we were at a standstill he wanted to come anyway to have a look at the operation. He was brought to the Bastion one evening. He wasn't told the results of our tests. We just let him walk around the roof. After a short while he called us together and pointed to chamber six.

"There is a very bright aura down there. Also there is a lesser aura over here," he said as he pointed to chamber two. He described the aura as a yellowish light, and said it meant there was gold.

That kind of proof wasn't going to get us another extension but it helped bolster our sagging morale. Olof stayed a week. He visited a few other sites and spent some time with Pedro, Pol, and Ben. Pol and Ben remembered him from 1975, and they considered him as something just short of a god. Before he left he said he was certain we were going to be successful, but he didn't say when.

On Wednesday afternoon, 25 January, I received another letter from the Office of the President. It was dated 16 January and had been sent by registered mail but somehow it got lost and didn't arrive until the twenty-fifth. It read, "Please be informed that after a thorough consideration of the matter, this Office is not inclined to extend your contract anew. Accordingly, your request is denied."

It then ordered us to turn over the restoration work of the Bastion to the Intramuros Administration Committee already set up for that purpose. This letter had been expected since the day

Noel was asked to resign. I think in deference to Noel they kept delaying it, hoping something might happen. The resignation was a political necessity for the president. This did not mean they were not friends. Noel was still very close to her and he still had a lot of backers in the palace. It was an open secret that we were still digging and everyone kept hoping we would hit.

We had stopped work on the roof of the Bastion as ordered, but not in the dungeon. Only a few people were aware that we were even working there. A magnetometer test had been conducted in that area at the same time we tested the roof of the Bastion because the eye-witnesses insisted that some treasure had been buried below the floor of the dungeon in front of the Bastion.

The test had picked up some very good readings in two places, one at about three meters underneath the floor and the other at about six meters. At first the crew didn't want to work. They had heard so many stories of what a fearful place the dungeon was and of so many people dying down there. But we finally convinced them that it was just another excavation.

Archival documents had noted that at high tide prisoners in the dungeon had to stand on tiptoe in order to keep their head above water but we didn't know which dungeon they referred to. The one in the Bastion itself had a watergate which controlled the flow of water, and the cells were underwater at high tide. But we wondered if there were a lower level underneath this dungeon.

The crew jackhammered a hole in the floor. Underneath, as expected, we encountered the water table. What we didn't expect to find is that this level had been filled to the top with sand, so a pump was brought in. That's the reason we kept working here. Technically we were restoring, not excavating, by pumping out the sand.

As the sand level went down hundreds of wooden stakes could be seen in the lower level, arranged in a pattern of sorts. The stakes were sent out for testing, but they got lost and we didn't get any results before we vacated the site. Not until two years later did Orly Obiñon, head of the National Museum laboratory, test more of the stakes. They were carbon dated at 300 years, plus or minus sixty years, which means they were definitely placed there by the Spanish. Those stakes, along with the sand, were probably the foundation on which that part of the Bastion and dungeon were built. If that were true then there was no lower level in this dungeon. If the Japanese put anything there they had to dig into the same sand we did.

Olof was invited to see this excavation, and confirmed there was an aura there also. The crew seemed to take this as absolute confirmation and stepped up the tempo of work. But we had been digging on borrowed time, and time ran out.

I drove out to the fort in the afternoon and called the guards and the crew together. They saw the look on my face and knew it was over. I told them to stop the pumps and start policing the area. We finished the cleanup in silence. The men were paid, the last of the equipment was loaded onto the truck, and everyone left.

After they were gone I walked around to make sure nothing was left behind. My footsteps echoed in the dungeon. It was so peaceful now, and dark. I bent down, duck-walked through the small opening which was the entrance, and came out in front of the Bastion. I crossed the road and entered the torture chamber. This had been my office and second home for a year. Now it was empty. The fading light cast shadows of the trees on the floor and the walls. When the wind blew the leaves rustled and the shadows changed shape. I never noticed that before. A superstitious person might imagine that the spirits which dwelt here had come back to reclaim this chamber. Maybe one of them was the ghost of Yamashita.

I walked out and climbed the steps to the roof of the Bastion to watch the sunset on Manila Bay. It was spectacular this time of the year. This was the nicest part of the day. A gentle breeze. A setting sun. We were so close. So close. Now we'll never know, I mused. The fort's secrets were intact.

The breeze whipped up. I adjusted my hat. A few drops of water splashed at my feet, trickled over to the holes made by our drill rigs, and disappeared. We had made a lot of holes, I noticed, but the old fort still stood. She endured our assault just like she endured the typhoons, earthquakes, rebellions, and battles of her storied past. And she had protected the treasure in her bosom just like she protected herself all those years. Maybe she didn't like us clawing out her innards. Perhaps it wasn't meant to be. I decided then and there to just leave this grand old lady alone. She had earned her peace and dignity.

The rain fell steadily, the last downpour of the season. The last sliver of sun sank beneath the waves. The light faded fast. Darkness came quickly in this part of the world, like someone threw a black cape over the sky.

Something rubbed my leg and I looked down. It was the cat. She had stayed with us through it all. I reached down and picked her up. The first time I tried that, almost a year ago, she bit me and I needed a tetanus shot. We kept feeding her but left her alone until months later she began to sidle up to us. Her offer of peace was accepted and we became friends. Now she was purring in my arms. "Come on, cat," I said. "Let's go see Bando and find you a home."

CHAPTER FIFTEEN

The Swiss Connection

On 2 July 1990 Imelda Marcos received an unexpected present on her sixty-first birthday. "Not guilty!" the jury foreman announced. Imelda's friends in the court room tried to muffle their squeals of delight. Imelda hugged Gerald Spence, her lawyer, and hurried over to St. Patrick's Cathedral on Fifth Avenue. There she knelt and crawled on her knees down the center aisle to the altar to give thanks while photographers recorded the event. She knew of course this would be on the 6:00 o'clock news.

She had been indicted two years earlier, along with her husband and several others, including the flamboyant jet-setter Adnan Kashoggi. Marcos had died so he was no longer a part of the indictment. Only she and Kashoggi stood trial. One defendant, the California Overseas Bank, had already pleaded guilty to wire fraud. Another defendant, Rodolfo Arambulo, former president of that bank, had pleaded guilty to a charge of racketeering. The others stayed out of the U.S. to avoid prosecution. Kashoggi was also found not guilty of mail fraud and obstruction of justice.

Imelda had been charged in U.S. District Court in New York with taking part in a racketeering conspiracy. The indictment stated that they stole more than $100 million from the Philippine treasury and secretly brought it into the U.S. In addition, two American banks and an insurance company were also defrauded of $165 million. This money was used to purchase an art collection, jewelry, and real estate. Kashoggi and others were used to conceal the ownership.

During the trial the testimony flowed in day after day, showing how Marcos used his dictatorial powers in ordering that the money be taken from this institution or that bank. It also showed Imelda's voracious appetite for spending it.

Her defense was that Marcos kept her in the dark about his activities. She also claimed that then vice president George Bush suggested that Marcos invest the so-called Communist Takeover Fund in the states instead of keeping it in the Philippines. This didn't seem to fly. Nobody in government ever heard of such a fund before, and even if it were real that didn't justify hidden bank accounts under all those fake names.

Then the defense suggested that Marcos' wealth came from the Yamashita treasure. That may have been true also, but it had nothing to do with Marcos looting his own treasury. The next tack was more plausible if not any more believable. Investments were made by Marcos during his presidency but he made them on behalf of the country and not merely for his and Imelda's benefit, the defense claimed. There just wasn't any concrete proof that all those investments would inure to the country.

But there was proof that Marcos accepted kickbacks and bribes. Not true, said the defense. His commissions from such deals were legal because he had made it legal. During his dictatorship he signed Presidential Decree 579 into law, which legalized his right to receive 2 ½ percent from corporate deals. That was interesting also since nobody ever heard of that decree. Nor had they heard of his accepting a measly 2 ½ percent. He was called "Mr. Ten Percenter," but never to his face of course. While he was in power Marcos swore that he took no kickbacks or commissions from anyone.

During the trial things didn't seem to go well for Imelda. No matter what she said or did it seemed to reverberate against her. She tried to play the role of the destitute widow. "I am actually on the welfare of family and friends right now," she said.

The prosecution painted a different picture. They presented evidence showing that she visited New York three or four times a year from 1980 to 1984. While there she stayed at the Waldorf Astorial Hotel in the $1,800 a day presidential suite. On each visit she called the Philippine National Bank in New York four or five times and ordered them to deliver an average of $100,000 to her at the hotel. The amounts totalled $22 million by 1983, when the New York state bank examiners threatened to close the bank. There was also the mountain of evidence which showed her insatiable appetite for expensive jewelry.

But in the end all the shenanigans her defense lawyer tried didn't make any difference. Marcos had obviously raped and pillaged the country, but he was dead and couldn't be prosecuted. Imelda was alive, but spending wasn't a crime. And the prosecution failed to prove that Imelda had knowledge of Marcos' misdeeds. So she walked away a free woman.

Now she turned her attention to another matter. Halfway around the world someone had begun to talk about a bank vault holding some of Marcos' gold. .

The lights from the television cameras were so bright it was difficult to read my statement to the committee. "I was the manager for the gold recovery project . . ." I read on trying to concentrate while the cameras rolled. There could be no mistakes this time. A one-hundred peso ($5) theft could get you ten years in prison in the Philippines. I was accused of stealing billions.

Before the Fort Santiago treasure hunt ended another treasure site had been located and excavation begun secretly in May 1988. It was at the base of an old bridge abutment on the Pasig River. Before and during World War II there was an electric train that ran from Manila to an outlying area in Rizal province. The train crossed the Pasig River on this bridge. It was destroyed by the Americans during the liberation of the Philippines in 1945. One of Ben's maps indicated that treasure had been buried below this abutment. Pedro and Pol claimed to have witnessed this burial. Pedro's regression confirmed this. (My notes of this regression were mentioned on pages 91-92.) We called it the bridge site although there was no longer a bridge. When the closing of the Fort Santiago site was imminent I was asked by two friends, who were not associated with IPM, to continue with the bridge site. If I would, then they would fund it, so we became partners afterward. This project didn't last much longer though. The last contract extension expired on 5 February and we decided not to request another, so I went home. But after about six weeks rest I was on a plane headed back. The investors wanted to continue with the treasure hunt.

One morning the phone rang at 6:30. "You're not going to believe what's in the papers," Noel said without even a

"Good morning." He read the article over the phone. I sat up in bed.

"How much?" I asked. "Who?" Noel repeated some of the article. "Okay, let's meet at 10:00." I hung up and laid back down. In the past year I had been charged with smuggling, money laundering, murder, and a few other minor crimes that escaped me at the moment. All charges had been investigated and subsequently dismissed. Now 1989 brought a new charge.

Noel, Mario, and I had stolen 340 tons of gold, worth $4.5 billion, according to the newspapers. Three army trucks had come to the bridge site in the middle of the night and secretly spirited away the treasure. There were eye-witnesses to this crime, and a statement had already been given to the palace.

We met at Mario's office that morning. Noel had resigned as National Security Director a few weeks earlier but he still had plenty of contacts where it counted. He produced a copy of the statement. As we read it things became clearer.

The statement had been made by Clyde,* one of the IPM investors that had come over and worked with us at the fort for a few months until the site was closed. For some reason he just could not get along with the rest of the workers. He was a nice enough guy but he had a touch of paranoia. He always seemed to be worried that a recovery would be made and then kept secret from him. The workers picked up on this and made a joke of it. That made it worse. He started accusing them of misleading him or, worse, hiding the treasure.

There were frequent complaints about Clyde from the workers at the fort. I had thought about doing something but the site was closed, so the problem took care of itself. Then he came to the bridge site and the complaints started all over again. Most of our workers at the fort were transferred to the bridge, so maybe he just didn't trust them. But something had to be done.

One day I called him in, explained the matter as best I could, and said that it would be best if he stayed away from the site. He seemed to take it good-naturedly, and said he planned on returning to the states anyway.

* Not his real name

A month.later we made plans to close that site because, through further regression, it was determined that the actual burial site was fifty meters from the bridge abutment which placed the treasure about thirty meters into the Pasig River below the river bed. Marcos had the Pasig River widened and deepened at this point ten years before. He probably recovered the treasure at that time. And even if he hadn't, tunnelling under a river required technology we didn't have. A recovery of that type was estimated to cost over a million dollars. We decided to try and recover somewhere else first and then return to the site when we could afford it. There was also another reason for closing the site. An incident had occurred a few days before the permit expired on 5 February.

A car pulled up at the bridge site and three people got out. One of them was George Wortinger; another was a Filipino named Ben (not Valmores, the eye-witness) who had recently been appointed the new IPM representative in the Philippines. With him was another Filipino carrying a radio and trying to act tough by showing a gun in his belt.

Ben had come to the site before uninvited. When we politely asked him to leave he had become obstinate but he finally left. Although we had promised all IPM investors a share in the bridge site if we recovered, this wasn't an IPM site and he had no business being there. Besides, we were already aware of who he was. He had been vice-governor of some province under Marcos. He was used to getting his way. If he didn't his favorite negotiating ploy was a threat. There was no subtlety to the man at all. We knew he liked to boast about his knowledge of treasure hunting. The day after we asked him to leave the bridge site, reporters showed up at the gate, but our security wouldn't allow them in. We suspected that he had leaked our location to the press.

George stayed behind while Ben and his armed friend came to the gate. Despite a warning from our guards, they opened it and forced their way in. The guards yelled at them to halt but they kept going. There was one other American, Ernie, on the site operating the drill rig. He rushed over and yelled, "What the fuck are you doing here?"

Ben was carrying a closed umbrella. He swung it and hit Ernie on the side of the head. Eight of our twelve guards had surrounded the two uninvited guests. When Ernie was hit the guards stopped yelling. Instead pistols were cocked and rifles were aimed. For a moment it looked like Ben and his friend were going to die and they knew it. He dropped his umbrella and just stood there looking very worried. His friend raised his hands over his head and visibly started shaking.

"What's going on here?" Lieutenant Foja yelled as he ran up. Foja was in charge of security. "Lower your weapons," he ordered as he broke through the circle of guards. "Sir, you two are under arrest for trespassing. Please come with me." Foja escorted the two men out the gate and back to their car a few meters away.

"You will remain here until I have contacted my headquarters and get instructions on what to do," said Foja. He posted four guards at the car, then requested some identification from each man, and walked away.

Ben opened the back door of the car and sat down. He left the door open and his legs dangled outside. Just then Ernie came running up and kicked the car door as hard as he could, slamming it against Ben's legs. The crunching noise it made sounded as though both his legs had been broken. "Aaayyy!" he screamed.

"Take that, you son-of-a-bitch," Ernie yelled. The guards reacted by doubling up with laughter.

Despite his pain Ben had to wait another hour for Foja to finish his report. The three were finally allowed to leave after getting a final warning from Foja. Later George told me he had just come along for the ride. George was a friend and had been allowed on the site before. Ben probably thought George could help get them on the site this time.

We thought Clyde had already packed up and left, but he hadn't. He was hiding across the river watching our every move with binoculars. What I didn't know was that before I spoke to him and he decided to leave, the workers pulled another joke. December 7 was the anniversary of the Japanese bombing of Pearl Harbor. Ernie jokingly referred to it as Slap-A-Jap Day. When Clyde heard him say "I slapped a Jap," the workers told him that Ernie's comment was a code meaning he had found the treasure.

When we decided to close the site Clyde was convinced that we had recovered the gold and were keeping it all to ourselves. He decided something had to be done, so he contacted Ben, who was still smarting from the incident at the site. He helped Clyde swear out a deposition accusing us of stealing the gold. It was delivered to the palace on 21 February, shortly before Clyde left for the states. Ben then leaked copies to the press.

After we all finished reading the statement Noel said, "The president has ordered an investigation."

"Maybe we should cut her in," I said. The looks that Noel and Mario shot my way told me this was not a joking matter.

"There's something else," Mario said. He handed me an envelope. "We're all invited back to Congress."

It was Fort Santiago all over again. The media had picked up the ball and ran with it as far as their imagination allowed. Treasure stories always sold well. The facts didn't get in the way before and they didn't this time either. So when our car pulled up to Congress that morning we were once again overwhelmed with reporters and television cameras. Still not used to this, every time I said, "No comment," I felt important, until I remembered that if they didn't believe my story then the next stop could be jail.

We all sweated under the television lights as we took turns reading our prepared statements and then submitted to the questioning of the committee. The questions weren't that hard and the panel was polite. But it was obvious that a few of them believed the media hype and were convinced that we had four and a half billion bucks hidden somewhere.

The deposition that started it all was, under scrutiny, ridiculous. According to it, we used three army trucks on three different nights to move the treasure. This was true. We had used those vehicles, but it was a practice drill to determine the best route to the Central Bank once we recovered. The palace was aware of this drill and our efforts to formalize our recovery procedures. The logistics required in taking 340 tons of gold out of our hole, which was fifty meters deep, and then transporting it to a secure place for safekeeping were complicated enough without trying to steal it. Besides it didn't take a genius to figure out that three trucks making one trip at night for three nights could not haul that much gold.

In addition to Noel, Mario, and I, the military commander of the region where the bridge site was located was also questioned.

He was Foja's commanding officer, and provided our security and the trucks we used. A no-nonsense colonel loyal to the president, he obviously could not have had anything to do with such a scheme.

What really galled us was that we could not face our accuser. Clyde had stated in the deposition that he would return to the Philippines with more evidence about our theft. He must have changed his mind. He didn't come back for the hearing, and he didn't offer any more evidence.

The hearing took all morning and part of the afternoon. When the panel finished with their questions we were free to go. There were no arrests and no indictments. We all shook hands, smiled for the photographers, and went our separate ways. One more potentially explosive episode was defused. Another day in the life of the *Americano* treasure hunter was over and he wasn't dead or in prison, so it was a good day albeit a wasted one.

The intrigues were endless. There was always at least a story or two going around about a recovery we made on this mountain or in that jungle. People were constantly using my name, either to raise money for non-existent projects or to get access to treasure hunting sites.

The gold scams continued. Some were funny and some were not. An American by the name of Arvey Duane Drown was picked up by the Communist New People's Army in Cagayan province in northern Luzon in October 1990. He was carrying a million pesos (US$50,000.00) in cash. The Filipinos were released and one of them, the driver of the jeepney vehicle Drown had rented, reported the incident. He said Drown had been approached by a Filipino who claimed to be a geodetic engineer. The engineer convinced Drown to come with him and bring the cash. It was unclear whether they were going to a treasure site or to purchase gold bars already recovered, another popular scam. The driver said that about twenty men claiming to be NPA intercepted the jeepney and took them hostage. The next day the Filipinos were released but Drown was held. After twenty months of tedious negotiations he was finally released on 30 June 1992.

That kind of scam had been around for a long time. Another engineer, a friend of George's by the name of Joel, had a friend called Manny. He claimed a tribal chieftain in Mindanao had shown him some gold in a cave. Mindanao was the largest island in the Philippines located about 800 kilometers (496 miles) south of Manila. The chief wanted to sell it and would offer a large discount.

George made the offer to my group. After discussing the matter with Noel we agreed to bring the chief here, along with one bar of gold for assaying, and provide security for his trip. The chief turned down our offer, so we decided against it. The security involved in transporting gold from there to Manila was just too difficult, and we couldn't involve the military without showing proof of at least one bar.

About every two of three months Clyde would return to the Philippines and snoop around to see what we were doing. At the same time he would catch up on the latest treasure hunt gossip to find out who was digging where. Sometimes, if he were busy, he would ask his father in law to go. It was on one of those trips, in August 1989, that he heard about the chief's offer. He returned to the states and told Clyde.

Clyde jumped on the offer. A friend of his knew James "Bo" Gritz. Gritz was a retired Green Beret lieutenant colonel who was a legend in Vietnam but more recently he was known for his work involving prisoners of war. Gritz was asked to come to Manila and set up their security. He was busy at the time but he agreed to help by providing one of his associates, Gary Goldman, an ex-Green Beret captain.

The first week of September they returned to Manila, met up with Joel, Manny, and three others — two more Filipino friends of Joel and Manny, and a nameless American friend of Clyde's — and the group left for Mindanao. Their destination was Cagayan de Oro City in Misamis Oriental province. (This city is not connected with Cagayan province. They are 1,200 kilometers [744 miles] apart.)

There Manny introduced them to Ruth. She was the chief's contact. After staying overnight she and the team took a bus and headed south to a town called Malaybalay, the capital of Bukidnon province. One of the team recalled the trip: "It was like a scene out of Indiana Jones. A hot, dusty two-hour ride in an old bus, with people, chickens, and pigs on top and hanging off the sides."

Malaybalay would be their base, Ruth said. She instructed them to wait there while she arranged a meeting. They rented some rooms and waited. There wasn't much else to do. It was the rainy season. It rained everyday. Ruth finally returned and took Goldman, Joel, and Manny to meet the tribal people and their chief. Clyde decided to remain in the background.

The chief was not exactly the epitome of a tribal leader. A leathery old man who spoke no English, few people in the world cared less for riches, or so it seemed. He wasn't that anxious to sell. There were a lot of meetings, held mostly at night and lasting until the wee hours of the morning. It kept raining, and the meetings went on for three weeks. Goldman and Joel became the negotiators. At each meeting they asked to see the gold and were turned down, but finally the chief agreed.

Goldman and Joel rented a truck. The chief and his tribesman pointed the way, and they drove south. For about an hour the road was passable until they passed through a small village. For the next thirty minutes the road got gradually worse, degenerating into ruts which were barely passable. Then they turned off that road onto an even smaller path and drove another three kilometers to the base of a mountain. They got out and walked about five meters through some trees. All of a sudden they were standing before a cave. "Because of the heavy underbrush you couldn't see it until you were right on it," one of the group commented later.

The chief led them inside. It was dark but he seemed to know every twist and turn. Finally he halted, said something, and pointed over in the corner. A few meters away were stacked some bars. They were difficult to see clearly but they had the burnished sheen of old gold. After a few moments the chief turned and headed back out of the cave. Everyone quickly followed not wanting to be left behind in this dark maze.

Back in town the group was told about the cave and the gold. Everyone was excited and anxious to conclude a deal. At the next meeting the chief agreed to sell fifteen bars, at six kilograms per bar, for five million pesos ($250,000), but there could be no inspection of the gold beforehand. Depending on the purity and the price of gold at the time, ninety kilograms could be worth fifteen million pesos. Clyde accepted the chief's offer.

The group jumped into action. They purchased a cattle truck and compartments were welded underneath to hide the gold. The group checked their equipment, which included night vision goggles and Armalite rifles. At the appointed time they all piled into the truck and drove to the meeting place. There they picked up some of the chief's men, who directed them to the site. As soon as they arrived they were informed the sale was off.

They returned to Malaybalay wondering what went wrong. Later they found out. The chief was expecting three men, unarmed, not seven armed to the teeth. It took another week of discussions to convince the chief that the group meant no harm, that the weapons were for the protection of the gold they were buying. Finally the chief gave in. The group met some of his men, who took them to the site. They arrived around midnight.

They didn't go to the cave this time. Instead they were led through the trees and underbrush to a hole in the ground. Looking down they could see one of the chief's men. Stacked off to the side were the bars. The excitement grew as the group set up the tripod they had brought and lowered the bag down the hole. They let out twelve meters of rope before the bag hit the floor. They yelled down to the man to send up five bars and they would throw down a bag containing ₱1.5 million ($75,000). For some reason he hesitated and wouldn't load the bars in the bag.

Just then one of the group which had been posted as a lookout ran up and said, "Two soldiers are coming." Everyone scattered and hid. The soldiers walked up to the hole, looked down, talked to each other in whispers for a few minutes, and then walked away. This was strange, considering they were out in the middle of nowhere.

When the group reformed at the cave the chief's men that had acted as guides were gone, but the man was still in the hole. Now there was a sense of urgency in everyone's voice bordering on panic. "Let's hurry," one said. "There may be more soldiers out there." "Yeah," said another. "This could be an ambush."

Goldman yelled down in the hole, "Move your ass out of the way." Then he threw two of the bags, each containing ₱1.5 million into the hole. "Now load the gold," he yelled. And waited. And waited. And waited.

"I'm going down," said Goldman. He was lowered into the hole. The man was gone but the bars were still there. They were put in the bag and pulled up. Then Goldman was pulled back up. As soon as he got to the top he said, "Let's get out of here."

The bars were loaded on the truck. Everyone jumped in and the truck took off. As soon as they were on the way someone told him, "That can't be gold. It isn't heavy enough."

The next day Joel and Manny took some filings from the bars and left for Manila to have them assayed. They never came back or called to give the group the results. The rest of the bars were assayed and found to be brass. They wanted Ruth to find the chief for them but she had disappeared also. Then they heard the colonel in charge of the local military detachment was looking for them, so they packed and left hurriedly.

Later Goldman took some men back to the area, found the cave, and explored it. It was two and a half miles long and had nine openings. None were visible from the road. The surrounding trees and brush camouflaged the openings very well. No gold or anything else of value was found, and the chief and his people had disappeared. At first Goldman and Clyde thought Ruth, Joel, and Manny were in on the scam, but later decided they weren't. They were just too embarrassed to face their friends. The old chief, on the other hand, was wiser in the ways of the world than anybody could have ever imagined. Clyde was out three million pesos ($150,000) but at least he wasn't kidnapped or hurt.

The incident with Congress did not seem to bother my financiers. If anything it convinced them that there really was a treasure and I just had to keep looking. Noel and Mario joined me in the search, not as full-time treasure hunters but as advisers. They had access to the myriad civilian and government authorities needed in order to operate legally. A successful recovery would entail a lot more than digging a hole, finding it, and getting it out of the ground. Obtaining a government or private permit required some legal footwork and coordination with the government authorities. The service and maintenance of our sensitive equipment required access to the state university and government institutions. Security requirements had to be provided or approved by the military. The removal of the treasure from the site to the Central Bank had to be coordinated with that institution.

For every legitimate treasure hunting group who followed the rules, there were a hundred illegitimate ones who disregarded all advice and did things their own way. The government's attitude seemed to be live and let live. If a recovery were successful and they found out, then they would step in and claim all of it as a penalty to that group for not doing it legally, they claimed. The authorities would intervene beforehand, however, if a complaint were registered or an accident occurred. Usually it was an accident that called attention to an illegal excavation.

The stories usually appeared on page five or six of the local newspapers. Only if Americans were involved would the story be moved to the first page. Every week or so they appeared to announce "Cave-in Buries Two," or "Five Found Dead of Asphyxiation." Somebody had been buried alive in a tunnel under a house, a pit in the middle of the jungle, or a cave on the side of a mountain. Another version of the same story might tell of finding several people dead in a tunnel from breathing the fumes put out by a gas-operated water pump. Whether it was improper ventilation or lack of shoring, ignorance more than anything else killed a lot of innocent people.

What most of them didn't realize was that digging a hole was a dangerous undertaking. Anything deeper than a man required at least the advice of a mining engineer and geologist, and it usually required more. A ten-meter hole that required shoring could easily cost $25,000. And if the treasure were buried deep enough to lie below the water table the hole was even trickier, and demanded more expertise and even more financing. But the rewards were just too great not to take a chance. That was the problem. The treasure hunters could not see the danger. They only saw the gold, silver, diamonds, and jewels. Or, rather sadly, they imagined they saw them.

And there were the con men. They were everywhere with various schemes. Some brandished maps; others showed old rocks as markers; and still others carried photographs of gold bars stacked beside a newspaper showing a recent date. Some of these photos were ridiculous. One color picture showed bars that were painted a bright canary yellow, definitely not the color of gold. Another had a skinny little man holding up a fifty kilogram bar with one hand and the newspaper with the other. Now that was a strong fellow. As far as could be determined, there was no major group controlling these schemes, just a lot of people running around with their own secret agenda looking for gullible, greedy foreigners. With that in mind I wondered if the eye-witnesses Pedro, Pol, and Ben had their own hidden agenda. Why hadn't they ever found anything?

The evidence indicated they saw some treasure buried. If they didn't then they had found a way to beat the system, to fabricate evidence, and even fake the truth under hypnosis. Two lines of Sir Walter Scott rolled over and over in my head:

> *Oh, what a tangled web we weave,*
> *When first we practice to deceive*

In May 1991 David Castro, PCGG chairman, announced that some gold which had been smuggled out of the Philippines by Marcos had been found in Switzerland.

At first the newspapers reported there were 300 bars but Castro corrected them and said that there were 325 tons, not bars, valued at $3.5 billion. He added a little more information, saying that the bars bore the Central Bank of the Philippines hallmark, and were kept in the storage vault of a bonded warehouse managed by Union Bank at the Kloten airport near Zurich. The man responsible for this discovery was an intelligence agent of the PCGG whom Castro would only identify as RJ. The media now had a mystery man to write about, and they did so with gusto.

RJ wasn't that mysterious and was even quite well known over at the Philippine Plaza. That hotel was a haven for treasure hunters, heavy breathers, and gold groupies of all sorts. On any given morning there might be a half-dozen mixed groups of foreigners and Filipinos sitting around different tables drinking coffee and talking about buried treasure as if they were discussing the weather. Reiner Jacobi was familiar to most of them. He stood 1.75 meters tall, weighed seventy-eight kilos, and had blue eyes and salt and pepper hair.

Jacobi's first contact with the Philippine government was Vicente Reyes, the Philippine consul general in Hong Kong. Jacobi had provided some documents about the Marcos gold to Reyes in 1989. When Colonel Cecilio Penilla, his military attache, delivered the documents to Castro in Manila, Jacobi accompanied him. He met Castro for the first time that December and offered his services for free.

Jacobi claimed that he had come to Manila to try and gather information about 3,000 tons of gold that had disappeared from the Central Bank during Marcos' time. The bank had never reported more than fifty tons as international reserves, so where Jacobi obtained his information isn't known. In 1988 the PCGG, in a third amendment to its racketeering case against Marcos, alleged that 800,000 troy ounces was diverted from the Central Bank reserves in 1973, but that was less than twenty-three tons.

Jacobi posed as a gold buyer. His European accent was perfect for this image. He stayed for almost a year. George Wortinger was staying there also. Eventually he and Jacobi met and became partners. He introduced Jacobi to several prospective sellers but they all turned out to be heavy breathers. Then one afternoon in November 1990 Jacobi introduced George to someone — the infamous Mama Mary.

A close — some said intimate — friend of Marcos since she was a teenager, Maria I. Gosilatar was now in her fifties. Imelda called her the "Midnight Lady" for her propensity to visit Marcos at unusual hours. Everybody else called her Mama Mary, and she claimed to know a lot about Marcos' gold. She said the "Blue Book" was once in her possession but she had to give it back.

The Blue Book allegedly contained a record of all the Marcos gold shipments to various banks and their account numbers. Mama Mary had talked to a number of gold buyers, real and otherwise, about this but thus far had not entered into a serious transaction. Now it was Jacobi's turn to court her. One day she brought along a friend, Adoracion Edralin Lopez. Lopez, a relative of Marcos, had an interesting story to tell.

She claimed to be one of the three signatories when gold was deposited in the bonded warehouse at Kloten airport in 1983. The other two signatories were a Filipino and a foreigner, both living outside Switzerland, but she wouldn't divulge their names. The gold was deposited at the airport so it wouldn't have to be registered at customs. She said that Marcos had rented the space for ten years.

Marcos died in September 1989. Lopez flew to Zurich sometime in 1990 to inquire about the gold. That's when she found out her name had been removed as signatory without her permission. Her objections at the bank fell on deaf ears. She knew the power of the people she was dealing with so she came home to Manila to try and think of a way to reclaim her rights. Eventually she and Mama Mary crossed paths.

Mama Mary took her to Jacobi. Lopez told her story and even described the vault. She told them how the gold was laid out and, in one tantalizing detail, said that passengers arriving at the airport on Concourse B were literally walking over the gold. Jacobi took her to Castro and she agreed to help the PCGG. Castro in turn promised to grant her and Marcos' heirs their share if they were able to recover.

In early 1991 Jacobi, Castro, and Lopez flew to Switzerland together. On 5 February, in the Zurich office of Doctor Franz Reichenbach, one of the Philippine government's lawyers in Switzerland, Lopez issued a Deed of Assignment to Castro. It stated that the gold was in vault number 88-RW-RP, and that the account number was G-72570367-d-UBS.

Jacobi continued to assist Castro and reported that Imelda was hiding $1.3 billion in two secret bank accounts in Credit Suisse. The bank denied this. Until then Swiss banking officials had only identified $350 million in Swiss bank accounts suspected to be Marcos' money, and only $16 million had been returned in an out of court settlement with Roberto Benedicto, an associate of Marcos. The Philippine government already had knowledge of sixty-three corporate, seventeen foundation, and twenty-three individual accounts belonging to Marcos, his family, and associates. The two secret accounts Jacobi alleged to were not part of these.

The PCGG requested a freeze on these new accounts identified by Jacobi. The Swiss district court inquired as to how they obtained this information. Jacobi claimed that he had a computer expert who had cracked the bank's computer codes. In Switzerland this really wasn't the right thing to say. The court ordered an investigation into the matter. According to George, a computer expert called "Fritz" had received help from a disgruntled employee of Credit Suisse, who provided the daily bank codes. There was no way to confirm Jacobi's or George's claims, however.

While this was going on Jacobi asked Castro to officially engage him as an agent of the PCGG. In May he was appointed "as consultant on intelligence and security matters related to the Marcoses in Europe." There was no background check.

On 11 July, Jacobi was arrested in Munich, Germany. Fritz and another associate were arrested in Zurich on the same day. All were charged with violating Swiss banking secrecy laws. Jacobi was freed a week later by a German court when it was ruled that the charge for which he was arrested was not a crime under German laws, so he could not be extradited back to Switzerland. Fritz and his associate were also released. Jacobi left for Hong Kong shortly afterward.

After the arrest in Munich, Jacobi's name was released to the public. Castro was publicly criticized for hiring him. The other PCGG commissioners disavowed the matter, claiming that Jacobi was hired by Castro personally and not the PCGG. Then Peter Cosandey, the district attorney for the canton of Zurich, announced that he wouldn't provide any further legal assistance to PCGG because Castro used illegal methods to obtain information. There were calls for Castro's resignation but President Aquino said she had no intention of accepting it if he resigned. Under pressure, Castro terminated Jacobi on 22 July. Eventually Cosandey resumed his cooperation with the Philippines.

Things died down for awhile. Then on 27 July, Interpol, acting on a request by the U.S. Drug Enforcement Agency, arrested Jacobi in Hong Kong. The U.S. government requested his extradition to the states. He and an associate had been indicted in Miami for conspiring to import and distribute drugs.

Jacobi decried his innocence. He was no drug trafficker. To the contrary, he helped the U.S. Bureau of Customs catch a man, Dennis Marks, who had transported ten tons of hashish into Spain. He did this while working as an undercover agent for Customs. He said the DEA had a turf war with Customs. His arrest was the result of this vendetta, he claimed.

Some nasty rumors were floating around Manila and Hong Kong during this time, that Imelda was behind all this. It was no secret that she had hired two former employees of the CIA. They were masterminding the persecution of Jacobi, the rumors went. The situation did fit the pattern of past incidents during the Marcos era. If someone crossed Marcos or Imelda back then, the least that person could expect was the total, and public, ruination of their reputation. No concrete evidence could be found to substantiate that Imelda had anything to do with Jacobi's arrest. Jacobi compounded his problems, however, by talking to the media.

He gave an interview to the Hong Kong press, and a television crew from Channel Seven in Manila were sent over. Jacobi said he was forty-nine years old and a Swiss born Australian. He was the half-brother of Klaus Jacobi, deputy chief of the Swiss Foreign Ministry but they grew up separately. He was adopted by an American general who worked in intelligence. He admitted occasionally working undercover with the CIA. He was a licensed private investigator, and had his own security firm in British Columbia.

That was Jacobi's background, according to Jacobi. And almost all of it was false. According to the DEA's files he was born in West Germany, not Switzerland, on 24 June 1942. He carried two passports — one Australian, N314062, and one Canadian, K773292. He also had several aliases — Rolf Gerhard Koenig, Reinhardt Koenig, Rex Johnson, Dirk F. Stoffberg, and Herbert Solomon.

A spokesman for the Swiss foreign ministry said that Jacobi's claim that he was related to Minister Klaus Jacobi was "complete nonsense." And the solicitor general's office in Victoria had a similar comment, replying that there was no licensed private investigator by the name of Reiner Jacobi in British Columbia.

Jacobi was also confused about his role in the arrest of Dennis Howard Marks. A combined task force of agents from the DEA, Customs, IRS, Naval Investigative Service, and the U.S. Attorney's office was formed and led by DEA Agent Greg Lovato. He code-named the project Operation Eclectic. Scotland Yard and Her Majesty's Customs were involved. The Spanish police also assisted when Marks was arrested at his home near Palma on the Spanish island of Majorca in the Mediterranean on 25 July 1988.

Marks fought extradition for over a year but he was finally brought to the states. After he saw the evidence he pleaded guilty to one count of conspiracy and one count under the RICO (Racketeering Influenced Corrupt Organizations) statute. On 13 July 1990 he was sentenced to twenty-five years in prison.

Jacobi had played no role in this masterful piece of multinational police work. To the contrary, he was a friend of Marks. When Marks was arrested the first time, and tried for drug smuggling in London in 1981, Jacobi helped fabricate his defense. Marks was found not guilty. A book was written about this called *High Time — The Shocking Life and Times of Howard Marks*. In it Marks' bragged that he was too smart to get caught. Those remarks made Marks a marked man.

Jacobi did work as a confidential informant for the U.S. Bureau of Customs. Lawrence Ladage, then Special Agent in Charge of Customs at Portland, Oregon, was his benefactor. He claimed that Jacobi had an impressive track record of providing accurate information on European terrorists and the illegal export of high-tech equipment from the states. It was during this period as an informant that Jacobi and an associate, Thomas Sunde, bragged on numerous occasions that they worked for the CIA. To enhance this image both took to wearing blue bomber jackets emblazoned with a discreet seal of the United States. During Operation Eclectic, Jacobi and Sunde wanted to join the investigation. Customs didn't mind but the DEA did because they suspected they were spying for Marks. This disagreement did cause a row between the two agencies. But Grand Juries don't return indictments based on inter-agency feuds.

Now Jacobi's credibility was in serious jeopardy, but Castro still believed in his agent. He decided it was time to go public with some more information, and called a press conference.

He produced documents showing the serial numbers of gold bars which were released by the Central Bank's minting plant for shipment in 1983 and 1984. These bars were not part of the Central Bank's official inventory, he announced, and he showed a copy of the receipt for the bars signed by Tomas Rodriguez, operations manager of Tamaraw Security Agency. Rodriguez had come forward and admitted that Tamaraw, which was owned by Ver, Marcos' former Chief of Staff, had picked up the gold and taken it to the airport. The serial numbers of these bars matched those stored in the warehouse in Switzerland. Not only that, Castro said, he had met one of the pilots who flew the bars to Switzerland after the assassination of Ninoy Aquino in 1983.

Castro had actually known about the existence of those gold bars before Jacobi and Lopez had entered the scene. The first leak about those shipments came from the wife of an army officer close to Ver, who knew Guillermo Carague, minister of the budget and management under President Aquino. The lady had provided the Tamaraw documents to Carague, who turned them over to Adolfo Azcuna, Aquino's legal adviser. Azcuna, in turn, gave them to Castro. They remained in the PCGG files until some individuals approached Castro with copies of the same documents seeking a reward.

They had one additional piece of evidence — Rodriguez himself. He admitted his role in the matter, and testified to the authenticity of the documents. Now Castro knew that a smoking gun existed, or rather smoking bars, but he didn't know where they were. Then, as if on cue, Jacobi appeared one day with Lopez.

Lopez' credibility was questioned when she had a dispute with the law a month after Castro went public with her name. She was arrested in Manila by the National Bureau of Investigation and charged with writing bad checks. After posting bail she went into hiding. She sent a message to Castro, claiming that she was being harassed and pursued by friends of Marcos and Imelda who wanted to do her harm. Castro promised to protect her.

Lopez' fear for her life was justified, as was Rodriguez,' who was in hiding also. There were too many instances of people who wound up dead or missing after criticizing the Marcoses. Doctor Potenciano Baccay was one of Marcos' kidney specialists. On a trip to the states in 1985 he had revealed to journalists of the *Pittsburgh Press* that Marcos had kidney transplants in August 1983 and November 1984. Marcos always denied rumors of his ill health. After Baccay returned to the Philippines he was abducted at his house late one night. His body was found later with nineteen stab wounds. The killers were never caught.

Primitivo Mijares disappeared in January 1977 after defecting in the U.S. and publicly criticizing Marcos and Imelda. Five months later his fifteen year old son disappeared and was later found murdered.

At Imelda's recent trial in New York several witnesses talked of their own experiences with Imelda and her friends. An employee of Sotheby's International Realty, Thomas Bryan, testified that in 1982 Imelda was interested in purchasing the Leslie Samuels' apartment at 660 Park Avenue in New York along with its contents of art works and furnishings. To hide her ownership a friend, Gliceria Tantoco, tried to buy it, but the cooperative's board rejected her. When this hit the newspapers the next day Tantoco called Bryan. "She said," Bryan related to the court, "that if any additional information becomes public, I should fear for myself and my family."

Another witness, former Philippine National Bank vice president Oscar Cariño, testified that, when Imelda visited New York, he was the one who had to take $100,000 in cash to Imelda four or five times each trip. When asked why he cooperated, Cariño admitted Imelda had paid him commissions to facilitate the release of funds. But he said he did it not for financial reward but for fear of being "finished off" if he resisted Imelda.

Amnesty International documented thousands of cases of "human rights abuses" during the Marcos reign, but the term did not adequately describe the emotional impact of a veiled threat or warning made by Marcos, Imelda, or their associates. How many other witnesses were out there wanting to help the government but were just too afraid?

Like the dog that didn't bark in a Sherlock Holmes mystery, the witness that didn't testify at Imelda's trial spoke volumes. In Europe, Gliceria Tantoco finally reached an agreement with the U.S. Justice Department. She would cooperate and testify against Imelda. In return certain charges pertaining to her and her husband would be dropped. Her testimony was important. One of Kashoggi's lawyers said, "Had Mrs. Tantoco stepped into the courtroom, she could have changed the complete face of this case for both Adnan and Mrs. Marcos. That's how vital a witness she can be for the prosecution."

Tantoco was about to board a plane for New York to testify when she received the news that a kidnapping attempt on her grandchild had occurred in Manila. That did it. She fled, and went into hiding. When chief prosecutor Charles LaBella was asked who may have planned the kidnapping, he replied, "I will leave that to your imagination. It has to be a party who knew she was going to testify and who knew her testimony could have nailed those two defendants."

The PCGG filed an application for legal assistance to verify the existence of the gold deposits in the vault at Kloten. In the application they estimated that as much as 5,000 tons might be stored there. Union Bank denied that they held such a deposit. The district attorney said this was an old rumor that had prompted an official inquiry during the 1980s which yielded no evidence of gold smuggled out of the Philippines by Marcos. Besides, he said, "that amount was beyond the capacity of the Philippines to produce." That remark seemed an odd rebuttal to the PCGG's request.

Except for the Union Bank denial, the evidence seemed irrefutable. The bars did exist, were not part of the Central Bank's inventory, were taken out of the Central Bank and flown to Switzerland, and the serial numbers matched those at Union Bank. That sounded like an airtight case. Simple? Never. Not in the mystical world of Swiss high finance and legal maneuvering that could confuse a rocket scientist.

Attorney Antonio Coronel, Imelda's lawyer in the Philippines, attacked immediately. That gold doesn't belong to the Central Bank, he told the PCGG. It came from the Central Bank mint, not the treasury, and it was privately minted. The gold never belonged to the treasury, so the government has no basis for demanding it back. Besides, Coronel said, "all this talk about intelligence officers is pure baloney." He said that the information on the gold could have been obtained from one of the witnesses at Imelda's trial.

So what, the Philippine government countered. If the Central Bank refined it then where did it come from. And besides, the burden of proof of ownership rested with Imelda. Hmmmm, exclaimed the public.

Hong Kong refused to extradite Jacobi. He was subsequently released, but he was still considered a fugitive by the U.S. government.

The battle over the 325 tons continued. It seemed odd that no one ever reported it missing. That much gold didn't disappear from some bank vault without the word getting around. But what if it had disappeared a half-century ago?

On Sunday, 4 November, the circus came to town. That's how the palace described Imelda's return to the Philippines. Tax evasion and other charges had been filed against her by the solicitor general's office, and the government allowed her to return to answer the charges. She had always said that she would come back, and she did. She wasn't allowed to bring her husband's body home. Still it was a triumphant return of sorts, after the not guilty verdict in New York.

She rented sixty rooms of the Philippine Plaza Hotel for her entourage, which included four of her American lawyers, twenty American security guards, and several members of a Washington-based public relations firm. "I come home penniless," she tearfully said on arrival, and then repaired to her own suite which cost $2,000 a day.

Two months later she declared her intention to run for president. She lost. The people were not ready for another Marcos. But during her whirlwind campaign she admitted that Marcos had recovered some buried treasure while he was president. She never said how much.

CHAPTER SIXTEEN

Enrique Zobel

On 2 January 1942 the Japanese army entered Manila. The populace, in shock, stood mutely by as the invaders occupied the city. At the Polo Club along Dewey Boulevard, soldiers took one look at the polo ponies and conscripted them for their own use. As the handsome animals were led out of the stables, the members stood by mutely. All except one, a fifteen year old boy. When he saw two of his favorite ponies being led away he tried to stop the soldiers and take them back. The soldiers reacted by picking up the boy and taking him to Fort Santiago.

Things didn't look too good. It was a time when Filipinos were executed for the least offense in order to set an example. The boy was questioned by an officer who, rather than being hostile, was amused by his spunk and daring. But the officer didn't believe anyone with light skin and blue eyes could be a Filipino. After the boy explained his ancestry he was released. That's how Enrique Zobel met the infamous Lt. Colonel Seichi Ohta, head of the *Kempei Tai.*

Later Ohta summoned the young Zobel and asked about his father, who was imprisoned at Capas, Tarlac. Zobel doesn't recall what he actually said to Ohta. He only remembers Ohta's reply. "Okay, you go and pick him up. Use my car."

Zobel, scion of the Roxas-Ayala-Zobel clan, smiled when he recalled the incident and admitted it was a little foolish. But it only underscored the remarkable life of a man who made a career of defying the odds and winning. His ancestor, Domingo Roxas, founded the family's first trading company in the Philippines in 1834. Today it's a billion dollar empire.

By the time Marcos came to power, Zobel was one of the richest men in the Philippines. He wasn't a crony and he had not made his fortune by raping and pillaging the country. To the contrary, he was a man of enormous vision whose success came from hard work and astute business decisions.

Short, stocky, and competitive, Zobel's first love was polo. One of his polo-playing friends was the Sultan of Brunei, the tiny oil-rich nation to the south. Zobel lived in style on a 650 hectare (1,600 acres) ranch, Hacienda Bigaa, 97 kilometers (60 miles) south of Manila where he kept sixty polo ponies. Driving through his mango orchards one might encounter a herd of exotic Rusa deer, a gift from the Sultan of Johore.

Zobel had rich and powerful friends all over the world. That may have been why Marcos left him alone. Other wealthy and successful businessmen weren't so lucky. If Marcos saw something he liked, especially if it made money, he usually took it.

Zobel could have played the role of landed gentry and polo player but that just wasn't his style. He was an aggressive and successful businessman. Chairman of the board, president, and director of dozens of corporations, his financial and managerial prowess could especially be seen in the Bank of the Philippine Islands, which he took over in the mid-seventies and built into one of the nation's largest financial institutions. He also built Ayala Corporation into a billion-dollar real estate and industrial conglomerate.

By the early eighties Marcos and his cronies had effectively destroyed the Philippine economy. Zobel agonized over what was happening to the country. Upset at such heavy-handed tactics, he eventually resigned from both Ayala Corporation and the bank, and began concentrating his efforts on businesses outside the Philippines through another of his companies, Ayala International.

In 1985 he told the *New York Times*, "If you had money to invest in Southeast Asia, the Philippines is the last place I would tell you to put it now." He was one of the few that could say something like that and not risk the ire of Marcos, who knew how influential Zobel was. Six months later, Zobel supported him in the 1986 snap election. But this time powerful friends couldn't help.

Tragedy struck in May 1991. Zobel was thrown from his horse while playing polo in Spain, and was paralyzed from the neck down. In June 1992 he called a press conference in Manila. Now sixty-five years old and a quadriplegic, he wanted to make an announcement. He dropped a bombshell.

He said that Marcos had shown him some gold certificates in 1988. The value was estimated at $35 billion, and Marcos wanted to give most of it back to the Filipino people. They had worked to set up a foundation for this purpose but Marcos died in September 1989 before the papers could be signed.

There had been other similar public disclosures before the Zobel announcement, but never from a man so prominent worldwide. And never this large an amount.

In March 1988 Marcos secretly offered the Philippine government $15 billion if he could return. President Aquino turned it down and made a counter offer which Marcos never responded to.

Four months later, in July 1988, Marcos made another offer. This time the amount was $5 billion. The offer was leaked to the newspapers and Marcos reacted by denying the whole thing.

After Marcos died in 1989 everything was either forgotten or filed under "What Might Have Been" for history enthusiasts. Zobel made his disclosure then. Something could still be done, he said, if the Marcos heirs would own up.

·

When Marcos arrived in the states in February 1986, he was shocked to find out President Reagan would not or could not protect him. His legal mind told him that as a former head of state he should be immune to litigation. But his political savvy told him it would be unwise to hang around to argue the point. Quietly he put out the word. Find another safe haven.

It was an exercise in frustration. His powerful connections in other parts of the world could no longer help. One by one the replies came back, couched in diplomatese, that he wasn't welcome. Spain, Mexico, Singapore, Panama, Ghana all said no. Tonga and Paraguay were more receptive, but it was obvious they were more interested in his money than in him or his family. There was nowhere to go.

The legal battles started almost immediately. It was an emotional roller coaster. On 5 June a judge ordered that U.S.

Customs release Marcos' money, jewelry, and belongings. The family rejoiced, but a timely government appeal prevented their release. Then the attorney general in New York announced that Marcos and Imelda were being investigated for alleged violations of the RICO law. The Philippine government followed suit by filing several civil cases in the U.S. Subpoenas began to arrive. Ver decided it was time to leave. He said goodbye to Marcos and slipped away one night in June, flying out of the country on a newly purchased passport.

On Sunday, 6 July, in Manila heavily armed Marcos loyalists, led by Arturo Tolentino, Marcos' vice president elect, occupied the Manila Hotel. He declared himself acting president in Marcos' absence. He had hoped that this would spark a revolt across the country and that millions would rise up and demand Marcos' return. An excited Marcos was constantly on the phone with Tolentino keeping abreast of developments. But the millions never materialized and the revolt fizzled.

Marcos became a natural target for con men. They came from all over suggesting grandiose schemes for his return to the Philippines. Of course they asked for huge sums of money. Colonel Dulay came in August 1986 with two former CIA employees. They made a lot of promises and asked for a lot of money. Neither were delivered. Then two retired Philippine military colonels showed up in October with a proposal costing P400 million. They were shunted aside also, but others with bigger and better, and costlier, schemes replaced them, and on and on *ad nauseam*.

On 30 September 1986 Marcos was questioned by Philippine and American lawyers representing the Philippine government. He took the Fifth Amendment (the right against self-incrimination) 197 times. The next day Imelda followed suit, taking the Fifth 200 times. Both had to be worried about all the documents found at the palace and the new evidence gathered by the PCGG. Despite having the best lawyers that money could buy it was obvious that sooner or later they would wind up in court.

Nothing had gone right in 1987. In January they were subpoenaed to testify in the investigation of kickbacks paid in the sale of weapons to the Philippine military. They fought it, claiming Marcos was too sick to travel. Finally they agreed to produce documents in their possession without having to go before the Grand Jury.

The military coup had failed in January also, and the 707 was found on the runway waiting to fly Marcos and his entourage back to the Philippines. Even more embarrassing were the tape recordings of Hirschfield, which caught Marcos shopping for weapons and planning another coup in May.

Marcos had kept an avenue of approach open to Aquino but it seemed more a ploy than anything else. The first legitimate plan to return to the Philippines was hatched in 1986 by three Filipinos in Hawaii — Francisco S. Ugale and Alfonso Adeva, businessmen, and Jiamil Dianalan, a Muslim Filipino who had served in parliament under Marcos. It was code-named Sheraton Project. Sheraton was given added prestige in 1987 when Hawaiian Senator Daniel Inouye agreed to meet with Marcos after the negotiating points had been agreed upon. Aquino's cousin, Congressman Emigdio Tanjuatco, Jr., acted as mediator. He finally flew to Honolulu and met with Marcos on 21 January 1988, but Marcos ended these discussions shortly afterward and began to deal with Francisco Sumulong and Roquito Ablan.

About this time Marcos must have realized he was running out of time. All his plans had come apart and the New York Grand Jury indictment was looming ever larger on the horizon. There was a chance he could become the first head of state to be convicted of criminal charges in the U.S. He decided he had better work out a settlement with Aquino to end all this litigation and go home, no matter what it cost.

In February, about the time IPM commenced digging for treasure at Fort Santiago, Sumulong and Ablan visited Marcos, who surprised them by saying he was prepared to make a compromise agreement. In March they returned to Honolulu and Marcos presented his offer. If he and his family were allowed to go home, he would give $15 billion to the Philippine government. Five billion dollars was to be spent for infrastructure projects in the Philippines; $5 billion would be used to reduce the nation's foreign debt, which was $27 billion at the time; and $5 billion would be given to Aquino's family for the suffering they endured under Marcos during martial law.

They returned to Manila and presented the offer. Aquino was receptive at first, according to Sumulong. But when the family met to discuss it they turned the offer down and instead made a counteroffer. This was relayed to Marcos but he didn't respond. Neither Sumulong nor Ablan would say what the counteroffer was. But they did say that Marcos admitted the $15 billion was still in the Philippines and only he knew where it was hidden. Sumulong was later quoted in the newspaper as saying, "*Sayang, napakinabangan na natin sana 'yung pera.* (It was a pity. We could have used the money.)"

This was the second time Marcos admitted that he still had gold buried in the Philippines. He mentioned on the Hirschfield tapes that $14 billion in gold was still buried there.

On 27 April, Marcos and Imelda were subpoenaed to produce their fingerprints and other items. They appealed. On 11 May, Marcos' mother, Doña Josepha, died. Marcos appealed to Aquino on humanitarian grounds and asked that he be allowed to attend her funeral. He was turned down.

On 22 June in Washington, the Center for Democracy hosted a breakfast for five Philippine legislators. Ablan and Sumulong were in attendance. They told Professor Allen Weinstein that Marcos would return substantial assets to the Philippines if he were allowed to go home, and asked Weinstein if he would help. He agreed to assist, so Marcos wrote a letter to him dated 11 July, stating that he would give $5 billion to the government if the following conditions were met: 1) He, his family, and his delegation could return to the Philippines and Ilocos Norte (his home province); 2) He and his family would have diplomatic and political immunity; 3) The Philippine government would drop all cases presently pending against him in the Philippines and any other country; 4) He would agree not to engage in political activities; 5) He and his family would be issued Philippine passports and could travel freely inside and outside the Philippines. Whether or not this was related to the previous counter offer wasn't known.

There was a follow up letter to Weinstein dated 5 August in which Marcos stated that he would prove his sincerity by immediately transferring the Swiss bank accounts under dispute to the Philippine government. Weinstein flew to Honolulu on

7 August to meet with Marcos and discuss the details of the proposal. Consul General Gomez was kept appraised of the situation throughout these negotiations. He in turn advised Aquino. The press somehow got word of this development. Aquino issued a statement that Marcos had to deliver the $5 billion first before negotiations could begin. Marcos reacted by denying he ever made the offer, and negotiations ceased again.

Nandeng Pedrosa, a former banker whose father was secretary of finance under President Quirino, was in Taipei in 1988 as a consultant to a Taiwanese group. While there he was asked by one of the group to help in another matter because he spoke English fluently. That is how he met Robert Kerkez.

Kerkez was from Las Vegas and was in Taiwan to try and negotiate a deal involving a gold certificate for fifty tons of gold. He wanted five years advance interest at 10 percent a year, for a total of 50 percent of the value of the certificate, discounted by 30 percent. In that way, if the value of the gold ever fell below 70 percent of its present value then the gold would be sold to pay off the loan. At the time gold was selling for about $400 an ounce, so the money involved was approximately $246,400,000. Pedrosa and the Taiwanese who was acting as Kerkez' broker put together a loan proposal. Soon afterward an agreement with one of the banks was ready to be concluded.

During the negotiations, which took place over a three week period, Pedrosa met with Kerkez four or five times. He described him: "Bob seemed to be a nice man. He wore cowboy boots and his suits were cut in the Texas style. He was well-mannered but a little too outspoken. He said he was just a middleman, that the authority to release the funds would come from the head of a bank in San Francisco. He also said that he was there to negotiate as many certificates as the banks in Taiwan could handle. 'How many do you want? Twenty? Thirty?' he said."

While this was going on the story about Marcos $5 billion offer to the Philippine government came out in the newspapers. Pedrosa read about it and was aware that twenty-one of Kerkez' certificates, if they existed, would be worth over $5 billion if they were negotiated in this manner. He was anxious to ask about this at their meeting that morning but Kerkez didn't show up. That afternoon the

Taiwanese called and said that Kerkez had pulled out of the deal
and left abuptly for the states. Pedrosa never heard from him again.

Later in Manila the PCGG invited a retired colonel and two
foreigners for questioning. They were allegedly engaged in trading
huge volumes of gold bars believed to be part of Marcos' gold hoard.
One of the names given was Robert Kerkez. The colonel's name
was Enrique Pimentel. Pedrosa had seen it on the gold certificate
that Kerkez had with him in Taiwan. The third man was a Lebanese
financier by the name of Ibrahim Dagher, who was already well
known to the PCGG. He was a friend of another Marcos associate,
Michael de Guzman.

After the Weinstein mission failed, Marcos tried another tack.
Harold Ezell was the Immigration and Nationalization Service
commissioner for the Western Region which included Hawaii. He
had been cordial to Marcos and Imelda during their stay in
Honolulu. On 2 August a group called The United Filipino Council
of Hawaii honored Ezell with a dinner. The party was held at
Marcos' home. He presented a plaque to Ezell in appreciation for
his services to the Filipino. Unfortunately the gesture backfired.
Ezell landed in hot water with his superiors when news of the party
hit the newspapers.

A few weeks later Marcos' hopes were raised when a Philippine
court ruled he could come to Manila for Baltazar Aquino's testimony
scheduled for November. Aquino (no relation to the president) was
cooperating with the PCGG and agreed to testify in one of the
numerous civil suits being brought against Marcos. He had been
Marcos' highways commissioner and had gone to Hong Kong on
at least ten occasions between March 1975 and July 1976 to collect
"commissions" owed to Marcos by Japanese suppliers of the
Philippine Highways Ministry. They totalled $4,539,786.60, and
were deposited in Marcos' account, number 51960, at the Swiss Bank
Corporation in Hong Kong. Despite the damming evidence, Marcos
was excited about being able to return.

His next move was to ask Enrique Zobel for a loan of $250
million. Whether or not this was connected to his anticipated return
in November isn't known. But in October 1988 Marcos asked
Doctor Lourdes Pascual, a family friend, to prepare a promissory
note and deliver it to Zobel in Manila. The note was prepared but
its delivery was delayed by more pressing matters.

On 21 October the Grand Jury in New York handed down an indictment against Marcos, Imelda, and nine others. It set off a flurry of legal histrionics that took up most of Marcos' time. It also prevented him from returning to the Philippines for Baltazar Aquino's testimony.

On 14 November the U.S. Supreme Court ordered Marcos and Imelda to report to the FBI in Honolulu for fingerprinting, palm printing, photographing, and to produce a sample of their handwriting and recordings of their voices. The previous July they had been subpoenaed and ordered to sign consent directives, authorizing the foreign banks to turn over their financial records. They appealed, claiming they were entitled to their Philippine constitutional rights. This motion was denied. They were ordered to comply by 8 August 1988. They then claimed head of state immunity. This motion was also denied and they were ordered to comply by 18 August. Another appeal was filed, and denied on 19 October. The case was elevated to the Supreme Court. They lost, and were ordered to report to the FBI.

Pascual finally flew into Manila in late November and met with Zobel. She showed him the note and asked if he could loan Marcos $250 million to pay off the accumulated salaries of his supporters and staff in Hawaii. The note had been antedated to 17 October, *before* the indictment was handed down, to protect Zobel. Signed by Marcos, it stated that "In consideration of this loan I promise to deliver three million ounces of gold within three years after I return to the Philippines." Zobel told Pascual he would fly to Hawaii and meet Marcos in December.

Marcos encountered more setbacks before Zobel arrived. On 29 November the court-appointed doctor announced that Marcos was well enough to travel to New York for his arraignment. On 1 December an Appeals Court upheld the decision to freeze his assets worldwide. A few days later his own doctors issued a report that described him as chronically ill with multiple abnormalities of the kidney and heart.

On 8 December at seven in the evening, Zobel met Marcos for dinner. He noticed that Marcos hardly ate and looked very tired and weak. Marcos asked for the promissory note that Pascual left with him. He had left it at his residence ten minutes away, so he had to go and get it.

On returning, he told Marcos he didn't have $250 million available, but he asked how the loan would be repaid if he could arrange it. Marcos asked his nurse, Teresita Gallego, to fetch a folder. Zobel leafed through it. It was about an inch and a half thick and full of deposit certificates for gold stored in various banks all over the world — Switzerland, Monaco, the Vatican, the Bahamas, and other places. He didn't have time to add up the total but estimated that, at $400 an ounce, the price of gold at the time, the value was roughly $35 billion.

Some of the certificates were dated in the forties after the second world war. Marcos explained that he began accumulating gold toward the end of the war. He found some treasure, and also bought gold bars from soldiers that had found them in the debris of Yamashita's retreating convoy. He reminted the bars in Hong Kong in 1946, and accumulated more through various treasure hunts. The reason he kept it secret until now, Marcos said, was because other countries could have a legal claim to it until 1985. The statute of limitations in international law was for a forty-year period.

To most people that knew Marcos this story sounded a bit odd. He came from a poor family and he made his first million as a first-term congressman in 1949 and 1950 selling import licenses. He bought a Cadillac to celebrate his new status. Before then, there was no outward indication of any wealth. When he courted Imelda in 1954, he brought her to a bank vault and showed her stacks of hundred-dollar bills, but no gold bars. Records found in the palace after he left showed that he didn't open his first bank account abroad until 1967 when he deposited $215,000 in Chase Manhattan Bank in New York. Not yet accustomed to hiding money, he used his own name.

Marcos may have had some dealings with Minoru Fukumitsu and Venancio Duque in the fifties, but he didn't start his serious treasure hunting until he became president in 1965. It wasn't until five years later that he announced that he had found the Yamashita treasure.

Nevertheless, Imelda had shown others some gold certificates of the same description — yellowed with age and dated 1946 to 1948. She claimed she was going to present them at her trial but she never did. Her lawyers also considered flying to Manila to obtain Orlando

Dulay's deposition in prison as proof that Marcos found the treasure but this wasn't done either. Dulay waited until the trial was over before he told David Castro and the PCGG about Marcos finding $40 billion in gold.

Over dinner, Marcos said he wanted to help the Filipino people. Zobel suggested that he set up a foundation. Marcos asked him to head it. Zobel demurred and suggested instead that the Vatican or its representative head it.

Marcos agreed, and decided that the Roman Catholic church would receive 10 percent of the gold for use in its foreign missions. Another 10 percent would be retained by his family. Seventy-nine percent would go to the foundation set up for the benefit of the Filipino people. And one percent would go to pay his debts, with the balance to go to his loyal staff and his doctors and nurses.

According to Zobel, Marcos rattled off the percentages without hesitation, as if he had planned the whole thing in advance. He may have. Zobel was the god-father of Greg Aranetta at his wedding to Irene, Marcos' daughter, in June 1983. Since the early eighties, when the economy went into a tailspin, he had pressured Aranetta to convince Marcos to return the treasure and help the country.

Zobel found out Marcos was flying gold out of the country in 1972. As a pilot in the air force reserve, qualified in fixed wing and rotary, he had a lot of friends that flew. Some of the Ilocano pilots (Marcos preferred to trust military from his own province of Ilocos Norte) had talked about flying C-130 aircraft loaded with gold to Zurich.

Marcos was aware of Zobel's constant pleadings to Aranetta. Just why he finally decided to give in and up the ante will never be known. Maybe he knew he was a very sick man, and was even more desperate to go home. Whatever the reason, he decided to give away most of a treasure he had always denied having.

Marcos said that in future communications he would use the code name Gandhi, and asked that they meet again after he had discussed the plan with his lawyers. He suggested 23 or 24 December but Zobel said he couldn't make it until after Christmas.

Zobel left around 11:30 that evening. A few hours later Marcos was taken to St. Francis Hospital complaining of chest pains. On 18 December he was allowed to leave and spent Christmas at home.

On the twenty-eighth he was rushed back to the hospital with a high fever. The December meeting was called off. He went home again on 4 January 1989.

From Honolulu, Zobel went to San Francisco and then Europe. He returned to Manila on 3 January, in time to celebrate his birthday on the seventh. On 12 January he invited Pedro Cojuangco, the president's brother, and Mrs. Dely Castillejo, Cojuangco's sister-in-law, to his residence. He told them about Marcos' desire to set up a foundation and asked that Cojuangco tell Aquino.

Marcos was taken back to the hospital on 15 January. He fell into a coma four days later. From then on he would only have brief moments of consciousness. On 16 January, Zobel had breakfast with Vice President Laurel at Laurel's residence and told him about the proposed agreement. To try and convince Aquino that Marcos was only coming home to die, they devised a plan to send two doctors to Hawaii to independently verify his state of health. Laurel said he would ask Aquino to approve it. Later that evening he called Zobel to say it was okay.

Zobel flew into Hawaii on 18 January. The next day he heard that one of Marcos' lungs collapsed but doctors were able to inflate it. Around midnight, Laurel called and said that the two doctors had been stopped at the Manila airport and prevented from departing by Aquino's minister of health.

Marcos was still too sick to see Zobel, so on 22 January he met with Imelda and told her about Marcos' wishes for a foundation. The next day he met with Pascual, his lawyer, and one of Marcos' assistants to discuss how the trust agreement should be drawn up. It was decided that the Papal Nuncio in Manila, Bruno Torpigliani, would serve as principal trustee. The other trustees would be Father Rogelio Alarcan, Rector of Letran College, Pascual, and Zobel. Zobel agreed to serve on the condition that no compensation would be paid to the trustees for their work.

Before leaving, Zobel contacted John Fulks, head of the FBI in Hawaii. He wanted it known that all his dealings with Marcos and the Philippine government were above-board, and asked that the FBI make sure no one saw him and Marcos together when they met. A few days before, a television reporter had showed up at his house and asked him if he were in town to negotiate a deal with

Marcos. He denied it, but worried that the plan might be jeopardized if it were made public. Fulks said he would take care of it. Zobel then called a friend, Frank Yturria, in Washington and asked him to brief Secretary of State James Baker on the situation.

A lot of very important people knew what Zobel was doing. They were not that surprised. Long before meeting with Marcos on 8 December, he had taken an interest in finding a way to pay off the foreign debt of the Philippines, and had discussed the matter with friends in high places. Being a banker himself with worldwide connections, he occasionally met with some of the country's creditors. When the talk came around to that subject Zobel would ask, "How much discount would you give if I could pay off all the debt?"

They replied that they would accept forty-eight cents on the dollar. That meant the government only had to repay about $13 billion instead of more than $27 billion. This was in the back of Zobel's mind all the time.

Zobel flew to San Francisco on 27 January and met with Eduardo "Dandeng" Cojuangco Jr., Aquino's first cousin, Eduardo Romualdez, a cousin of Imelda and former ambassador to the U.S., Greg Aranetta, and two of Imelda's lawyers, John Bartko of San Francisco and Richard Hibey of New York. After the plan was explained to them, Cojuangco, Romualdez, and Aranetta expressed their own desires to serve as trustees. Zobel said that the final decision would have to come from Marcos.

He returned to Honolulu on the twenty-ninth and went to the hospital at noon but was still unable to see Marcos. That evening he met with Imelda and Bong Bong at the hospital, and showed them a draft of the trust agreement. Bong Bong remarked, "See, mother, father never told us these things."

Bong Bong's statement could be interpreted many different ways. It could mean that he was unaware of Marcos' gold hoard. This is unlikely. It probably just meant that he was unaware of the foundation that Marcos wanted to set up. That Imelda had known for a week and not told him was just another curiosity in a family known for its intrigues.

The next afternoon Zobel went back to the hospital. Marcos opened his eyes once, and seemed to smile at him, but he went back to sleep and no documents were signed.

The next day Zobel gave Imelda and Bong Bong four copies of the trust agreement. Bong Bong agreed to get his father to sign them when he could. Zobel departed Honolulu on 1 February. When he arrived in Manila he heard that Marcos had undergone a tracheotomy. He wondered how much time Marcos had left. On 3 February he met with the Papal Nuncio and Alarcan and gave them a copy of the trust agreement.

Marcos' medical condition was rapidly deteriorating. In April the court-appointed doctor reversed his decision and announced that Marcos was medically unfit for travel to New York. In June the doctors removed the kidney that had been transplanted four years earlier. From there it was all downhill. Marcos turned seventy-two on 11 September. He died seventeen days later shortly after midnight. He never signed the trust agreement.

In deference to Marcos' death, Zobel did not bother the family in mourning. He heard from Pascual that Bong Bong retrieved the folder containing the gold deposit certificates from Marcos' nurse.

He quietly pursued the matter, hoping that Imelda and Bong Bong would follow through with Marcos' plans. In November 1989 he attended the Volvo Golf Tournament in Spain with Rainer E. Gut, chairman of the board of Credit Suisse. He asked Gut if the Swiss banks would release the gold if the foundation presented two letters of authority — one signed by President Aquino and one signed by the Marcos heirs. Gut replied it could be done.

The year 1990 came and went. Imelda spent most of the time defending herself in a New York courtroom, so Zobel didn't push her on the foundation idea. But he wouldn't give up. In January 1991 he had lunch with Cardinal Sin and four Jesuit priests and told them what Marcos had planned.

Zobel had his accident in May 1991. It took a long time to get over the emotional trauma of going from a dynamic human being to a cripple. Imelda returned to the Philippines in November. She never contacted him, so he wrote her on 20 April 1992 and asked that she set up the foundation and "never let [Marcos'] dream die with him." He ended the letter by stating, "I hope that we can begin to work something out within a week after the elections." The elections were held on May 11. He waited for a reply, but one never came.

He anguished over whether or not he should go public. All his close friends and advisors were of one voice. Don't do it, they said. There's just no way you can prove your story. The media will crucify you. In typical Zobel fashion he did it anyway. On Thursday, 4 June 1992, he called a press conference. He followed up with two television appearances the next day.

Why, the reporters asked, did he wait until now to say anything? Zobel replied that he thought he was dying and wanted to announce sooner, but he didn't want to interfere with the elections.

Aquino at first denied knowing anything about it, then later changed her mind and admitted she was aware of the discussions between Marcos and Zobel. But her overall reaction seemed to be of disinterest. This led Zobel to comment that her main agenda in matters concerning the return of Marcos' gold was that if it would make him look good then she was against it no matter how much the country benefitted. Imelda chose not to respond. She sent several messages to Zobel saying she would meet with him but she never did.

The family kept quiet about the gold deposit certificates. If they were real then Marcos found at least some of the treasure. But just how much did Marcos accumulate? In addition to the certificates that Zobel saw, the Hirschfield tapes mentioned $14 billion in gold and Sumulong mentioned $15 billion *still in the Philippines*. Was there a total of $50 billion?

Despite all the intriguing evidence, no Swiss bank ever admittted holding any gold for Marcos. Some admitted they held his dollars, but not his gold.

There were whispered rumors that Imelda and Bong Bong hired extra lawyers to verify the gold certificates in the file folder. To add to the confusion, each certificate was reputedly in the names of three trustees, and they were not anxious to give up their potential wealth.

There was talk of a will dated 23 June 1988, in which Marcos left half his estate to Imelda and half to his children. The family said nothing and made no move to probate it. With or without a will, under Philippine law, after all of Marcos' obligations were settled Imelda was entitled to one-half of the balance as her conjugal share. Then the rest of the estate would be taxed at 60 percent, and what was left would be divided according to the will. If there were no will, Imelda would receive another one-fifth share and each of the four children a one-fifth share.

Estate taxes could amount to a lot of government revenue if Marcos left billions behind. The Bureau of Internal Revenue would probably intervene also to get their share because he did not pay income tax on that money. So the family probably wasn't in a big hurry to settle the estate.

There was no hurry. In Switzerland there was no law of escheat regarding bank accounts. Simply stated, if Marcos hid gold in a bank account in the states, and there was no activity in that account for ten years, then the account would inure to the state. That law would not apply to banks in Switzerland, however. Adhering to their code of secrecy, even if an account had no activity it would remain on the books indefinately. If someone proved himself or herself to be the heir of the account holder, then the account would be turned over.

Most stories about golden treasure are fairy tales, but this one isn't. The poor people of the Philippines don't live happily ever. They are still starving. But there is hope. As Zobel noted in his public appeal:

> It is not yet too late...Perhaps if the next president of the Philippines and the Marcos heirs can come to an amicable settlement of the issue, we can all benefit from it. Otherwise, our people stand to lose all of the wealth that Mr. Marcos apparently had deposited in various parts of the world, with his bankers being all the richer for it and us all the poorer.

Right now that's the way it is.

Notes

Gustavo Ingles was interviewed in 1986 and 1991 for his recollections as a survivor of Fort Santiago.

The palace museum offered daily tours (except Wednesdays when the cabinet met) of Malacañan Palace. You could see where General Ver planted the bombs in President Marcos' office, the bedrooms of Marcos and Imelda, and their vaults. They no longer contained the filing cabinets or jewelry, but there were pictures of the way they were found after Marcos left. You could also see the room where Marcos' and Imelda's clothes and shoes were still on the racks.

The details of Marcos' abrupt departure and flight to Honolulu via Clark Air Base and Guam are contained in a report by the Readiness Subcommittee of the Committee On Armed Services, House of Representatives, dated May 1986, and entitled "Investigation of the Costs Involved in Moving Former President Marcos and His Party from Manila to Hawaii."

The details about Imelda's jewelry being found in suitcases in Dasmariñas Village, Makati, and in suitcases at the airport being carried by a Greek jeweler are well documented in newspapers and magazines of that time. One example is *Mr. & Ms.* magazine, dated March 20-26, 1987, "A Gem of a Story."

The raid on Imee Marcos' office was also well publicized at the time since it was one of the first carried out, and yielded quite a bit of information. Journalist Phil Bronstein, reported the story for the *San Francisco Examiner*, entitled "Jackpot for 'Raiders' of the hidden holdings," on 9 March 1986.

Cesar Parlade was assigned to the legal department of the PCGG when I first met him in 1986. He, along with Congressman Boni Gillego, provided me with the documents and advice which started me on this journey.

The book on Marcos' war exploits published by the Philippine government, Office of Media Affairs, during the Marcos era, was entitled *Documents on the Marcos War Medals*.

Although his selective memory presents a distorted and somewhat obfuscated version of many events, Colonel Arturo Aruiza, a military aide to Marcos, wrote an interesting book, *Ferdinand Marcos: Malacanang to Makiki* that provided some background information about Marcos' last days in the palace.

Chapter 2   The Central Bank

The details of Marcos' stay and his security at Hickam Air Force Base are given in the May 1986 report mentioned in the Chapter One notes.

The information about Michael de Guzman's attempt to transfer Marcos' Credit Suisse deposits to his own bank came from the Philippine Senate's transcript of the testimony of Michael de Guzman and others.

International Financial Statistics, March 1988, pp. 407-408, published by the International Monetary Fund, provided the information about the status of gold reserves at the Central Bank. Mrs. Ophelia Soliven graciously assisted me at the Central Bank when I needed some clarification.

The Dewey Dee scandal was well known in the Philippines. What wasn't well known was that he was the catalyst for the collapse of the government's precarious financial system.

The information about the 525 tons of gold was first brought to light in April 1982 by the *Far Eastern Economic Review* in its article, "Golden Fleece." Michael Young was interviewed by Guy

Sacerdoti and Gary Coull. A palace source provided a copy of the Mercantile Insurance Company letter.

John Lutley, of the Gold Institute, Washington, D.C., and John Lucas, Bureau of Mines, Washington, D.C. told me about the *Gold Ingot Hallmark Book.*

The 1991 edition of the *Guinness Book of World Records* (page 194) provided the information about the amount of gold mined.

The information about KLM flight 864, the Korean Airlines flight, and the 707 flight from Amsterdam was contained in an undated confidential memorandum obtained from U.S. government sources. The data on Ron Lusk was found in this memo and another source which has to remain confidential.

The Gapud telex, the Interpol cable, the secret U.S. Treasury Report, and the computer printout of the $94 million sent to Swiss banks was obtained from the PCGG.

The foreign debt escalation data was obtained from the *Philippine Statistical Yearbook*, published annually by the National Economic and Development Authority.

The statement that "the Philippines was the only country in the world that compiled and published accurate information about its foreign debt," appeared in a paper, "The Philippine Economy: Policies and Development, 1975-1982," published by the Central Bank in 1983.

The Luxembourg sales agreement and other documents relating to this was first reported by the *Philippine Free Press* magazine. The PCGG and the magazine provided copies of these documents.

The information about Dacus came from a memorandum published by the Center for Constitutional Rights in the U.S. and from a deposition of his testimony in the trial of Roger Roxas and the Golden Buddha Corporation vs. Ferdinand and Imelda Marcos, Case No. 88-0522-02, First Circuit Court of Hawaii.

The information on Cruz-Cruzal's arrest was also contained in the undated confidential memorandum obtained from U.S. government sources. An interview with Frank Higdon confirmed the details.

Higdon and former Attorney General Edwin Meese were interviewed about the meeting with the professor of economics in Manila.

Chapter 3   The Gold Deals

I interviewed Dulay at New Bilibid prison outside Manila. His mother-in-law, Mrs. Ladra, also helped a great deal delivering messages back and forth. His lawyer, Mario Ongkiko, PCGG Chairman David Castro, and Solicitor General Frank Chavez were also interviewed.

Philippine journalist Julie Amargo obtained a copy of the KLM waybill. The Central Bank provided a copy of its article, "CB's Gold and Silver Reserve Management: Clearing the Doubts."

The information about the missing 13,915 pounds of gold came to light after Marcos fled in February 1986, and was first reported in the *Los Angeles Times* on 16 March 1986.

Interviews with Pedro, Pol, and Ben provided most of the information about the alleged gold recoveries.

The telex from the Archdiocese of San Francisco, the papers of Great American Management Corporation of Houston, and the information about the 7.5 tons in the Quezon City house came from the PCGG.

The *Sunday Telegraph* in Australia reported the story of T.C.B. "Andrew" Tan trying to sell 2,000 tons of gold. It was reprinted in the *Daily Inquirer* newspaper in Manila on 21 April 1986. The English language newspaper in Tokyo, *Yomiuri Shimbun*, reported the twenty tons of gold being sold by Marcos aides. It was reprinted in the *Manila Journal* newspaper on 5 January 1988.

Adnan Kashoggi told about Marcos' shipload of gold in his testimony during the 1990 trial of Imelda Marcos.

The transcript of the taped interviews which Robert Chastain and Richard Hirschfield had with Marcos was printed in the *Philippine News* newspaper in San Francisco.

Conrado Limcauco, head of television Channel Four in Manila, was empowered by the government to conduct his own private investigation into Marcos' treasure recoveries. He was the first to explain Operation Umbrella to me. The PCGG documents and other information helped corroborate his information.

Geoffrey Greenlees and David Castro were interviewed about the Munich gold deal.

Chapter 4 The Legend

Yamashita's execution was described in newspaper accounts of the period: "General Yamashita Met Slow Death in Black Gallows," *Manila Chronicle*, 26 February 1946, and "Yamashita's End," *Philippine Free Press*, 3 March 1946. I talked with several village elders in Los Baños who lived there during that time.

The trial of Yamashita was documented in *The Yamashita Precedent: War Crimes and Command Responsibility*, by Richard L. Lael, and *The Case of General Yamashita*, by A. Frank Reel.

The Los Baños prisoner of war camp and its liberation was described in *Escape at Dawn*, by Carol Terry Talbot and Virginia J. Muir.

Philippine historian Teodoro A. Agoncillo published several books about the wartime situation in the Philippines that were helpful: *The Fateful Years*, volumes 1 and 2, and *The Burden of Proof*.

The war in the Pacific was documented in *American Caesar*, by William Manchester, and *Eagle Against the Sun*, by Ronald H. Spector.

Yamashita's retreat was described in *Tiger of Malaya*, by Aubrey Kenworthy.

Philippine animosity toward Japan after the war was described in *War Reparations & Peace Settlement: Philippine-Japan Relations, 1945-1956*, by Takushi Ohno. The data on the salvaging of Japanese ships lost during the war was also documented in this book.

Ernesto Rodriguez' book, *The Bad Guerrillas of Northern Luzon* described Marcos' experiences as a guerrilla during the war, and how he was arrested by the U.S. forces.

Minoru Fukumitsu's claim that there was no Yamashita treasure has appeared in numerous periodicals. A few examples are: "There Is No Yamashita Treasure," in the *Panorama* magazine of the *Philippine Daily Express*, 17 July 1982, and "War Treasure Still Sought In Philippines," *Los Angeles Times*, 28 May 1978.

I interviewed Houston Turner, Sheldon Empol, and Andy Aquila, three survivors of the Bataan Death March, on May 12, 14, and 15, 1992, respectively, at the fiftieth anniversary convention in Burlingame, California.

Chapter 5   The Evidence

The *Awa Maru* incident is well known. My information was taken from a book, *The Awa Maru Incident*, by Minoru Fukumitsu. It was published in Japan, and no English version is available. Fukumitsu could not be reached for an interview.

In 1976 several newspapers carried articles about the Awa Maru when Commander Loughlin and several others applied for permission to salvage the vessel: "Sunken Ship May Hold $5 Billion Treasure," *San Francisco Chronicle*, 18 November 1976, and "A Treasure Hunt for $5 Billion," *San Francisco Examiner*, 19 November 1976.

A fictional account of the sinking of the *Awa Maru* was published in 1981, entitled *In Pursuit of the Awa Maru*, by Joe Innis.

Three books provided the information for the nostalgic glimpse of Manila just before the war. Florence Horn's *Orphans of the Pacific*, published in 1941; Lewis Gleeck's article, "American Life Styles In Colonial Philippines," In *Pammadayaw: Philippine Studies by International Authors, In Honor of Dr. Marcelino Foronda, Jr.*; and Beth Day Romulos's *The Manila Hotel*, published by the hotel on the occasion of its Diamond Jubilee.

Soldiers of the Sun: The Rise and Fall of the Imperial Japanese Army, by Meirion and Susie Harries provided excellent insights into the Japanese military machine before and during World War II.

The story of the silver pesos being dumped in Manila Bay off Corregidor is well known. Manchester mentioned it in *American Caesar*. Ben Waldron, a Corregidor veteran, also mentioned it in his book, *Corregidor: From Paradise to Hell*.

Pedro, Pol, and Ben provided the information on how the treasure was buried. I wrote the British government and the Singapore archives. They both denied the story about shipping Her Majesty's treasures to Singapore.

The story about the Money Pit on Oak Island has appeared in *Readers Digest*, "Assault On A Treasure Island," by Douglas Preston, September 1988, 24-29, and the *Asian Wall Street Journal*, "Adventurers Still Seeking Bottom of Fabled Money Pit," by D'Arcy O'Connor, 29 July 1987, p. 1.

Chapter 6   The Eye-Witnesses

Pedro, Pol, and Ben's stories were told by themselves. The trip to Japan in 1968 was confirmed by several sources: Reverend Simeon Lepasana, who served with Colonel Villacrusis on one of the Task Forces; Johnny Wilson, the historian of the Task Force; and Tabo Ingles, who was a friend and classmate — Philippine Military Academy, Class of 1945 — of Villacrusis.

The Japanese atrocities committed as the Americans were retaking the Philippines were detailed in Lieutenant Colonel Aubrey Kenworthy's book, *Tiger of Malaya*.

The number of people killed in Manila was never accurately determined. Both Manchester (*American Caesar*) and Breuer (*Retaking the Philippines*) estimated that as many as 100,000 died. Kenworthy's book noted that a Manila undertaker buried 8,000 bodies. The official history, *U.S. Army in World War II: Triumph in the Philippines*, estimated that between 30,000 and 40,000 died in Manila and southern Luzon during that brief period.

Pedro Lim was from Calamba. I talked to him and several of his town mates who survived the Calamba massacre.

Chapter 7   Father Bulatao

Father Gabriel Casal introduced me to Father Bulatao in January 1989. In addition to the dozens of regressions, we spent countless hours together discussing his favorite subject, the altered state.

Prince Chicibu's military career was mentioned in the excellent history, *Soldiers of the Sun: The Rise and Fall of the Imperial Japanese Army*, by Meirion and Susie Harries.

The military attache at the Japanese Embassy in Manila, Colonel Shuzo Yamamoto, was interviewed regarding the relatives of the Imperial family that served in the military in the Philippines during the war. He said there were none. This contradicts Ben Valmores' claim that he saw Prince Chichibu on one occasion in 1944.

The National Institute for Defense Studies in Japan tried to track down the various people mentioned in the stories of Pedro, Pol, and Ben. Friends at Reuters News Agency in Tokyo assisted me in tracking the royal family. They were unable to confirm the existence of a Lord Ichivarra. The U.S. Army Library was checked to make sure the names I inquired about did not exist. The German War Ministry assisted me in the search for Von Dauden.

Congressman Boni Gillego helped with his recollections of Pol Giga. Efforts to locate Jose Castillo, Julio De Guzman, and a Filipino-Japanese named Okusura proved futile.

Chapter 8   The Treasure Hunts

Marcos' announcement that he was giving away all his wealth on New Years Day 1970 made all the newspaper headlines in Manila at the time, as did his announcement that he had found the Yamashita treasure. Imelda's medical problems were well known. That they only happened at critical periods of Marcos' political career was also well known. A typical story appeared in the *Philippine Herald*, on 29 May 1968. "Doctors Set More Tests For Imelda" was the title of the article. It was on page three. That a story about the first lady only made page three is indicative of how serious the press took such announcements.

Copies of Marcos' and Imelda's signature cards for their Swiss bank accounts were found in the palace after the revolution. Marcos' use of the name William Saunders dates back to World War II. That name came up while I was researching Marcos' war record. A letter dated 26 July 1944, addressed to Major Bernard Anderson, an American guerrilla, was found in the Whitney Papers, MacArthur Memorial Archives. It requested arms, ammunition, money, and other items, and was signed "William Saunders." It was written on *Ang Manga Maharlika* stationery. That was the name of the guerrilla group which Marcos claimed to have led. On the back of the letter was handwritten, "14 Aug 44, Req. fr Col. Fertig, Dec 43, Ferdinand E. Marcos w/Gen Capinpin." Capinpin was Marcos' commanding officer in the Twenty-first Infantry Division.

I interviewed Roger Roxas numerous times over a two-year period. In addition, Roger took me to the site to explain how the digging and the recovery took place. In the course of our interviews Roger was regressed to recall specific points about the excavation and the discovery in order to accurately portray his experience.

The civil action, Roger Roxas and the Golden Buddha Corporation vs. Ferdinand and Imelda Marcos (Case No. 88-0522-02), First Circuit Court of Hawaii, is sheduled for 1993.

The courageous story of Quintero's decision to expose Imelda for handing out envelopes full of cash at the Constitutional Convention is documented in *The Weekly Nation*, "The Ordeal of Quintero," 12 June 1972, pp. 8-9.

Marcos' claim that Yamashita surrendered to him appeared in the *Asia* magazine on 12 September 1971. Vicente Barranco questioned this fact in his own article, dated 23 October 1971, in *Philippines Free Press* magazine, "Did Yamashita Surrender to Marcos?"

In addition to Pedro, Pol, and Ben, several others related stories about various other treasure hunts that had been undertaken in the Philippines. These included Johnny Wilson, Simeon Lepasana, Cesar Leyran, and some former military officers who preferred to remain anonymous.

Father Baudenbrock's death was also mentioned by Sofia Adamson, the wife of the founder of Adamson University in Manila, in her memoirs entitled *Gods, Angels, Pearls, and Roses*. She recalled that the priest was murdered by the Japanese.

Johnny Wilson, Pol, and Ben all related the story of the meeting at the bowling alley. Johnny told me about Venancio Duque being a part of the task force in an interview on 18 September 1988. Simeon Lepasana provided me with a copy of the 2 May 1973 letter which was signed by him, Villacrusis, and Ramos.

Pol explained the codes and symbols of the maps to me just like he explained it to Cesar Leyran. I still have his scribbled notes.

Don Paquito Ortigas related the stories of how Marcos took over part of his property. Ninoy Aquino's name was mentioned by Nandeng Pedrosa, Cesar Leyran, and Johnny Wilson, among others.

Several former members of the Leber Group, including Cesar Leyran and Olof Jonsson told me they saw the "flags" that Ben and Pol gave Villacrusis. A picture of Ben's flag appeared in the *Philippines News* when it ran the 24-part series about the Leber Group treasure hunt.

Chapter 9   Leber Group

The Leber Group story was told first by Steve Psinakis in the *Philippine News* in 1978. At the same time the *Las Vegas Sun* picked up the story and reported it in some detail. Bob Curtis' own voluminous files on the treasure hunt, which included tape recordings, photos, engineering drawings, and newspaper clippings, added considerably to its credibility.

Olof described his meeting with Marcos in 1974 and the visit to the summer palace where the Golden Buddha was seen. The first meeting of Leber Group was described by Olof, Curtis, Cesar Leyran, Ben, and Pol in my interviews with them.

The visit of the survivors and relatives of the *Nachi* was widely reported in the press. One such article appeared in *New Philippines*, in March 1975. The fate of the *Nachi* was reported in *History of U.S. Naval Operations In World War II*, volume 12, p. 239.

The exact location of the Nachi was obtained by ordering from the National Archives a copy of the log of the USS *Chanticleer*. A good resource book on Japanese ships sunk in World War II was *The End of the Japanese Navy*, by Masanori Ito.

Members of the Leber Group that were interviewed included Curtis, Olof, Cesar, and the eye-witnesses Pol and Ben. I met Amelito Mutuc in 1987 but no details of Leber Group were discussed. Several others associated with the excavation were also interviewed: Doctor Eduardo Escobar, the owner of Age Construction Company who stored Curtis' refining plant; Sapro Santos, the lieutenant assigned by Ver as a driver for the Americans; and Steve Psinakis.

The November 1975 issue of *Cosmopolitan* reported that Imelda was one of the ten richest women in the world.

Raul Manglapus provided a copy of his letter and the newspaper article about the attempted assassination of the Movement For Free

Philippines members. Simeon Lepasana took me to Teresa to see the weed-covered excavation site on the property of Raymondo Francisco.

John Lucas, at the U.S. Bureau of Mines in Washington, D.C., was my resource person for the technical aspects of gold bullion.

Chapter 10   Nippon Star

General Singlaub was interviewed several times by telephone. In addition he faithfully answered all the questions that I mailed to him. He explained how the Nippon Star operation was set up, including the Phoenix, Helmut, and Geomilitech connections. He also told me the story of how he was first contacted by John Harrigan. I read a fascinating autobiography of Singlaub, *Hazardous Duty*, just published.

I interviewed Cesar Leyran dozens of times over a three-year period. He and Pol told me about the Calatagan Bay operation. He and Mrs. Villacrusis told me how Colonel Villacrusis died.

I met John Voss, Tom Polk, and Allan Forringer in Las Vegas in 1987. They corroborated the stories of the others.

I obtained a copy of Nippon Star's status report on their four sites. Cesar took me to the two sites at U.P. Los Baños. Pedro took me to the site at Majayjay on Mount Banahaw.

I met Al Meyer in Manila. He told me about his treasure hunting exploits but he never demonstrated his metal detector.

The two Jack Anderson columns that mentioned Meyer appeared in the *San Francisco Chronicle* on 10 November 1986 and 21 November 1986.

The meeting in Hong Kong was described to me by Curtis and Singlaub. The two versions were contradictory, but the basic facts were the same. *The Philadelphia Inquirer* story appeared on 17 February 1987.

Noel Soriano confirmed that the Nippon Star operation was not sanctioned by the palace, and that President Aquino was not aware of the operation. John Lemmon told me about the day

Nippon Star was ordered off Corregidor, and that their permit
was fake.

Chapter 11   Corregidor

I kept a daily log of our 17-18 September meeting in Las Vegas
with Curtis.

I have a copy of the letter Curtis sent to Aquino.

Noel related to me the details of the meeting with President
Aquino when he asked to go to the states. He also told me about
the trip to London to discuss Aquino's security two years later.

The best book ever written about Corregidor during the war,
according to James Black, the preeminent expert of Corregidor in
the Philippines is *Corregidor: The Saga of a Fortress*, by James H.
& William M. Belote.

Ben Waldron provided a first-person account of Corregidor
before and during the war in *Corregidor: From Paradise to Hell*.

I kept a log of the meetings in Las Vegas, 26-29 October 1987.
Each evening we all met for dinner. I met John Voss and Tom Polk
at that time. I also met Allan Forringer at the same meeting. We
discussed Nippon Star then, and several times after that in Manila.
Forringer died in the Philippines in 1991.

I also maintained a daily log for personal use and submitted
weekly status reports to Curtis on the Corregidor operation.

Chapter 12   Return To the Fort

Houston Turner, one of the Bataan Death March survivors,
pulled guard duty at Fort Santiago just before the war started. He
provided some fascinating details about the fort and Bastion de
San Lorenzo.

I kept a daily log and submitted weekly status reports during
the Fort Santiago operation. These helped refresh my memory of
the incidents mentioned. From the files of the National Historic
Institute, Director Quiason provided letters and data about other
attempts to excavate the fort in the last twenty years.

Newspaper and magazine accounts of the fort operation are too numerous to mention. Beginning in February 1988, when the cavein occurred, over two dozen local magazines and newspapers wrote stories almost daily for about a year. The operation had exposure in the international media also. *The New York Times, Los Angeles Times, Asian Wall Street Journal*, and *International Herald Tribune* among others printed front page stories.

Chapter 13   The Digging Continues

The story about the incident at the palace regarding the commissioners was related to me by Mario Ongkiko and Amado Dizon, one of the commissioners. Only recently did those involved feel safe enough to talk about the threats they received.

Noel, Mario, and George Wortinger refreshed my memory on some of the details of the strategy sessions. Mario helped recall details of the hearings. In addition to the weekly reports rendered to IPM, occasionally I had to render a report to the Office of the President when IPM requested an extension of its permit. This report showed progress to date and justified the need to continue with the excavation. I maintained copies of these also. They helped to recall the details about the gold flecks and the core which held the marble fused to the railroad tie. The gold flecks were assayed at the U.P. The core was turned over to the palace along with a report.

Jun Orobia, Felix Imperial, Gabe Casal, Serafin Quiason, Ernesto Sonido, and Ben Austria were interviewed and provided specific details about their roles in the operation. Sonido and Austria introduced us to the high-tech approach to treasure hunting.

Aida Alejandrino told me the story about Villacrusis and how she got him the permit. She still has the scrapbook, and she loaned me the maps of Fort Santiago so that the pictures could appear in this book.

Pedro, Pol, and Ben provided their recollections when I wrote this chapter. I have Pol's original sketch showing the number of vaults used and where the gold came from.

"Marvin" hated publicity and asked me not to mention his name. Okay, Marvin, but thanks for helping.

Chapter 14   The Con Man

The FBI report to the NBI was somewhat brief. The Federal
Archives and Records Center in San Bruno, California, provided
a complete record of Curtis' indictment and trial. Case number
77-00066 refers to the U.S. versus Curtis criminal action.

Pedro provided the originals of all his sketches. After they were
analyzed we worked with copies of the originals so as to prevent
further deterioration.

Doctor Sonido introduced us to geophysics and the various
tests which could be performed to determine how to locate buried
metal. The test results were contained in official reports to the Office
of the President.

After Phil Bronstein showed me the article about Curtis' class
action suit I wrote to the Federal District Court in Reno, Nevada.
The Court Clerk there graciously provided me with summaries of
Curtis' other two lawsuits. Case number 307152 refers to his Class
Action suit. Case number 313689 refers to his Judgment by Consent.

Olof's visit to the roof of the fort and his pointing to the gold
aura was witnessed by Pedro, Pol, Noel, and myself.

Chapter 15   The Swiss Connection

The indictment against Imelda Marcos and the other
defendants was filed before the District Court, Southern District
of New York, and is a matter of record. The trial began on
20 March 1990 and ended on 2 July 1990.

Mario Ongkiko and Noel Soriano helped me recall the details
of the operation at the bridge site. In addition I kept a daily log
during the project.

George Wortinger helped recall the incident regarding Ben and
the guards at the bridge site. George was also on good terms with
"Clyde" and his father in law, and kept me apprised of their trips
to the Philippines.

The kidnapping of Arby Duane Drown was a matter of real
concern to the Philippine authorities. Government and church
officials helped negotiate his release, which occurred on

30 June 1992, the day Fidel Ramos was sworn in as the new president.

The scam involving the chief was first related to me by George Wortinger, who put me in contact with the third American — the one I called anonymous — involved in the operation.

David Castro, PCGG chairman, was interviewed regarding the proof of the gold bars. He related how the documents from the Tamaraw Security Agency were first given to the palace and then to him. He has interviewed Tomas Rodriguez and others who took part in this, but none of them would agree to an interview. I managed to contact one witness but he would not talk because he feared for his life.

Jacobi's exploits with Dennis Howard Marks are chronicled in a book, *Hunting Marco Polo*, by Paul Eddy and Sara Walden. Jacobi's indictment is Case No. 91-0220, United States District Court, Southern District of Florida.

Chapter 16   Enrique Zobel

Lt. Colonel Seichi Ohta was head of the *Kempei Tai* in the Philippines from December 1941 to October 1942. The role of the *Kempei Tai* during the Japanese occupation of the Philippines is documented in *The Kempei Tai in the Philippines: 1941-1945,* by Ma. Felisa A. Syjuco.

Baltazar Aquino's Second Supplemental Deposition, dated 9 January 1986, in PCGG Civil Case No. 1, People of the Philippines versus Ferdinand E. Marcos et al. identified the deposit receipts of the monies he deposited for Marcos.

All the newspapers carried accounts of the Enrique Zobel press conference. The most thorough was a three-article series published by the *Daily Inquirer* on 5, 6, and 7 June 1992.

Joan Orendain, Zobel's public relations manager, provided me with a copy of his statement, the letter to Imelda, and the promissory note. I interviewed Zobel on 30 July 1992. He graciously provided more details of his meeting with Marcos and his subsequent attempts to set up the foundation.

Marcos' $5 billion offer was reported widely in the media in the Philippines and abroad. A copy of the letter that Marcos sent Weinstein was published in the *Philippine News*.

Francisco Sumulong went public with his story about the $15 billion offer in June 1991. The *Daily Globe* newspaper reported the story in an exclusive interview with Sumulong.

I interviewed Nandeng Pedrosa on 6 April, 14 April, and 31 August 1990. A fourth interview was arranged but his untimely death of a heart attack precluded such a meeting. He provided me with a copy of the gold certificate which Bob Kerkez was trying to negotiate. Kerkez' summons by the PCGG made the newspapers: "PCGG Summons Trio Dealing in FM Gold," *Philippine Daily Inquirer*, 13 September 1990, 7; "3 Marcos Treasure Hunters Being Hunted By Military," *Daily Globe*, 13 September 1990, 6.

Colonel Aruiza's book *Ferdinand Marcos: Malacañang to Makiki* helped me reconcile the dates of Marcos' hospitalization.

Enrique Zobel and the clan are in *Fortune* magazine's list of billionaires. (*Fortune*. 7 September 1992, 130.)

Swiss Bank of New York kindly provided me with information about the Swiss Civil Code and its banking laws regarding escheat.

Select Bibliography

BOOKS

Adamson, Sofia. *Gods, Angels, Pearls, and Roses.* El Monte, California: American International Publishing Company, 1982.

Agoncillo, Teodoro A. *The Burder of Proof.* Metro Manila: University of the Philippines Press, 1984.

_____ . *The Fateful Years.* 2 vols. Quezon City, Philippines: R.P. Garcia Publishing Co., 1965.

Agoncillo, Teodoro A., and Miligross C. Guerrero. *History of the Filipino People.* 5th ed. Quezon City, Philippines: R.P. Garcia Publishing Co., 1977.

Agustin, Conrado Gar. *Sketches In Japanese Prisons.* Manila: Intramuros Archives, 1979.

Aruiza, Arturo C. *Ferdinand E. Marcos: Malacañang to Makiki.* Quezon City, Philippines: AC Aruiza Enterprizes, 1991.

Bain, David Howard. *Sitting In Darkness.* Boston: Houghton Mifflin Company, 1984.

Belote, James H. & William M. *Corregidor: The Saga of a Fortress.* New York: Harper & Row, 1967.

Beyer, H. Otley. "A Brief History of Fort Santiago." Manila: Intramuros Archives, 1943.

Breuer, William B. *Retaking the Philippines.* New York: St. Martins Press, 1986.

Circuit Court, First Circuit, State of Hawaii. Civil Case Number 88-0522-01. Roger Roxas and the Golden Buddha Corporation vs. Ferdinand Marcos and Imelda Marcos. *Deposition of Norman Dacus.* Taken on 27 March 1992, at 530 Las Vegas Boulevard South, Las Vegas, Nevada 89101.

Edwards, Jack. *Banzai You Bastards.* Hong Kong: Corporate Communications, n.d.

Eddy, Paul, and Sara Walden. *Hunting Marco Polo: The Pursuit of the Drug Smuggler Who Couldn't Be Caught By the Agent Who Wouldn't Quit.* Boston: Little, Brown and Company, 1991.

Fukumitsu, Minoru. *The Awa Maru Incident* (in Japanese). Tokyo: Yomiuri Shimbun, n.d.

Gatbonton, Esperanza B. *Intramuros, A Historical Guide.* Manila: Intramuros Administration, 1980.

Gleeck, Lewis E., Jr. *The American Governors-General and High Commissioners In the Philippines.* Quezon City, Philippines: New Day Publishers, 1986.

Gopinath, Aruna. *Manuel L. Quezon.* Quezon City, Philippines: New Day Publishers, 1987.

Harries, Meirion and Susie. *Soldiers of the Sun: The Rise and Fall of the Imperial Japanese Army.* New York: Random House, 1991.

Haydock, Tim. *Treasure Trove.* New York: Henry Holt & Co., 1986.

Horn, Florence. *Orphans of the Pacific.* New York: Reynal and Hitchcock, 1941.

Hunt, Ray C., and Bernard Norling. *Behind Japanese Lines: An American Guerrilla In the Philippines.* Lexington: University Press of Kentucky, 1986.

Innis, W. Joe, with Bill Bunton. *In Search of the Awa Maru.* New York: Bantam Books, 1981.

International Monetary Fund. *International Financial Statistics.* Washington, D.C., March 1988.

Ito, Masanori. *The End of the Imperial Japanese Navy.* New York: W.W. Norton. Jove Books, 1962.

Jesswani, Jesus, ed. *A Look At Philippine History.* Manila: St. Paul Press, 1989.

Karnow, Stanley. *In Our Image*. New York: Random House, 1989.

Kenworthy, Aubrey S. *Tiger of Malaya*. New York: Exposition Press, 1953.

Lael, Richard L. *The Yamashita Precedent*. Wilmington, Delaware: Scholarly Resources, Inc., 1982.

Lindholm, Paul R. *Shadows From the Rising Sun*. Quezon City, Philippines: New Day Publishers, 1978.

Manchester, William. *American Caesar*. Boston: Dell Publishing Company, 1978.

Manila Merchants Association. *Manila: The Pearl of the Orient*. Manila: Manila Merchants Association, 1908.

Morrison, Samuel Elliot. *History of U.S. Naval Operations In World War II*. vol 12. Boston: Little Brown & Co., 1966.

National Archives. 37th Infantry Division and 129th Infantry Regiment Records. Army Records Division. Record Group 407. Washington, D.C.: National Archives.

National Economic and Development Authority. *Philippine Statistical Yearbook*. Manila, various years.

National Historical Commission. *Fort Santiago and the Rizal Shrine*. Manila: National Historical Commission, n.d.

National Historic Institute. *Fort Santiago and the Rizal Shrine*. Manila: National Historic Institute, 1987.

Office of Media Affairs. *Documents On the Marcos War Medals*. Manila: Republic of the Philippines, 1983.

Ohno, Takushi. *War Reparations & Peace Settlement: Philippines-Japan Relations, 1945-1956*. Manila: Solidaridad Publishing House, 1986.

Onoda, Hiroo. *No Surrender: My Thirty Year War*. Trans. Charles S. Terry. New York: Kodasha International, Ltd., 1974.

Quirino, Carlos. *Chick Parsons: America's Master Spy In the Philippines*. Quezon City, Philippines: New Day Publishers, 1984.

Quito, Emerita S., ed. "American Life Styles In Colonial Philippines." In *Pammadayaw: Philippine Studies by International Authors, In Honor of Dr. Marcelino Foronda, Jr.* Manila: De la Salle University Press, 1987.

Reel, A. Frank. *The Case of General Yamashita.* Chicago: University of Chicago Press, 1949.

Rodriguez, Ernesto R., Jr. *The Bad Guerrillas of Northern Luzon.* Quezon City, Philippines: J. Burgos Media Services, 1982.

Romulo, Beth Day. *The Manila Hotel.* Manila: The Manila Hotel, undated.

Singlaub, John K. With Malcolm McConnell. *Hazardous Duty.* New York: Summit Books, 1991.

Smith, Robert R. *U.S. Army in World War II: Triumph in the Philippines.* Washington: Government Printing Office, 1963.

Spector, Ronald H. *Eagle Against the Sun.* New York: The Free Press, 1985.

Steinberg, David Joel. *The Philippines: A Singular and Plural Place.* Boulder, Colorado: Westview Press, 1982.

Sullivan, William H. *Obbligato.* New York: W.W. Norton & Co., 1984.

Syjuco, Ma. Felisa A. *The Kempei Tai In the Philippines: 1941-1945.* Quezon City, Philippines: New Day Publishers, 1988.

Talbot, Carol Terry and Virginia J. Muir. *Escape At Dawn.* Wheaton, Illinois: Tyndale House Publishers, 1988.

Toland, John. *The Rising Sun.* New York: Bantam Books, 1970.

U.S. Congress. House. *Investigation of the Costs Involved in Moving Former President Marcos and His Party from Manila to Hawaii.* Report prepared by the Readiness Subcommittee of the Committee On Armed Services. 99th Cong., 2d sess., 1986. Committee Print 20.

Villamor, Jesus A., as told to Gerald S. Snyder. *They Never Surrendered.* Quezon City, Philippines: Vera-Reyes, Inc., 1982.

Villarin, Mariano. *We Remember Bataan and Corregidor.* Baltimore: Gateway Press, 1990.

Waldron, Ben D. and Emily Burneson. *Corregidor: From Paradise to Hell.* Freeman, So. Dakota: Pine Hill Press, 1988.

Wilcox, Marrion, ed. *Harper's History of the War in the Philippines.* New York: Harper & Brothers Publications, 1900.

Zaide, Gregorio F. *Jose Rizal: Life, Works, and Writings*. Manila: C.P. Villanueva, 1981.

ARTICLES

Barranco, Vicente. "Did Yamashita Surrender to Marcos?" *Philippines Free Press*. Manila, 23 October 1971.

"Billionaires, The." *Fortune*. 7 September 1992

Central Bank. "The Philippine Economy: Policies and Development, 1975-1982," Manila, 1983.

"Fort Santiago." *Sunday Tribune*. Manila, 23 July 1933.

Lyon, Eugene. "Track of the Manila Galleons." *National Geographic*. September 1990.

Maidenflores, Jaime. "Our Friend, the Enemy." *Panorama*. *Philippine Daily Express* newspaper, Manila, 17 July 1978, 14-19.

Malone, William Scott. "Greed: The Golden Fleece." *Regardies*. October 1988.

"Manila's Historic Walls." *Sunday Tribune*. Manila, 18 August 1929.

McDougald, Charles C. "On the Hunter's Trail." *Mr. & Ms.* Manila, 4-10 July 1986, 14-16.

Moraes, Dom. "The Cool Couple." *Asia*. Manila, 12 September 1971.

Nuyda, Doris G. "A Gem of a Story." *Mr. & Ms.* Manila, March 20-26, 1987, 14-19.

Preston, Douglas. "Assault On A Treasure Island." *Readers Digest*. September 1988, 24-29.

Sacerdoti, Guy, and Gary Coull. "Golden Fleece." *Far Eastern Economic Review*. Hong Kong, April 1982.

"Survivors Continue Search For Pacific War Dead." *New Philippines*. Manila, March 1975.

"The Ordeal of Quintero." *The Weekly Nation*. Manila, 12 June 1972, 8-9.

"There Is No Yamashita Treasure." *Panorama*. *Philippine Daily Express* newspaper, 17 July 1982.

Villanueva, Felicia Pamela A. "CB's Gold and Silver Reserve Management: Clearing the Doubts." *Central Bank Review*. Manila, June 1986, 8-10.

Winchester, Simon. "After dire straits, an agonizing haul across the Pacific." *Smithsonian*. April 1991.

Index

9 780940 777088